Yemen

a travel survival kit

Pertti Hämäläinen

الجمهورية اليمنية

Yemen – a travel survival kit

2nd edition

Published by
Lonely Planet Publications Pty Ltd (A.C.N. 005 607 983)
PO Box 617, Hawthorn, Vic 3122, Australia
Lonely Planet Publications, Inc
PO Box 2001A, Berkeley, CA 94702, USA

Printed by
Singapore National Printers Ltd, Singapore

Photographs by
Pertti Hämäläinen & Tuula-Maria Merivuori
Front cover: The Bridge of Shihara, built in the early 1600s
Back cover: Feeding Cows in Dhafar

First Published
January 1988

This Edition
October 1991

Although the authors and publisher have tried to make the information as accurate as possible, they accept no responsibility for any loss, injury or inconvenience sustained by any person using this book.

National Library of Australia Cataloguing in Publication Data

Hämäläinen, Pertti
    Yemen – a travel survival kit.

    2nd ed.
    Includes index.
    ISBN 0 86442 114 1.

    1. Yemen – Description and travel – 1981 – – Guide-books.
    I. Title.

915.3320432

text © Kwayyis International Oy 1991
photos © photographers as indicated 1991

Pertti Hämäläinen

Pertti Hämäläinen was born in Turku, Finland and lives in the capital of the country, Helsinki. Pertti has an MSc in Applied Mathematics from the University of Turku and works as a data communications specialist with a company importing computer equipment and software.

He was introduced to travelling by his wife Tuula in the late '70s. Her great interest in Islamic architecture first led them to Southern Arabia in 1984 and they have kept returning to the Yemen to research this book. Pertti is a member of die Deutsch-Jemenitische Getsellschaft eV and the American Institute for Yemeni Studies.

From the Author

This book is dedicated to the memory of my mother.

From the Publisher

Diana Saad and Alison White edited and proofed this edition. Chris Lee Ack was responsible for design, Jane Hart and Peter Flavelle drew the maps, and Jane also designed the cover.

This Book

Updating the Yemen guide for this edition has been somewhat of a challenge. While the first edition was written and used in the final years of Yemeni separation, our 1990 research trip for the second edition was done during the month of the official unification of the two Yemens. We entered the People's Democratic Republic of Yemen, travelled to the Yemen Arab Republic to witness the unification festivities, and finally left the unified Republic of Yemen!

While working on the text, bad news kept arriving at an accelerating rate from the Middle East, causing constant changes. Iraq invaded Kuwait in August, Saudi Arabia cut all development aid to Yemen and expelled all Yemeni nationals in October. By December 1990, most Western development

workers, not to speak of tourists, left the Middle East (including the Yemen) in anticipation of a devastating war in the region. Fortunately the Yemen was not a participant in the military crisis and remains one of the most peaceful destinations in the Peninsula.

We've received lots of letters from the readers of the first edition, ranging from hurried travellers rushing through the country in a couple of weeks to workers residing or having resided in the country for several years. With thanks to everyone, and apologies to those left out, I'd like to credit:

Stephanie & Stephen Adams (NZ), Mirella Alessio & Luke Villata (I & A), Marie-Louise Archer (UK), John di Benedetto (Y), Warwick Ball (UK), Andrew Bastram (UK), Carla Bellot (S), Philippe H. Bonhoure (F), Wim Bos (NL), Michael McGrath (A), Maurizio Dall'Olio (I), Gill Farjounel (F), Janice M. Flaherty (US), Barbara Gaffin & Doug Cahn (US), Mary Hebert (US), Patrice Legeay (F), Gianfranco & Manuela Lovison (I), Els Mourits (NL), Kathleen & Jens Munthe (US), Kenneth J Oberembt (E), Jean Christophe Richar (F), Fred Sargent (A), Catherine Scauflaire (B), Karl-Heinz Schwarz (G), Ursula Schwendener (S), Mark Sedgwick (E), Robert Steinglass ((US), Hugo de Vrion (NL).

A- Australia, B - Belgium, E - Egypt, F - France, G - Germany, I - Italy, NL - Netherlands, NZ - New Zealand, S - Switzerland, UK - United Kingdom, US - United States, Y- Yemen

But more than to any single individual, thanks should go to all the friendly people of the Yemen, especially those under 15 years of age. Without their overly eager assistance in daily situations I would never have got in the mood for writing this book.

Warning & Request

Things change – prices go up, places open and close. So if you find things better, worse, cheaper, more expensive, recently opened or long ago closed please write and tell us. As usual good letters will be rewarded with a free copy of the next edition or an alternative Lonely Planet guidebook.

Contents

Introduction

The Republic of Yemen was formed on 22 May 1990 by the spectacular merger of North Yemen (the Western-oriented Yemen Arab Republic, or YAR) and South Yemen (the People's Democratic Republic of Yemen, or PDRY, 'the first and only Marxist Arab state in the world'). The event ended a separation that had lasted for hundreds of years. The unification, which anticipated that of Germany by more than four months, became possible when the PDRY modified its leftist doctrines following the global demise of Soviet influnce and financial support in the late 1980s.

However, the world took hardly any notice, even though the country was a member of the United Nations Security Council at that time. In the ensuing months,

7

during the crisis leading up to the Gulf War, Yemen attracted a lot more attention because of its awkward attempts to strike a balance between the UN resolutions against Iraq and the powerful notion of the all-embracing Arab Nation.

This was history repeating itself. During the past decades, the Yemens have often made negative headlines in the Western press: revolutions and civil wars in the 1960s, border clashes, assassinations of presidents and the hosting of Palestinian and Western terrorists in the 1970s, economic catastrophes and riots in South Yemen in the 1980s.

Good news was rare: a few cultural and historical TV documentaries and books, produced by people who had visited the country and fallen in love with it, presented an unlikely wonderland of biblical-oriental flavour. It has been aptly said that only a few explorers, dreamers and scientists visited the region before the 1980s, with the dreamer's viewpoint most apparent in works describing Yemen.

However, this image of Yemen conveys only a tiny fraction of the truth. For most visitors, Yemen is a very positive experience – even seasoned travellers are impressed by the country's beauty and friendliness.

The separation that preceded unity was nothing new: the historical Yemen was never a single state. The region inhabited by people who today regard themselves as Yemenis ranges from the Najran oasis and 'Asir area in south-western Saudi Arabia to the Mahra region in easternmost Yemen. In ancient times, around 1000 BC, this part of southern Arabia was divided into warring kingdoms and, later, into rival Islamic imamates. Moreover, the region fell frequently (though always temporarily) under foreign occupation. The last colonists withdrew only in the 20th century – Turkey from the north in 1918 and Britain from the south in 1967.

While foreign powers left their mark on Yemeni society, they were unable to uproot the original culture – a culture that had survived intact under the rule of local sheikhs and imams for more than 1000 years. Although this policy had the positive effect of reinforcing national identity during and after occupation, it also isolated the Yemeni people from the outside world. Today, Yemenis uphold their cultural heritage with pride while striving furiously to modernise their society. It is the privilege of today's traveller to witness the endurance of the world of 'a thousand and one nights' in the grip of the abrupt modernisation that began barely a generation ago.

Yemen is more accessible today than it has ever been. Modern air traffic has brought this remote area within everybody's reach and recent developments have removed most of the barriers erected by local rulers to keep outsiders away. After the revolutions and civil wars, the two Yemens started to welcome tourists in the late 1970s and, while the flow is not yet a flood – a few tens of thousands visitors each year – it has grown steadily.

The Yemenis have even tried to develop a flourishing tourist industry but these attempts have largely failed, at least when compared to countries such as Morocco, Tunisia and Egypt. There are no holiday resorts in Yemen, Western-style hotels are rare and many attractions are inaccessible. If you're an individual traveller looking for adventure, you'll enjoy Yemen as it is today. If you prefer to travel in groups, the country is still highly recommended, though costly. If, however, you're after an inexpensive tour within a comfortable framework, you should look elsewhere. Don't expect to make your way through Yemen without some difficulties – but, then, it certainly is worth the effort.

Facts about the Country

HISTORY

Yemen is one of the oldest inhabited regions in the world. According to tradition, Shem, the son of Noah, founded the city of San'a (hence the improbable name 'Sam City'). Whether this is folklore or historical truth, we do know that the Yemen's history dates from the very dawn of humankind.

Pre-Islamic Kingdoms

The earliest known civilisations in southern Arabia existed more than 1000 years before Christ. The kingdoms around the region occupied by today's Yemen sometimes existed side by side, sometimes one after another.

Very different information can be gathered on when these kingdoms were founded or destroyed, their inhabitants, their means of livelihood and the faiths they professed. Modern Western research has concentrated on cultures closer to European ancestry, and much of Arabia's prehistory has remained obscure despite the many ruins, inscriptions and other information about them. And although the Yemenis are proud of their ancient origins, local research concentrates on the Yemen's Islamic period as research into pre-Islamic history is discouraged.

The Frankincense Trade The ancient kingdoms based their existence first on agriculture in the valleys and deltas of the greater wadis and, second, on trade. The trading communities were able to accumulate greater wealth than those communities

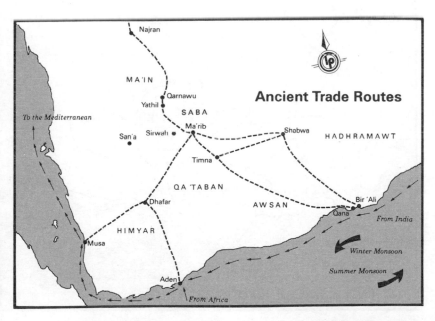

Ancient Trade Routes

9

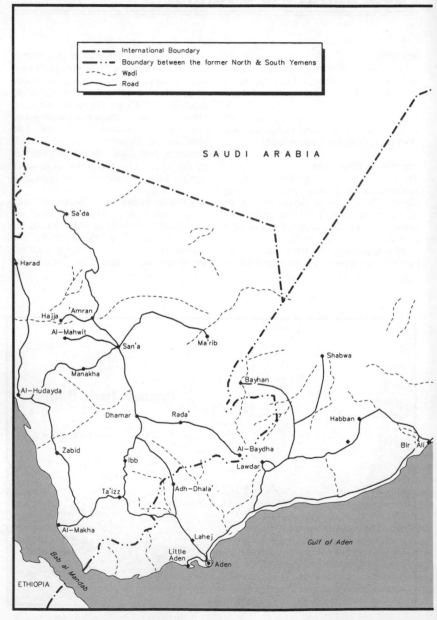

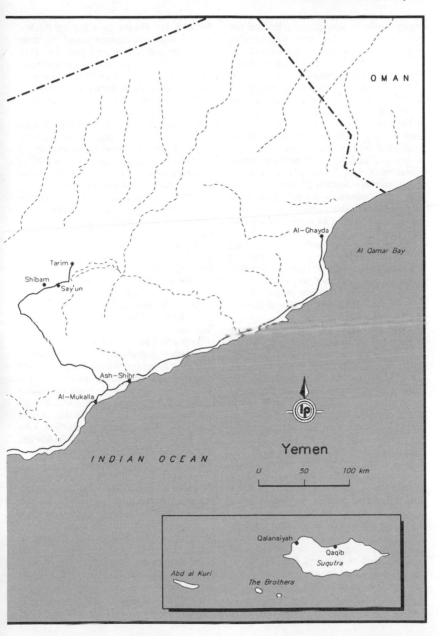

engaged only in agricultural activities; the settlements along the main trade routes became mightier than the others – or perhaps it was the mighty kingdoms that dictated the course of the trade routes.

In ancient times, the most important commodities produced in southern Arabia were myrrh and frankincense, the resins of trees of the Commiphora and Boswellia genera growing only on the southern coastlands of Arabia and on the northern coast of the Horn of Africa. (Frankincense is produced today in western Oman, Yemen and, to a lesser extent, northern Somalia.) These aromatics were highly valued everywhere in the civilised world for the pleasant odours they release when burned as incense. They had great ritual value in many different cultures – from the Egyptian to the Greek and Roman. The oldest Egyptian scriptures describing frankincense date from the 15th century BC; myrrh oil was also used to perfume royal mummies. As the Christmas gospel shows, the Jews, too, valued myrrh and frankincense as highly as gold.

These commodities were carried by sea or by land, and the land routes through Arabia were the first ones to be used on a large scale. Originally, donkeys and mules predominated but, around the 11th century BC, the introduction of camels made transport much more effective. Camels can walk much longer distances without rest or water than donkeys and this meant that the routes could be plotted through dry lands, with only a few stopping places needed for food, water and lodging along the way. From the important frankincense production area of Qana (today's Bir 'Ali) on the shore of the Arabian Sea, it became possible to reach Ghaza, Egypt, in a matter of two months.

The caravans were huge and a single convoy could involve thousands of camels. In addition to fragrances, they carried commodities, such as gold and precious items, that came to Qana by sea from India. As demand for myrrh and frankincense increased around the Mediterranean, all kinds of trade flourished.

Saba & Its Rivals In southern Arabia, several mighty kingdoms along the trade route rose and fell within a period of 1500 years. The most important of these was Saba, which existed for at least 14 centuries from about 1000 BC. Sometimes it was conquered but, most of the time, it was the strongest power in the region.

Saba had been a flourishing kingdom long before written history began. It is first mentioned in the Old Testament description of the visit of the Sabaean queen Bilqis to King Solomon. Obviously, it had became necessary to cement friendly relations between the two powerful rulers, one of whom controlled the southern end of the frankincense road while the other held sway at the northern end. The mission was successful and precious presents were exchanged in an abundance that aroused great admiration among the Biblical chroniclers. Arabian tradition has it that Menelik, the son of King Solomon and Queen Bilqis, became the ruler of Aksum, today's Ethiopia. His ancestry was then claimed by all Ethiopian leaders up to Haile Selassie.

Saba was initially founded in Sirwah but the capital was eventually moved to Maryab, later to be known as Ma'rib. Both towns still exist in present-day Yemen as small villages. The location was strategic, since the natural land route from Qana to the north through the Hadhramawt valley eventually crossed this region. The agricultural wealth of Saba was based on the famous dam in Ma'rib, which was built in the 8th century BC and stood for well over 1000 years.

However, Saba had powerful rivals along the trade route: Najran (in what is now southern Saudi Arabia), Ma'in, with its capitals Qarnawu and Yathil (in the al-Jawf province of today), Awsan, with its capital Miswar (probably in the Shabwa Governorate of today), Qa'taban, with its capital Timna (near present-day Bayhan in the Shabwa Governorate), and Hadhramawt, with its capital Shabwa (in the Hadhramawt and Shabwa governorates). Between the 6th century BC and 2nd century AD, these states alternately fell under Sabaean rule and freed themselves from it.

In the 2nd century BC, still another rival kingdom emerged: Himyar, with its capital Dhafar (now a small village in the Ibb province). The Himyarites lived a little way off the traditional incense route but were closer to the Bab al-Mandab strait. By 50 AD, Himyar controlled the most south-western part of the peninsula and was established as an important regional power.

What helped the rise of Himyar over Saba was the progress of science in the Mediterranean area. In the 1st century AD, a seafarer called Hippalus (some sources cite him as a Greek, others as a Roman) not only discovered the secrets of monsoon winds but developed a practical application for them. 'Let the summer monsoon blow the ships south of the Red Sea and all the way east to India, and the winter monsoon bring them back', he said. According to the nature of each ship's business, it could stop in the port of al-Muza north of Bab al-Mandab (probably near present-day al-Makha) or in the port of Aden a little further off. The Himyarites, who controlled the ports in south-western Arabia, benefited from this development while the Sabaeans were faced with a decline in land-based trade.

External threats were not uncommon, either. The Romans tried to conquer Arabia Felix between 25 BC and 24 BC, sending an expedition led by Aelius Gallus, but were forced to retreat after reaching the walls of Ma'rib. In the 2nd century AD came the Ethiopians, who managed to occupy the region for a few decades. Meanwhile, the old Sabaean dynasty had been replaced by new rulers from the Yemeni highlands and, around 190 AD, the new Sabaean rulers were able to throw out the Ethiopians.

By the end of the 3rd century AD, Himyar had again risen to power and this situation lasted until the Ethiopians returned in 525 AD. Many important developments occurred in the region during this second period of Himyarite rule: the old gods of Saba were forgotten with the conversion of the Himyar kings to Christianity and

Judaism. These religions had greatly intensified their missionary activities in southern Arabia with the weakening of the once mighty kingdom of Saba. The Ethiopians were Christian, too, and many Christian churches were built in the 4th to 6th centuries AD.

The rise of Christianity on the shores of the Mediterranean also had a remarkable impact on life in southern Arabia. Christians did not want to use 'pagan' ritual fragrances, so the importance of the frankincense trade gradually diminished. This trend culminated in 395 AD when Theodosius ruled that Christianity was to be the state religion of the Roman Empire, thus completely halting the flow of frankincense to what had been its main area of consumption.

The Sabaean kingdom thus faced a decline in the foundations of its wealth and the deterioration of its traditional social base. Under these circumstances, maintenance of the great Ma'rib dam was neglected and it broke several times during the first few centuries AD. In 570 AD, the year Muhammad was born, the dam broke for the last time and the inhabitants abandoned Ma'rib, wandering the Arabian Peninsula to settle in new locations.

The year 570 AD is called 'the year of the elephant' because of a third important event: the Ethiopians, whose warring troops had based their superiority on elephants, were defeated at last. But the Himyarites did not benefit from the victory, since they had achieved it by allying themselves with the Persians; by 575 AD, the Persians had managed to subdue this region, as they had already done across the rest of the peninsula.

Medieval Islamic Yemen

In 628, Badhan, the Persian governor of Yemen, converted to Islam and the whole of Yemen soon followed. The expansion of Islam in the Yemen, as elsewhere in the Arabian Peninsula, was rapid because the local strongmen, the sheikhs, always had their whole tribes converted with them; the new religion thus quickly spread from the top of society to the very bottom. Prominent

Yemenis visited the Prophet Muhammad, and the newly established Islamic centre was quick to send preachers and missionaries to guide the new converts along the righteous path. It was during the Prophet's lifetime, in the early 630s, that the first Yemeni mosques were built in San'a, in al-Janad and near Wadi Zabid. The first two still stand today and the third later served to mark the site of the city of Zabid.

At the southern edge of the Islamic empire, Yemen was soon divided into provinces that actively participated in spreading the Islamic revolution. In 632, the year that the Prophet died and the rule of the first orthodox caliphs (the Umayyads) began, the Yemenis sent more than 20,000 troops to serve in the army of Caliph Abu Bakr and to bring Islam into the area now occupied by Syria and Iraq. That same year, Yemen was divided into three provinces: San'a, al-Janad and Hadhramawt.

Further developments within the Islamic empire caused the Yemen's importance to wane, especially when the empire's capital was moved away from the Arabian Peninsula. Soon after the Umayyad Caliphate was founded in 661, the capital was moved to Damascus, leading to the definition of Yemen as one province of the empire. When the Abbasid caliphs seized power in 750, they moved the capital to Baghdad and in 812 made Yemen one of their provinces. As a result of these developments, Yemen saw numerous small, shortlived, semi-independent states and kingdoms – a situation that makes a condensed account of the Yemen's medieval history seem very fragmented.

The Ziyadids In 819, the tribes in southern Tihama revolted against the Abbasid governor in San'a. The governor appointed an able man, Muhammad ibn Ziyad, to settle the dispute and become the new governor. In 820, ibn Ziyad founded the town of Zabid near the famous mosque of Abu Musa bin Asha'ir and, eventually, he made his realm virtually independent. The dynasty founded by Muhammad ibn Ziyad lasted several hundred years but gradually declined under his successors.

Ibn Ziyad turned the al-Asha'ir mosque into a 'university', which was to be one of the most important centres of Sunni teaching in the Islamic world for hundreds of years. The Zabid university was reportedly in operation as late as the 18th century but, today, only the al-Asha'ir mosque remains.

The Zaydis In 897, a descendant of the Prophet, Yahya bin Husayn bin Qasim ar-Rassi, was called from Madina to mediate a war between the Hashid and Bakil tribes in northern Yemen. He founded the dynasty that was to last longest in Yemen – the Zaydi dynasty of Sa'da.

Yahya bin Husayn preached the Shi'a teachings of Islam, claiming that the Muslims should be ruled only by men from an unbreakable line of infallible imams descended from the Prophet's cousin and son-in-law, 'Ali. The teachings of Yahya made a clear distinction between what belonged to the state and what was private, both materially and spiritually, and placed great emphasis on the art of war. These principles greatly contributed to the formation of an exceptionally stable state and sustained the Zaydi dynasty which, during the centuries, controlled various regions around Sa'da and was only temporarily conquered by foreigners.

The Zaydi state was at its largest from 1918 to 1962, when it was simply called the Yemen. The 1962 revolution replaced imamic rule with a secular government, ending a 1000-year era in Yemeni history.

The Najahids & Sulayhids In 1012, the Ziyadid dynasty of Zabid ended when its last ruler, ibn Salama, died and left an infant successor. After the ensuing power struggle, an Ethiopian slave called Najah rose to power in Zabid. He ruled for 40 years and founded a dynasty carrying his name.

Meanwhile, in the mountainous Haraz district, a devout Muslim by the name of Ali as-Sulayhi slowly gathered followers and, in 1046, founded the Sulayhid state on Mt

Masar. Over the next 17 years, this state extended its influence across the Yemen. Ali as-Sulayhi belonged to the Fatimid faction of the Ismaili group, part of the Shi'a sect of Islam (see the Population & People section in this chapter). Today, the remaining Yemeni Ismailis live near Manakha, close to the original birthplace of the Sulayhid state.

The Najahids and the Sulayhids struggled for control of the southern part of Yemen for the next 100 years. Often, the Najahids ruled the Tihama in summer, while the Sulayhids descended from the mountains during the cool winters to tax the Tihamese. In the mountains, Sulayhid rule remained largely undisputed.

In 1067, an exceptional thing happened in the history of Islamic Yemen: a woman became the head of the Sulayhid state when King Mukarram's widow, Queen Arwa bint Ahmad, succeeded her husband to the throne. Queen Arwa, an extraordinarily wise and well-educated woman, ruled the Sulayhid state until her death in 1138. She moved the capital south from San'a to the town of Jibla (near Ibb), where the mosque of Queen Arwa still stands in honour of her memory.

The Ayyubids & Rasulids After the demise of the Najahid and Sulayhid dynasties, there was a brief era of disorder in the Yemen. For about 50 years (from 1173) most of the country, excluding the Zaydi state in the north, was ruled by the Egyptian Ayyubids. The Egyptians were not particularly successful in controlling such a remote area and, finally, in 1229, the country was left to the rule of one al-Mansur 'Umar ibn 'Ali ibn Rasul, a man of Turkoman origin. The Rasulid dynasty had its capital in Ta'izz and remained in power for more than two centuries, until the year 1454. At times, the dynasty ruled most of the Yemen, from Hadhramawt to Mecca.

These times were beneficial for the university of Zabid, which was at its most active during the Ayyubid and Rasulid eras. Thousands of Yemeni and foreign students attended the more than 200 schools of the town.

The Tahirids & Kathirids The Rasulids were followed briefly by the house of at-Tahir from Lahej, who ruled the south-western part of the country from 1454 to 1526. In the Hadhramawt area, a new dynasty, the Kathirids, rose to power in the 15th century. They managed to stabilise the region and it remained under their rule until the 1967 revolution.

With the Zaydis, these dynasties were the last Yemeni houses to rule the country. From about 1500, Yemen was confronted by a totally new phenomenon: European colonialism.

Modern Yemen
In 1507, the Portuguese annexed the island of Socotra in the Arabian Sea. This event was not only important for the island (the population of which still is predominantly Christian), but it was also the start of an ever-increasing European presence in southern Arabia. This development was made possible partly by the general rise of Europe and partly by the gradual degradation of local Yemeni powers, who had exhausted themselves over centuries of hostilities. While there were still important centres of Islamic learning in the Yemen, the region as a whole had already ceased to play a major role in world history. The emerging colonial powers of Europe soon recognised the strategic importance of this slowly developed vacuum and were eager to take advantage of the opportunity.

The First Ottoman Occupation The Portuguese tried to extend their presence to mainland Yemen in 1513, when Affenso d'Albuquerque, who had led the invasion of Socotra, attacked Aden. His attempt failed, however.

The Portuguese operations prompted the Mameluke rulers of Egypt to protect their interests in the southern Red Sea. They sent a large fleet to Yemen and succeeded in taking control of most of the Tihama and large portions of the highlands. However, they too were unable to conquer Aden. The Mamelukes were supported by Ottoman Turks, who equipped them with modern firearms.

In 1517, the Mamelukes in Egypt were themselves dethroned by the Ottomans. The Ottomans, too, soon managed to conquer most of the Yemen: Ta'izz in 1545, Aden in 1547 and San'a in 1548. This was the beginning of the first period of Ottoman rule in Yemen – an era that lasted for a century.

Although the Ottoman occupation was a difficult time for the Yemen, the period also saw important economic developments. The coffee trade, which had started in the late 1400s, greatly expanded under Turkish rule. The town of al-Makha on the southernmost shore of the Red Sea became the most important coffee port in the world and, in 1618, English and Dutch traders opened coffee factories in al-Makha to refine coffee grown in the Yemeni highlands.

The Ottoman occupation ended in 1636 when the Zaydi imams finally fulfilled their dream of freeing all of Yemen from Turkish oppression.

Zaydi Rule (1636-1849) The prospects for the newly expanded Zaydi state seemed glorious indeed in the 17th and early 18th centuries. The realm extended from Hadhramawt in the east to 'Asir in the north and the coffee trade boomed in an unprecedented way. Belgian, French and Danish merchants were actively trading in al-Makha and, by around 1720, Yemen virtually had a monopoly on the world coffee market – merchants found it hard to meet the demand for coffee.

The situation changed rapidly, however, when the coffee plant was smuggled out of Yemen and replanted in Brazil and Indonesia. Demand for Yemeni coffee soon vanished after 1740. In addition, the Zaydis faced growing internal and external threats to their authority. The Sa'udi sheikhs invaded the northern Tihama several times during this period; the most serious assault occurred between 1805 and 1809 when the Wahhabis (from what is now central Saudi Arabia) looted the Tihama down to al-Hudayda, leaving hardly a house standing.

In the south, the Shafa'i sultan of Lahej, who belonged to the Abdali tribe, put an end to Zaydi domination in 1728. The Zaydi imams lost control of Aden and the coasts of the Arabian Sea. This event can be seen as the beginning of a process that culminated in the eventual formation of the two independent Yemeni states in the 20th century.

British Occupation of Southern Yemen In the 19th century, the British expressed growing interest in the region. Already in 1799, they had annexed the island of Perim near Bab al-Mandab and, in 1839, they conquered Aden. By 1843, Aden had become a fortress belonging to the British Raj in India. It was not only seen as an important port on a major sea route but was also highly valued for the artesian wells in Sheikh Othman, which provided plentiful supplies of drinkable water. The Kuria Muria islands were occupied in 1854.

Luhaya in 1763

A friendship treaty between Britain and the Sultan of Lahej was signed in 1857. Moves towards full colonisation of southern Yemen continued in the 1870s when Britain, worried by the Turkish advance in the north, signed more and more 'protection' treaties with local sheikhs. In addition to the sultanate of Lahej, 20 small states or sheikhdoms in the Adeni hinterlands and on the island of Socotra signed 'peace and friendship' treaties with Great Britain between 1880 and 1914, thus gradually forming what was to be known as the South Arabian Protectorate of Great Britain. The line between Turkish Arabia and British Arabia was drawn in 1905 and, with minor modifications, this so-called 'Violet Line' was to mark the boundary between the North and South Yemeni states of the 20th century.

Up to the 1950s, areas around Aden continued to be added to those under British control, with the eastern parts of the region the last to join. In the end, British South Arabia consisted of the Aden Colony, the Western Protectorate and the Eastern Protectorate.

The Second Ottoman Occupation The Turks returned to Yemen in 1849, first occupying the Tihama as a result of skirmishes with the British and the Egyptians. After the opening of the Suez Canal in 1869, the Turks were able to greatly strengthen their presence in the region. In 1871, they occupied Ta'izz, in 1872 San'a and finally, in 1882, even Sa'da, the Zaydi capital. From 1901 to 1905, the borders between Turkish and British spheres of influence were defined and the 1905 border agreement between the colonial powers drew the line that was later established as the boundary between the two Yemens.

Although the second Turkish occupation involved all of Yemen not under British rule, the power of the Turks was certainly not undisputed. The Turkish administration was notorious for mismanagement and oppression; local sheikhs frequently rebelled against the foreign authorities and several mountain fortresses were never conquered

by the Turks. Constant resistance effectively prevented Turkey from founding a stable province in the Yemen.

In 1904, the leadership of the Zaydis passed to Yahya ibn Muhammad, the son of Imam Muhammad ibn Yahya, from the highly respected Zaydi family of Hamid ad-Din. Imam Yahya quickly established himself as the undisputed leader of the Yemenis, organised a most efficient insurrection against the Turks and, by 1905, had succeeded in conquering almost all the Turkish garrisons. The Turks quickly deployed over 40,000 men to recapture the country and fighting continued until a peace treaty was signed in 1907. In the treaty, Turkey agreed to begin fundamental administrative reform in the Yemen.

Although a framework for peaceful coexistence had been agreed between Imam Yahya and the Turks, another source of rebellion arose – the 1909 uprising of several North Tihama tribes under the leadership of Sayyid Muhammad al-Idrisi, who was to play an important part in the subsequent developments. In 1910, Imam Yahya's troops in the highlands also took up arms after finding out that the Turks were unwilling to meet their treaty obligations.

In 1911, however, the Turks succeeded in reoccupying the garrisons seized by Imam Yahya. Negotiations between the warring parties produced the Treaty of Da"an, which gave Imam Yahya and his Zaydi rule certain autonomy in the Yemeni highlands. This treaty was observed until the end of the second Ottoman occupation.

Meanwhile, hostilities between the Turks and the Idrisi forces continued in the Tihama, with an increasing number of active players becoming involved before and during WW I. During the Turko-Italian War (1911-1912), all the Tihama ports were bombed by the Italians, who dreamed of making the Red Sea an Italian lake. In 1915, the Anglo-Idrisi Treaty guaranteed the Idrisi forces some support from the British in Aden. Imam Yahya remained neutral in the Turko-British conflict.

By the time the Turks finally retreated

from Yemen in 1919, WW I had stripped the Ottoman state of its imperial status. The country was left to Imam Yahya, who became king of Yemen and, in the Lausanne Treaty of 1923, Turkey officially relinquished all territories in the Arabian Peninsula.

The Imamate of Yemen The problems of the newly established Yemeni state, the Kingdom of Yemen, were still not over. Idrisi forces continued to occupy much of the Tihama and it was not until 1925 that Imam Yahya was able to seize al-Hudayda. From there, the imam's troops rapidly advanced north of Midi, very near the present border between Yemen and Saudi Arabia.

The declining Idrisi state had to ally itself with the head of the evolving Saudi state, ibn Sa'ud, whose goal was to annex the former Idrisi state (that is, all of the Tihama to the north of al-Hudayda). To the north, Imam Yahya had similar plans, claiming the 'Asir region. The conflict culminated in the Saudi-Yemeni war of 1934. The Saudi forces rapidly advanced to al-Hudayda, forcing the imam to sign a treaty on Saudi terms and leaving 'Asir temporarily under Saudi rule for 40 years. In 1974 neither side made any claims on the issue, and the border between Saudi Arabia and Yemen drawn by the Ta'if Treaty is still observed today.

After the Turkish retreat, the British did not lose interest in the northern part of the Yemen. The forces opposing Imam Yahya could freely use Aden as their stronghold and, in 1948, a group led by Sayyid Abdullah al-Wazzir succeeded in killing Imam Yahya. However, the imam's eldest son, Ahmad, was able to throw the insurgents out of the country.

Imam Ahmad moved the Yemeni capital from San'a to Ta'izz and cautiously began to open the country. Imam Yahya had secured his power by keeping Yemen in a state of extreme isolation and backwardness; Imam Ahmad used foreign aid to start some development programmes and also established the Yemen's first diplomatic relations with

countries such as Britain, the USA and Egypt in 1951 and the Soviet Union in 1956.

The Imamate of Yemen remained, however, an underdeveloped country. By the end of Imam Ahmad's rule, there were still no paved roads, no Yemeni doctors (and only a handful of foreign ones), no schools other than Koran schools (which were attended by only one child in 20), no legislation except the Koranic Shari'a law and no factories. Disease abounded, with around 50% of the population suffering from some kind of venereal disease and 80% from trachoma. In 1962, Yemen was probably the most medieval country in the world.

The 1950s saw frequent border disputes between Yemen and the Aden Protectorate. In 1958, Imam Ahmad sought protection from Cairo. These negotiations led to the foundation of the United Arab States, a union of Yemen and the United Arab Republic (Egypt and Syria). The pact had little practical significance and was formally dissolved in 1961 by the United Arab Republic (UAR). Nevertheless, it certainly served to promote Egyptian interests when revolution broke out in Yemen one year later.

Birth of the Yemen Arab Republic (YAR) Although Imam Ahmad had faced considerable resistance, including an assassination attempt in 1961 in which he was wounded in the shoulder, he stayed in power until his death in September 1962. He was briefly succeeded by his son, Crown Prince Muhammad al-Badr, but a group of army officers led by Colonel Abdullah Sallal started a revolution after only a week, actively backed by troops from the UAR. Many of the officers had studied abroad and were influenced by Nasserite Arab Nationalism. The new regime founded the Yemen Arab Republic. The YAR was soon recognised by the USA and the USSR and, early in 1963, became a member of the United Nations.

Despite this, Muhammad al-Badr was not defeated. He fled to the northern mountains and began a bitter, eight-year civil war backed by Britain and Saudi Arabia. The

Republicans, supported by Egypt and the Soviet Union, were able to hold their position against the Royalists but could not achieve a final victory. The battles were often fierce, with heavy casualties on both sides; it has been estimated that up to 4% of the North Yemeni population was killed in the hostilities and Egypt lost almost 20,000 troops – more than in the 1967 war against Israel!

The prolonged war did not yield any positive results for the Nasserites and, by 1967, competing views had evolved within the Republican party about the course the revolution should take. The faction that emerged as the winner held that the existence of the new republic could only be guaranteed by establishing a friendly relationship with the Saudis. This view was considerably at odds with the ideology that had spawned the revolution five years earlier and, indeed, in late 1967, President Sallal was exiled to Iraq. He was replaced by Qadi Abdul Rahman al-Iryani, with General Hassan al-Amri as the head of the Republican army.

At the same time, the Egyptians left the Yemen, defeated in June 1967 by Israel and disillusioned by the ideological unreliability of the illiterate Yemeni tribespeople, who tended to be 'Royalists by day and Republicans by night'. The situation was perhaps best reflected by the emergence of two new verbs in the Arabic language: *tamallaka*, 'to go Royalist', and *tajamhara*, 'to go Republican'.

The scene was thus left to the Yemenis. To the surprise of almost everybody, the Royalists were not able to defeat the Republicans after the Egyptians' departure, although they laid siege to San'a from December 1967 to February 1968. After this unsuccessful siege, the Royalist side seemed to run out of steam and the final battles were fought between different Republican factions.

Victory was won by General al-Amri, who allied himself with the tribal sheikhs to uproot the leftist elements from the army – the very same elements most responsible for starting the revolution in 1962. He simultaneously sought peace with the remaining Royalist forces, tribe by tribe and, backed by

the Saudis, was finally able to end the war in 1970. Imam al-Badr was exiled to Britain and, in July 1970, the Yemen Arab Republic was recognised by Saudi Arabia.

Birth of the People's Democratic Republic of Yemen (PDRY) Developments in the southern part of the country were also extremely violent during the 1960s.

Britain had certainly done little to develop its protectorate states in southern Arabia during its 100-year presence. The area had been ruled from Bombay until, in 1927, the hinterlands and, in 1937, the Aden Colony were officially proclaimed British colonies. The 31 small sultanates that formed the South Arabian Protectorate served as little more than a buffer against possible threats from the north – Britain had opted for 'indirect rule' through the Western and Eastern Arabian protectorates. This meant that Britain maintained a minimal presence outside Aden itself, intervening only when local power struggles and the frequent border disputes with the Kingdom of Yemen required it.

In the early 1960s, the British still saw Aden as one of their most important permanent bases and planned to unite it with the hinterlands via the newly established Federation of the Emirates of the South (renamed the Federation of South Arabia in 1962). However, nationalist spirit in the region had already awakened in the region – frequent strikes in opposition to British rule occurred in the colony as early as the late 1950s – and Britain faced mounting difficulties in controlling developments.

The final boost for the nationalist movement came from the 1962 revolution in the north. The British decision to back the Royalists there certainly helped spread Republican ideas to the south, particularly when a third of the Adeni population were migrant workers of North Yemeni origin. In 1963 and 1964, full-scale guerrilla warfare was in progress in the Radfan mountains. The strife spread to the city of Aden in the following years as the nationalists gained increasing support among the Yemeni population.

The principal force on the Yemeni side was the National Liberation Front (NLF), formed by Marxist and nationalistic militants who had gone north after the 1962 revolution. In contrast to what had occurred in the north, the Nasserite wing of the liberation fighters (FLOSY – Front for the Liberation of Occupied South Yemen) did not gain a strong foothold in South Yemen. The NLF was a far more left-wing organisation than any that could have developed in the Imamate of the north – Aden's status as a major port with trade unions and contacts with the outside world had created a group of freedom fighters with much more radical ideas.

By late 1966 and early 1967, the British finally began to make preparations for the independence of South Yemen, promising to withdraw from Aden in November the same year. However, in June, after Egypt's defeat by Israel, the date of withdrawal was pushed back to 9 January 1968. The Yemenis refused to wait that long. Intense fighting late in 1967 forced Britain to announce that British South Arabia would become independent on 30 November 1967. The NLF forced the last Britons to leave Aden by midnight on 29 November. The People's Republic of South Yemen was born.

The new republic, under the leadership of President Qahtan ash-Shaabi, found itself in a most difficult situation. External relations were in a very sensitive state, with Saudi Arabia naturally suspicious of a Marxist country on their southern border, open hostilities at the Omani border (where the NLF supported the guerrilla movement in the Dhofar region) and the YAR supporting a right-wing opposition. Internally, the final power struggles lay ahead. The economy was on the verge of collapse following the departure of the British and this situation was exacerbated by the closure of the Suez Canal that same year, which greatly diminished Aden's importance as a port. The country was able to survive only with economic support from Communist countries, especially the Soviet Union, China and East Germany.

The internal power struggle was resolved in June 1969 when the government moved even further to the left in the so-called Corrective Movement. Qahtan ash-Shaabi resigned, Salem Rubaya 'Ali was appointed president and a new constitution was drafted. In 1969, a major nationalisation of the economy left only the oil refinery of British Petroleum untouched and, in 1970, the name of the country was changed to the People's Democratic Republic of Yemen (PDRY).

The Two Yemens

At the beginning of the 1970s, there existed two independent Yemeni states. Both had emerged from very difficult conditions and faced the task of building modern states from scratch. Both had to rely on foreign aid; funds came to the PDRY almost exclusively from the Eastern bloc, while the YAR received developmental aid from Saudi Arabia, Western countries and the Soviet Union.

As if to emphasise the enormous problems faced by the two Yemens, the 1970s saw two short border wars between them. The first, in September 1972, was mediated by the Arab League. In the resulting Cairo Treaty, the two Yemens agreed to merge within 12 months to form the Yemeni Republic – a surprise announcement confirmed in November 1972 by presidents al-Iryani of North Yemen and Salem Rubaya 'Ali of South Yemen.

The unification was postponed, however, and relations between the countries gradually became more remote. In 1974, a bloodless coup in the YAR replaced President al-Iryani with Colonel Ibrahim al-Hamdi. This development steered the country further to the right and improved North Yemen's relations with Saudi Arabia and the USA. The PDRY continued to follow a leftist path and, although relations with its neighbours gradually improved (in 1976, Saudi Arabia finally recognised the country, and hostilities with Oman ended), the unification of the two Yemens still seemed improbable.

The late 1970s were a difficult time for the government of the YAR. In 1977, President al-Hamdi was assassinated, possibly by northern supporters of the former Imamate, and his successor Colonel Ahmad ibn Husayn al-Ghasmi ruled for less than a year before also being assassinated. Al-Ghasmi was killed by a bomb carried in a suitcase from Aden and, although there was no conclusive evidence on who had planned the operation, South Yemeni President Salem Rubaya 'Ali was ousted and executed in July 1978. Armed clashes between the two Yemens occurred immediately and were renewed for the last time in 1979.

The battles were to no avail – the largely undemarcated border between the two countries did not move a single centimetre.

YAR: Towards Stability The first 15 years or so after the revolution were tumultuous ones for the YAR, which faced both internal and external security problems during this period. When friendly relations with Saudi Arabia, the YAR's big neighbour, were finally secured by the pro-Saudi military government of 1974, the basic conditions for improved stability were created.

In 1978, Lieutenant Colonel 'Ali Abdullah Salah became president of the republic. Whether because of his personal capabilities as a leader or because of the weariness of opposing forces, the country enjoyed a period of increasing stability under his rule in the 1980s. The last serious unrest occurred in the Ta'izz, Ibb and Dhamar provinces in 1981 and 1982 when dissidents from the PDRY, in coalition with fundamentalist Islamic forces, urged rebellion against the central government.

The cabinet consisted of some 20 ministers and, in 1979, the Constitutional People's Assembly was expanded to 159 members, with the president as chair. It was this body that, in 1983 and 1988, elected Colonel Salah to his second and third five-year terms as president. No political parties were allowed in the YAR and all important positions were held by the army.

Conflicts between competing interest groups were increasingly contained within the army and cabinet stability was guaranteed by carefully choosing the ministers so that different tribes were equitably represented. President Salah himself belongs to the Hashid tribe, who saved him in the 1979 confrontation with the PDRY by quickly mobilising some 50,000 troops.

Under its constitution, the YAR was an Arab, Islamic and independent state which derived all its laws from the Shari'a, the Islamic law. Nevertheless, personal freedom, private property, freedom of speech, and the inviolability of homes, places of worship and centres of learning warranted special attention in the wording of the constitution. Indeed, life in the YAR was apparently based on a largely Western set of values in spite of the deep religiosity of the people. Some Western visitors have found this mix of modern Western and traditional Arabic attitudes disappointing and criticised the Yemenis for having blindly adopted 'Western-style consumerism'.

While it may be true that the government catapulted the YAR from the medieval system of the Imamate to the 20th century in less than 20 years, this was clearly the will of the Yemeni people. In the days of the civil war, the last tribes of the north only dropped their weapons to give the new central government a chance to fulfil its promise to turn Yemen into a state as advanced as those developed by oil-rich Saudi Arabia. It may be said that the vision of the welfare state earned the government the necessary support from the people.

PDRY: Continuing the Struggle From the very beginning, the development path chosen by the PDRY was diametrically opposed to that of its northern neighbour. Because the forces that expelled the British in the late 1960s were extreme leftist, the revolution in the south led eventually to the birth of the first and only Marxist Arab state. The ruling Yemen Socialist Party was seeking to steer a path between Chinese and Soviet influences, and its declarations on world affairs during the 1970s were further to the left than those of the leading countries in the Communist world, peaking in such publicity-seeking acts as offering political asylum not only to Palestinian hijackers but also to West European Marxist terrorists using similar methods.

The developments of the early 1980s had a somewhat moderating influence, while the government moved closer to the Soviet camp. The PDRY was one of the very few countries in the world with which the USA did not establish diplomatic relations throughout the 1980s. This may have been more the result of impassivity on the part of the South Yemeni side than a sign of active decision-making in Washington, but the effect was that the PDRY was generally regarded as ruled by an extremist, leftist government.

While the YAR was becoming a more stable and controlled society, the PDRY continued to be beset by internal and external conflicts. During the first years of independence, the young republic was engaged in exporting its revolution to neighbouring countries, leading to serious conflicts with Oman and Saudi Arabia. Once these problems were resolved in 1976, skirmishes with the YAR continued, culminating in the 1979 war.

During the 1980s, there were only minor clashes on the country's borders but internal problems were far from being resolved. Most of the conflicts were personified in two men, Abdul Fattah Ismail and 'Ali Nasr Muhammad, who competed for power during the late 1970s and alternately held the post of president after the execution of former president Salem Rubaya 'Ali. In April 1980, following the 1979 YAR-PDRY war, 'Ali Nasr Muhammad was finally nominated as president and Abdul Fattah Ismail flew to exile in Moscow.

Under the rule of 'Ali Nasr Muhammad the country appeared to steer a less isolated course and very gradually opened its doors to the outside world, especially to other Arab countries, while strictly maintaining its socialist doctrine. Although the country seemed to have entered an era of relatively stable development in the first half of the 1980s, tensions again surfaced after the return of Abdul Fattah Ismail in late 1985. In January 1986, fierce civil war broke out in Aden, destroying many buildings and killing thousands of people in just a couple of weeks (the official figure was 3000 while unofficial estimates spoke of up to 42,000 people killed).

As a result of this catastrophe, 'Ali Nasr Muhammad fled to Ethiopia and Abdul Fattah Ismail was killed. The new president of the republic was chosen from those who had watched the crisis from a safe distance; in February 1986, Haidar Abu Bakr al-Attash flew to Aden from Moscow to become head of state. From the outside, little seemed to have changed – the new cabinet initially continued to follow a strictly pro-Soviet foreign policy and an orthodox Marxist domestic course. The key questions in all these disputes may have been more tribal in nature; Abdul Fattah Ismail was born in a village that belonged to the YAR, while 'Ali Nasr Muhammad's birthplace was inside the borders of the PDRY.

One Yemen

However, global politics changed a lot in the last years of the 1980s. The Gorbachev era and the near-collapse of the Soviet economy dried up the flow of both ideological and financial aid to most of Moscow's Third World allies, forcing them to re-evaluate their situation. The government of the bankrupt PDRY had few friends to turn to: they chose the brothers next door, the YAR.

In fact, the quest for unification of Yemen had continued since the birth of the two states. It had already become a tradition that, after any armed conflict, the countries publish a declaration and sign an agreement of eventual unification. However, the practical questions were always left unresolved. For example, the 1986 agreement, signed in Libya, stated that one of its goals was a 'unified political organisation'. Whether this meant a no-party, one-party or multiparty system was not specified.

Apart from the economic disaster status of

the PDRY and the deep wish of the Yemeni people, there was another pressing reason for unification: in the mid-1980s, significant oil fields were discovered in the desert area between the countries, on both sides of the undemarcated border. The governments faced the choice of defining the boundary or forming a neutral zone to be used cooperatively. Sensibly, in May 1988, they chose the latter option, accelerating the progress towards unity.

On 30 November 1989, the leaders of the two countries agreed on a concrete, 14-month plan to complete the process of unification. According to the plan, the legislative bodies of the two countries were to complete a proposal for the constitution of the Unified Republic of Yemen within one year, to be approved through a referendum within two months after that. Thus, the new state should have been born on 30 January 1991.

There was both internal and external opposition, though. The religious elite of the north, centred in Sa'da, used the mosques to spread terror propaganda about the secular south, where 'women go unveiled and men go drunk in the streets'. They received considerable support from the Saudis, who had watched nervously as the YAR, a former satellite, gradually drifted out of the Saudi sphere of influence. With oil wells of its own now in production, the YAR had succeeded in diminishing its economic dependence on Saudi Arabia. In 1989, the YAR, together with Egypt, Iraq and Jordan, founded the shortlived Arab Cooperation Council, a move that was certain to make the Saudis worry about losing their dominance on the peninsula. A unified Yemen, with a population surpassing that of their own, and strategically located by the shores of the Red and Arabian seas in control of the Bab al-Mandab strait, was a nightmare to Saudi security analysts.

Opposition to the unification backfired, however. Facing the possibility of failure at the critical moment, the Yemeni governments decided to wait no longer. During the spring of 1990, several preparatory steps were taken in rapid succession: the border was demilitarised and opened, state security forces were dissolved, currencies were made valid in both countries. Free enterprise was legalised in the PDRY and political parties in the YAR. Then, suddenly, on 22 May 1990 and several months ahead of the schedule, the Republic of Yemen was declared, under a provisional constitution, 'with San'a as the political and Aden as the economic capital'.

In a referendum held on 15 and 16 May, 1991, the Yemenis voted for the new constitution. The main opposition came from the religious parties who in vain demanded that the constitution declare Islamic Shari'a as the 'sole' rather than the 'main' source of legislation.

During the 1990-91 Gulf crisis, Yemen adopted a moderate stand toward the Iraqi occupation of Kuwait. It favoured an 'Arab solution' and demanded the withdrawal of Iraqi troops from Kuwait and of Western forces from Saudi Arabia. This was badly viewed by the Saudis (and Kuwaitis), who soon expelled all Yemeni citizens and cut off all economic aid to the Yemen. The Western press also criticised the Yemeni position, which was interpreted as support for Iraq and even alliance with Baghdad. The benefits of the unification were thus quickly negated by developments Yemen had had no part in.

GEOGRAPHY

Yemen's Arabic name, al-Yaman, suggests its geographic location at the southernmost tip of the Arabian Peninsula. The early Muslims living around Mecca divided their lands into those lying northward, or *sha:man*, and those lying to the south, or *yamanan*. Even today, Syrians informally refer to their country, and especially its capital, as *ash-Sha:m*; while *al-yaman* became the official name of the Yemen. (Yemenis are eager to point out other derivatives of the root verbs in question, relating the name to prosperity, but this is not fair to the Syrians, whose country's name would then foretell calamity.)

Yemen lies between latitudes 12°40'N and 19°N and between longitudes 42°30'E and

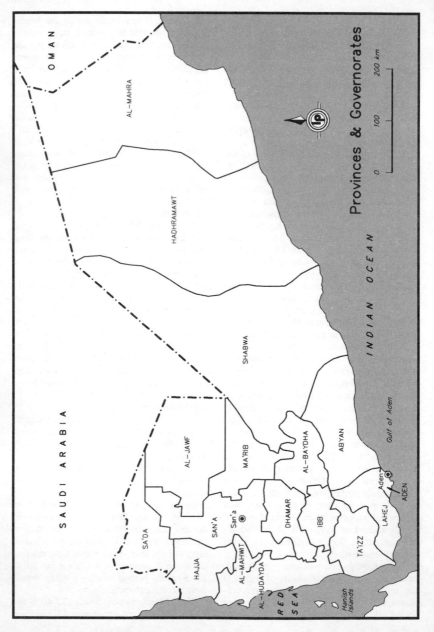

Provinces & Governorates

53°E on the shores of the southern Red Sea and the western part of the Arabian Sea, the Gulf of Aden. The seas are joined by the narrow strait of Bab al-Mandab ('gate of lament'), which separates the peninsula from the African continent.

If you look for Yemen in an atlas printed in the 1970s or 1980s, you may find different names for the countries. What may be called 'Yemen' or 'North Yemen' was officially known as the Yemen Arab Republic (YAR); 'South Yemen' was the People's Democratic Republic of Yemen (PDRY). If maps were the only source of information, you might be tempted to call the countries West and East Yemen, since the PDRY seems to stretch even further to the north than the YAR, while most of the area of the PDRY lies to the east of the YAR. The explanation is that most of the population of the PDRY lives in the coastal area south of the YAR, on the narrow strip of land extending as far west as the Bab al-Mandab strait; most of the eastern part of the country is desert.

Yemen shares borders with Saudi Arabia to the north and Oman to the east. The borders are largely undemarcated desert boundaries and you may find them drawn quite differently on maps; the countries involved refuse to draw them at all. There have been some disputes in the last decades but, by and large, the deserts have not warranted serious claims.

Some islands also belong to the Yemen. Kamaran and the Hanish Islands in the Red Sea and Perim in the Bab al-Mandab strait are relatively small, while Socotra, off the tip of the African Horn, is the largest and most important. The extremely poor Kamaran has some symbolic value for the Yemenis: in the early days of its independence, the PDRY claimed this poor island (together with the Kuria Muria islands off the Omani coast), hundreds of km out of its reach but only a few km off the coast of the YAR. Today, the most popular cigarette brand in the country is Kamaran.

Across the narrow seas are Black African neighbours: Ethiopia to the west, Somalia to the south and tiny Djibouti between them,

just across the Bab al-Mandab strait. Cultural exchange in the region has always been significant and the coastal areas of Yemen possess a distinctively 'African' flavour. The inland areas, on the other hand, have remained purely 'Arabic'.

Yemen's location by a major waterway has exposed the country to more remote influences, peaking with the colonisation of the northern parts by Ottoman Turks and of the southern parts by the English. Despite this history, Yemen has remained remote and isolated from the West and its extraordinary geography has greatly contributed to this. Indeed, understanding the landscape of the region is the key to understanding Yemen in other respects as well.

The Arabian Peninsula is an immense plate of granite, partly covered by shallow layers of younger sedimentary rocks. The plate is tilted, with the south-western edge, the Yemen, elevated and the north-eastern parts warped down. Accordingly, Yemen is sometimes referred to as the roof of Arabia or even the Tibet or Switzerland of Arabia, though the latter nicknames are misleading.

When looked at from west to east at the latitude of San'a, the topography of Yemen offers remarkable variety. The coastal strip (known as the Tihama) extends along the Red Sea from the southernmost tip of Yemen north into Saudi Arabia. This sandy plain, some 20 km to 50 km wide, is absolutely flat and has a tropical character. It ends abruptly at a steep, mountainous ridge known as the western mountains. Several of the peaks are well over 3000 metres and the highest point on the Arabian Peninsula, Jabal an-Nabi Shu'ayb, rises about 3700 metres above sea level.

Further to the east lie the fertile high plateaus for which Yemen is so famous. The Yemeni capital, San'a, is in the centre of the San'a basin at an altitude of 2250 metres. Mountains completely surround the plateaus. The eastern mountain ridge is somewhat less dramatic than the western, with fewer and lower peaks and a more gently sloping appearance. Several parts of the highlands are still volcanically active;

hot springs can be found here and the area is prone to earthquakes.

The eastern mountains slowly descend from above 2000 metres to about 1000 metres. At this altitude, the rocky landscape is transformed into the great sands of the vast Arabian desert, ar-Ruba' al-Khali, which extends its southernmost tip into the middle of the Yemen. The name means 'the empty quarter' and it is this quarter of the peninsula that so dominates the Western notion of Arabia. Well, you *can* find camels in Yemen. However, only around 1% of Yemenis are estimated to be nomadic – most of the population practise agriculture on the coastal plains, along the wadis of the mountain foothills or in the central highlands.

In the Yemen's southern part, a narrow coastal plain is occasionally broken by volcanic rocks extending right to the seashore. In western Yemen, the land rises rapidly inland in enormous fractures to the highlands of northern Yemen. Further to the east, the steepness of the terrain gradually eases and, at the Omani frontier, the highest point in the north-south cross section of the country is less than 1000 metres above sea level.

The vast mountain ridge that runs between the southern coast and ar-Ruba' al-Khali offers, for the most part, a very nondramatic landscape of arid tableland. Eastern Yemen does, however, have an important topographic feature – the valley of Wadi Hadhramawt. The valley is some 150 to 200 km inland and runs parallel to the coast (west to east) for half the width of the country before suddenly turning south-east to reach the sea. This fertile valley is an important part of Yemen and its inhabitants live in relative isolation from the rest of the country.

All this geographic variety is crammed into a country of only 532,000 sq km – smaller than France. At least two-thirds of this area is uninhabited; most of the Yemen's important centres are in the western coastlands and mountains.

CLIMATE & VEGETATION
Climatically, Yemen lies in the Sahel belt and shares many features with African countries

at around the same latitude. However, because of its topographic characteristics, Yemen has never been a country haunted by famine. The high mountain ridges trap moisture from the winds blowing in off nearby seas and, as a result, Yemen is the most arable spot on the Arabian Peninsula. Indeed, it is known as 'the green land of Arabia'.

Because of the extensive variations in its topography, Yemen has several distinct climatic regions.

The Tihama & Southern Coast
Despite the proximity of the sea, the Tihama and the southern coast form an arid zone. Rainfall is scanty – in most parts, between 100 mm and 200 mm annually. Most of the rain falls between late July and September, with only occasional showers during the rest of the year. Temperatures are high all year round. Night-time temperatures fall to between 18°C and 20°C from December to February and to about 27°C to 35°C in June and July. Maximum daytime temperatures range from 32°C in winter to 40°C or even 50°C in summer. Humidity is always extremely high and hot winds blow fine sand inland from the seashore. Indeed, the name Tihama means 'hot lands'.

Life throughout the Yemen, even in the Tihama, relies on the monsoon winds to bring ample summer rains from the south and south-west. (Winters are dry; the winter monsoon winds blow from the north and north-east, carrying cool, dry air from central Asia.) When the moist summer winds meet the western mountains, the air mass rises rapidly, cooling suddenly and freeing moisture in the form of torrential showers.

The rains are irregular and do not compare with the monsoon rains of, say, eastern India. In different years, the rains may come in different months and, some years, there may be no rain at all. The showers are very localised and often violent, causing strong erosion. When travelling along mountain roads during the rainy season, you may be forced to stop because of heavy streams flowing down the steep slopes, carrying huge rocks and sometimes destroying mountain roads altogether. Meanwhile, neighbouring villages only a km away may receive no rain at all.

The mountain rains give birth to perennial rivers flowing west towards the Tihama and the southern coast. Because of the extremely high rates of evaporation in the coastal areas, these rivers die in the sands and never reach the sea. Agriculture along these foothill wadis is intense, yielding up to four harvests a year. Ground water is also efficiently pumped in most parts of the Tihama. Some say that the pumping rate already exceeds the capacity of the replenishing water flow from the mountains, causing sea water to flow in and gradually endangering the agricultural potential of the plains.

The Tihama's vegetation varies from the mangroves and salt-resistant plants of the seashore to the sparse grasses and shrubs of inner Tihama's dune valleys. Further inland, the wadi shores and mountain foothills are moist enough to sustain evergreen plants such as palms and acacias; the level of human interference here is high, however, and most areas suitable for cultivation are used so intensely that there are few remaining examples of the natural vegetation.

The southern coast has a more varied topography. Volcanic rocks extend right down to the ocean at several sites, including Aden and Bir 'Ali. Cultivated areas are scarcer here due to infertile or scanty soils, although the climatical conditions otherwise correspond to those of the Tihama.

The Western Mountains

Rainfall is highest on the western slopes of the western mountains and in the southern part of the mountain area, where the province of Ibb is called 'the fertile province'. Around Ibb, it rains every month of the year – only a few mm in January but, in July and August (when there may be daily rain), a monthly rainfall of almost 500 mm is common.

The natural vegetation of the western and southern mountain slopes is tropical – evergreen forests of acacia, ficus and tamarisk. However, the impact of thousands of years of human settlement has left very little of the natural vegetation. Instead, there are vast open areas created by uncontrolled grazing and the cutting down of forests for firewood. Cultivation of dates, mangoes, bananas and papayas is common on the lower slopes. At higher altitudes (up to 1500 metres), wheat, maize, lucerne and especially sorghum are typical.

Higher in the mountains, on terraced slopes between 1500 and 2500 metres, coffee was formerly the Yemen's principal cash crop. Nowadays, it has largely been replaced by another mountain crop: qat (see later in this chapter). It is hard to tell which plants would constitute the natural cover of the land here, since every possible spot is under cultivation and only the steepest, rockiest slopes with their few small shrubs have avoided human exploitation.

The Central Highlands

Towards the north, the rains gradually diminish. In the central highlands, the summer is dry, with only a couple of showers a month. Most rain occurs in these regions in two distinct rainy seasons, the lighter in March and April and the heavier around August. In San'a, April may bring a rainfall of about 100 mm and August usually sees almost 200 mm of rain.

Temperatures in the highlands are mild and San'a's maximum daily temperatures range from 25°C to 30°C throughout the year. Minimum nightly temperatures are around 0°C in January and 10°C in July. In large areas of the Yemeni highlands, nightly frost is possible during winter but, because that happens to be the dry season, the Yemenis see no snow.

On the central highland plateaus, sorghum is widely cultivated at about 2300 metres above sea level. All kinds of vegetables abound, including potatoes, carrots, onions, garlic, lettuce and cabbage, as well as various spice plants. Even vineyards are a common sight; wine is forbidden in this Islamic country but raisins are popular.

The wadis and springs of the highlands provide a suitable environment for various fruit trees. Almonds, walnuts, peaches, apricots, pears, lemons, pomegranates and many others grow readily here.

In the highlands, there are elaborately built irrigation terraces of ancient origin. In many regions, the mountain slopes are covered by terraces, from the strands of the wadis to the tops of the hills. The high plateaus have also been converted to huge terraces. 'Rainwater harvesting' in Yemen takes two main forms. In *sawaqi* irrigation, farmers collect rainwater from areas not used for agriculture and channel it to their fields. In *sayl* irrigation, it is the run-off water from floods that is collected. Sawaqi irrigation is used on mountain slopes as well as on the plains while sayl irrigation is most frequently seen around the wadi villages. Rainwater harvesting is not limited to field irrigation – household water is also collected by these methods.

The Outskirts of ar-Ruba' al-Khali

To the east and north, the rains become scantier and less frequent, ceasing altogether in the northern central parts of the country, where the stony semideserts gradually turn into sandy deserts. Here, only a few shrubs and grasses survive. In the past, large wadis carried enough water from the eastern mountains to the desert to sustain entire civilisations. The famous kingdom of Saba owed its prosperity to a dam that collected water from the vast Wadi as-Sudd flowing in the north-eastern direction.

In the eastern part of the country, the huge Wadi Hadhramawt gathers the scanty rains that fall on the rocky area between the Arabian Sea and the central deserts of the Arabian Peninsula. This wadi, though sufficiently fertile to allow a sizeable population to derive a living from agriculture, never yields its waters anywhere near the sea. Date palm is the most notably cultivated tree here; the Hadhramis grow enough dates for export to other countries.

GOVERNMENT

On unification, the president of the former YAR, 'Ali Abdallah Salah, became president of the new state, while the PDRY president, Haidar Abu Bakr al-Attas, was appointed prime minister. The southern strongman, Yemen Socialist Party leader 'Ali Salim Al-Baydh, became vice-president.

Military governments had been the rule since the days of the revolutions – the governments of both Yemens had based their power on the army. In the hasty unification of 1990, the two cabinets were combined to form a new cabinet of 39 ministers. The parliaments, the north's 159-seat People's Consultative Assembly and the south's 111-seat Supreme Consultative Council, were strengthened by the addition of 31 members from the hitherto illegal opposition and became the new 301-seat Council of Deputies. Also important is the five-member Presidential Council, made up of the topmost officials.

The stated political direction of the new republic largely followed that of the YAR, both in internal and external affairs. Gone were the secular and Marxist ideologies of the former PDRY; Islam and free enterprise were to be the basis of the new state structure. The new Yemen also automatically became a member of those Arab state councils to which the YAR had belonged. Some important differences were spelt out, however, the most important being the pursuance of democracy. The multiparty system was new to Yemen and general elections – Yemen's first – were delayed to allow a 30-month transition period, during which the new state's legal and administrative structures were to be finalised.

In anticipation of the elections, more than 30 parties were quickly formed, making Yemen the first multiparty state in the Arabian Peninsula.

ECONOMY

By Western standards, Yemen is among the very poorest of the world's nations. UNCTAD's classification places Yemen in the group of the 40 least developed countries in the world, with an estimated per capita gross national product (GNP) of slightly over US$500 in 1990. However, the visitor to Yemen gets the impression that there is plenty of economic activity, especially in the northern part of the country, that does not get included in official figures.

The unified Yemen inherited two totally different economies: the bustling Western-style economy of the YAR, where the annual growth rate of the per capita GNP had averaged 6% during the 1980s, and the stagnating centrally planned economy of the PDRY, where the per capita GNP had been declining by 2% per annum over the same period.

The economies had evolved in isolation from each other after the 1962 and 1967 revolutions. Earlier, the British port of Aden had been central to the industrial and commercial development of the region. The British developed the port town from a mere fortification with little more than 1000 inhabitants to a bustling city of 150,000 people. Thousands had migrated from all over lower Yemen to take part in Aden's labour-intensive activities. One of the goals of the unification was to re-establish the port's status as the Yemen's economic capital, and to this end Aden was declared a free trade zone on 29 May 1991.

Agriculture

The backbone of the former YAR was agriculture, with industry accounting for less than 10% of the GNP. In the former PDRY, agriculture was also the main economic activity, employing some 75% of the population, but it provided only 25% of the GNP.

Only 2% of the area of the former PDRY is arable and even this limited potential has not been fully exploited; the country was self-sufficient only in vegetables and dates. In contrast, climatic conditions in the northern provinces are extremely favourable and the country should be able to grow all the food its people need. This has indeed been the case for 3000 years, since the early days of the Sabaeans, but the oppression of the second Ottoman occupation and the subsequent Imamate ended this kind of economic prosperity.

Restoring self-sufficiency in agricultural production has been the stated goal of the governments but, so far, the trend has been one of increased food imports. Glorious plans to develop Yemen into the granary of the Arabic world have so far been confined to the level of political eloquence.

Today, most agriculture is small-scale and intended for the sustenance of the family. In the former PDRY, the estates of sultans and other feudal landowners that had been transformed into state-run farms are now being privatised again.

The main output of Yemeni agriculture is cereals – sorghum, millet, wheat and barley, typically species that are resistant to drought. Bananas, grapes and dates are grown as cash crops along the wadis where the climate is warm enough, while coffee and qat are common in the highlands.

The Yemenis also breed livestock; cattle, sheep and chickens are a common sight wherever you go in the Yemen. With luck, you can come across migratory beekeepers hunting for flowering plants with their transportable beehives – honey is a highly valued commodity in Yemen.

The waters of the Red Sea and the Arabian Sea are rich in fish and the Yemeni fishing industry has great potential.

Labour Export

The most important export commodity of both Yemens in the 1970s and 1980s was raw, unskilled labour. The early 1970s oil boom in Saudi Arabia and the Gulf states created an unprecedented demand for manual labour. The newly opened YAR was especially eager to satisfy this demand. It has been estimated that, in 1975, at least 350,000 North Yemenis were working abroad; by the end of the decade, there were an estimated 500,000 to 1.5 million, most of them working in Saudi Arabia. Formidable figures have also been quoted for the PDRY, with even less precision. For the unified Yemen of 1990, the estimate was 2.5 million.

The significance of this labour migration lies in the fact that the workers sent the greater part of their earnings back home. In 1978, the peak year, some US$900 to US$1500 million flowed to the YAR in worker remittances, the latter sum being almost as great as the country's entire trade deficit. For the PDRY, it has been estimated that, between 1975 and 1987, about 70% of the GNP came from worker remittances, the highest percentage of all Arab countries.

This enormous influx of cash changed the YAR more profoundly than any revolution and gave the people a chance to buy imported commodities previously unimagined. Portable TV sets and stereos became a must. Donkeys and camels were carried to the market in Toyota jeeps instead of walking. The imported money greatly diversified the economy; returning workers invested their savings in small shops, handled the trade or maintenance of imported technological wonders or started working as taxi or truck drivers. The construction industry also boomed and, in turn, utilised more and more imported new materials. In other words, small-scale capitalism flourished in the YAR.

In the centrally planned PDRY economy, the flow of incoming money was more tightly controlled and the impact was less visible. Moreover, commodity goods were harder to obtain than in the YAR, where anything from radios to Toyota jeeps was smuggled in from Saudi Arabia with the silent approval of both governments. The economies of the YAR and Saudi Arabia grew so close in the late 1970s and early 1980s that the YAR can be said to have been a Saudi satellite. It was only in the late 1980s that the YAR began to distance itself from the Saudis. The governments also made an effort to end the smuggling.

During the 1980s, the demand for Yemeni labour in the Gulf states greatly diminished, partly because of the cheaper labour that began to flow into these countries from other parts of Asia and partly because falling oil prices forced the revision of construction plans. The worker remittances of both Yemens combined diminished to about US$300 million by the end of the decade.

Nevertheless, many Yemenis have chosen not to return home. Their previous abundant remittances caused severe inflation in the former YAR – almost 17% in 1988 – and have all but crushed the agricultural sector in many regions. There is also little demand for their labour. As a result, many continue living in foreign countries, starting small businesses after accumulating enough money.

Should all migrant labourers return, the already significant unemployment problem could become catastrophic. The danger is very real: in October 1990 Saudi Arabia expelled all Yemenis because of San'a's lack of support for UN resolutions against Iraq during the Gulf crisis. Within a month or so, 600,000 Yemenis returned to their newly unified homeland. The direct costs of the repatriation, combined with the lost remittances in the future, were estimated by the Yemeni government to cost the country the equivalent of 15 Yemeni annual budgets.

Development Aid
Both Yemens depended heavily on foreign development aid and the Republic of Yemen continues to do so.

In the YAR, all of the basic infrastructure built after the 1962 revolution was the result of development projects with industrialised states – for example, the asphalted roads were built with Chinese, West German, American and Russian aid, while East Germany helped build the telephone connections between San'a, al-Hudayda and Ta'izz.

Many projects were financed by oil-rich Arab countries, where several rich emirs trace their lineage to Yemeni tribes; the new US$90 million Ma'rib dam, constructed in the late 1980s, was personally financed by United Arab Emirates president Sheikh Zaid ibn Sultan al-Nahyan.

The YAR lacked not only industrial expertise but educated workers of all kinds. There are still very few Yemeni doctors and 90% of the country's teachers came from abroad, most from Arab countries such as Egypt and the Sudan. In fact, the Gulf crisis of 1990 caused a severe problem in the education sector: some 30,000 teachers were forced to leave the country after their salaries, which had been paid by the states of Kuwait and Saudi Arabia, were cut off.

In the PDRY, the whole economy was in ruins after the 1967 revolution. The closure of the Suez Canal had already cut off 75% of Aden's trade, the PDRY's main source of foreign currency. The British evacuation left 20,000 labourers without work and the complete withdrawal of British aid reduced the state's total budgeted income by 60%. With no agricultural or mineral exports, the country had to make do in conditions of extreme austerity.

With development aid from communist countries, the PDRY did survive and, with Arab countries later joining the ranks, the economy was gaining some balance towards the 1980s. In the late 1970s, the economy grew a massive 8% per annum and the main goal of the government – self-sufficiency – seemed closer than ever. However, internal political problems and the dwindling of the Soviet aid in the *perestroika* years of the late 1980s had disastrous consequences. The economy was actually shrinking at an average of 2% annually during the decade and, on the eve of unification, the state was practically bankrupt, with hordes of people in the cities queuing up for government-subsidised food.

Oil

Until the early 1980s, the Yemens were considered an oddity because they were on the Arabian Peninsula but had no oil. The oil industry was restricted to the formerly British Petroleum- owned oil refinery in Aden, nationalised in 1977. The shortage of crude oil plagued the plant, which was already making losses before the revolution. However, the refinery, operating with imported oil, accounted for 80% of the PDRY's industrial output.

In the mid-1980s, before the unification of the two Yemens, oil was finally found in the desert area between them. Commercial exploitation of the fields first began in 1986 in the YAR, in an area east of Ma'rib, using the expertise of Hunt Oil Company. Five oil wells were opened in the Ma'rib/al-Jawf region and a pipeline was built from the fields to the Red Sea coast. By 1989, output reached 200,000 barrels per day and the YAR became an oil- exporting country. Plans for developing the huge reserves of natural gas were also finalised.

In the PDRY, oil was first found near Shabwa in 1987 but the development of the fields was slow because the Russian partner company, Technoexport, had great domestic difficulties with the effects of perestroika and Soviet economic hardships. Oil was transported to Aden by road and output was limited to 6000 barrels per day in 1989. However, a pipeline to Bir 'Ali was completed in 1990 and total output was expected to reach 120,000 barrels per day in 1991.

The unification of the two Yemens will facilitate the exploration and exploitation of oil and gas reserves in the former border region. The unstable price of oil in the world market will remain an incalculable factor but domestic oil will at least keep the Toyotas climbing the Yemeni mountains, even if the rest of the economy founders.

POPULATION & PEOPLE

Statistics on Yemen are unreliable. The figures used in this chapter come from the 1986 population census, the most up- to-date official data available in 1990. Other sources give vastly conflicting figures. In general, the YAR published many more statistics than did the PDRY.

The 1975 census showed the population of the YAR to be about five million, while the 1986 census gave a figure as high as 9.3 million. The PDRY population was considerably smaller; figures ranged from 1.8 to two million. The population of the united Yemen was estimated at 12 to 13 million in May 1990. The figures should include more than two million Yemenis working abroad, a great source of inaccuracy.

Yemen is still a very rural country; in the mid-1980s, only 12% of the YAR's population lived in towns. In the area of the former PDRY, where only 2% of the land can be cultivated, one- third of the population lives in towns. Most of the population is scattered across the countryside in small villages or even smaller groups of houses. The biggest cities are San'a (population 450,000), Aden (400,000), Ta'izz (320,000) and al- Hudayda (300,000). At last count, the other towns each had a few tens of thousand inhabitants but they are growing fast.

Life expectancy was 43.8 years in the YAR and 46.5 years in the PDRY, and medical care remains very rudimentary. According to UNICEF statistics released in 1990, 192 out of each 1000 Yemeni children fail to reach age five – the 21st worst figure in the world. This, however, is a significant progress from 1960, when the Yemen's under-five mortality rate of 378 per 1000 was the third worst in the world. Some 50% of the population is under 15 years of age – a fact vividly illustrated by the hordes of curious children that surround you wherever you go.

On average, a Yemeni woman gives birth to 7.7 children during her lifetime. The annual population growth rate is 3.5%, doubling the population in only 21 years.

In the late 1980s, the average age at first marriage in the YAR was 18 years for women and 22 years for men. It is not uncommon for girls under 14 years of age to marry. Surprisingly, divorce is also common; according to the 1975 census, 2.1% of women were divorced. Many remarry and, according to some studies, as many as 15% to 20% of women in some rural regions are divorced at some time of their life. In this respect, Yemen differs distinctly from most Arabic countries, where divorce is a social catastrophe for a woman.

Religious Groups

Islam, like any major religion, is divided into different sects, or schools of thinking. The two main divisions, Sunnism and Shi'ism, are both represented in the Yemen. Most people in the former PDRY, the Tihama and the southern part of the highlands as far north as Dhamar belong to a Sunni sect called the Shafa'i, while the northernmost provinces are inhabited mainly by Zaydis, a Shi'a minority sect. The Zaydis make up one- third

to one-half of the Yemeni population. The division is by no means strictly geographical; rather, you will find a gradual transition from the dominance of one group to that of the other as you travel from south to north or vice versa. Still another Shi'a sect, the Ismailis, constitute barely a few percent of the population.

Shafa'is Sunnism is, in general, what might be called 'orthodox' Islam. There are four main schools within Sunnism: Hanafi, Maliki, Shafa'i and Hanbali. All derive their names from their founders, who lived during the first 200 years of Islam. Imam Muhammad ibn Idris Ash-Shafa'i, the founder of the Shafa'i school, died in 820 AD. The differences between the four schools lie not so much in questions of faith as in the interpretation of the Shari'a, the Islamic law, and all but the Hanbali school regard each other as equally orthodox.

Shafa'i teaching spread through most of the Arabian Peninsula and the eastern coast of Africa. Ash-Shafa'i himself travelled extensively and visited even the Yemen, but his teachings were ultimately implanted in Hadhramawt by his disciple, Sayyid Ahmad ibn 'Isa al-Muhajir, 100 years after his death. The learned Shafa'is in the Hadhramawt area still trace their origins to Ahmad ibn 'Isa. From Hadhramawt, Shafa'ism rapidly spread across the southern parts of the country, while Tarim and Zabid have been important centres of Shafa'i teaching.

Zaydis The other main sect of Islam, Shi'ism, developed during the very first decades of the new religion. Its founder, the Prophet's cousin and son-in-law 'Ali, was the head of his own party – *Shi'a* in Arabic. It was a doctrine of the party that leadership of the Muslim community rightfully belonged to the descendants of the Prophet. This view was not taken for granted by all believers, and during the first turbulent 120 years of Islam, the Muslims suffered three bloody and devastating civil wars. 'Ali became the fourth caliph but was assassinated in 661 AD; other direct relatives of the

Prophet were killed in 680 by the Umayyad Caliphate, which thus secured power for a few decades.

However, Shi'a opposition was not crushed and, in 750, they succeeded in destroying the Umayyads and enthroning descendants of the Prophet's uncle, al-Abbas. This was the beginning of the Abbasid dynasty on the Arabian Peninsula.

Gradually, Shi'ism also split into different sects. Major sects can be distinguished from each other on the basis of the number of imams they recognise. According to Shi'a belief, a secret interpretation of the Koran was transmitted from one successor of 'Ali to another; they thus became imams, considered some kind of superhuman beings. According to the biggest Shi'a sect, the Twelvers, the last imam was Muhammad al-Muntazar. He died in 873 but later returned to earth.

The Zaydis of Yemen recognise only four of the imams, all descendants of Zayd ibn 'Ali, in turn a direct descendant of Caliph 'Ali. Zayd ibn 'Ali was killed in Kufa in 740 while rebelling against the Umayyads. His followers founded the Zaydi branch of Shi'ism. Zaydism reached Yemen in the late 9th century and, in 901, a wise man named Yahya bin Husayn bin Qasim ar-Rassi became the first Zaydi imam after successfully mediating between warring Hashid and Bakil tribes.

Sa'da became the capital of Zaydi rule and teaching which spread over a territory that varied in size over the centuries. It continued uninterrupted in northern parts of Yemen and was at its zenith in the era of independent Yemen (from 1918) when the Zaydis ruled the whole country. Finally, the revolution of 1962 replaced the imam with secular rulers.

Although the Zaydi state no longer exists, people continue to call themselves Zaydis. There is no visible friction between Zaydis and Shafa'is in Yemen today, though you might expect it to exist when you remember the Iran-Iraq war, or the continuing confrontations between Shi'a and Sunni factions in Lebanon and in other parts of the modern Arabic world. Instead, these groups largely

inhabit overlapping areas and use the same mosques for prayer.

There are certain differences between the religious practices of the two groups but these are relatively minor, like the wording of the prayer calls. Other features are more prominent, such as the adherence to the traditional tribal structure, always much stronger among the Zaydis of the north than with the Shafa'is in the south. The social occupations of members of these groups also differ; the Zaydis have mainly distinguished themselves as fearless soldiers, while the Shafa'is have always been merchants and tradespeople and control most of the country's trade.

Ismailis The third religious group in Yemen is another Shi'a sect, the Ismailis. They recognise only the first seven imams, the last being Ismail, who died in 760 AD. The Ismaili movement flourished in eastern Arabia under the Qarmatians in the 10th century. It also thrived in Egypt during the rule of the Fatimid caliphs between 969 AD and 1171 AD.

In the Yemen, the first successful Ismaili expansion took place in 1061 AD in the form of the Sulayhi state, founded by 'Ali ibn Muhammad ibn 'Ali as-Sulayhi. The Ismaili kingdom lasted 79 years and had its capital in Jibla. Later, the Ismailis were oppressed by the Zaydis and many fled to India, where the community of Buhras still exists. Presently, the Ismailis make up only 1% to 2% of the population of the Yemen. Most live in or around the town of Manakha. The grave of an Ismaili saint, Hatim bin Ibrahim, in al-Khutayb in the Haraz mountains, is an important place of pilgrimage.

Tribal Groups

Next to religion, the most important factor dividing the Yemeni population into smaller units is the traditional tribal structure.

The basic building block of Yemeni society is the nuclear family, *'ayla* in Arabic. The family tends to be quite large by Western standards and averages 5.6 persons. Many women bear 10 or more children and some men have more than one wife. According to the Koran men can have four wives and, while this was in accordance with the legislation of the former YAR, polygamy was banned by law in the former PDRY.

The nuclear family never exists in isolation but is contained within the extended family. This is called *bayt*, meaning 'house'. The term can be taken literally; usually, each Yemeni house is inhabited by several generations of the same extended family. The archetypal bayt houses a man, his wives, his sons and his sons' wives and children.

The extended families form larger units by genealogy, *fakhdh* and *bayn* being the next groups in the hierarchy. The largest unit is called *qabila*, or 'tribe'. On a Yemeni map, you may find areas with names such as 'Bani Matar' or 'Bani Husayn'. The word *bani* literally means 'the sons of', so it is clear that all members of these units trace their origin to a common forefather.

Finding names of this kind on the map also suggests that, in traditional Yemeni society, the tribes and subtribes have always occupied a more or less strictly defined territory. This reflects the Yemen's dependence on agriculture, with economically independent tribes growing crops sufficient to feed their community. The static pattern of residence is very much true even today, since the buying and selling of land always takes place between members of the same tribe. An exception to this rule is the Bedouin tribes of the east; these nomads do not settle in a certain area but keep wandering along the outskirts of the big Arabian desert, forming a vast qabila of their own.

Belonging to a unit confers both rights and obligations. Conflicts are resolved within the smallest unit to which both participants belong and, the closer the opponents are to each other within the tribal structure, the smaller the number of people involved. If a *qabili*, or 'tribesman', kills a member of another tribe, everybody in his tribe is responsible for paying the compensation.

Over the centuries, many customs and external signs have evolved to distinguish members of different tribes from each other. An experienced observer can easily deduce the tribe to which a qabili belongs from the design of his *jambiya* (a ceremonial dagger worn by men at their waist), the way his *futa* (men's skirt) is made or the way he winds his headcloth. Women's clothing also varies considerably from tribe to tribe. Various ceremonies are held to mark events such as marriage, childbearing and so on. Some tribes in the Tihama practise the circumcision of women. Each tribe has a its own folklore, music and dances.

Every tribe elects a sheikh *(shaykh,* or 'the oldest one'), a respected and supposedly wise man who will resolve conflicts arising within the tribe according to Shari'a, the Islamic law. In the case of an unresolvable conflict with another tribe, it is the sheikh who is responsible for recruiting an army and leading the battle against the aggressor. His power is not absolute, however, and a new election may be held if he fails to live up to expectations.

The tribes form even bigger units that could be called tribal federations. Three such units exist in the northern part of Yemen today: the very strong Hashids and Bakils of the mountains and the Zaraniqs of Tihama, whose power was crushed after the 1934

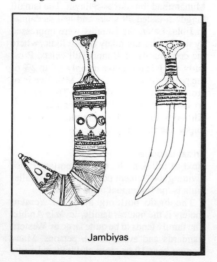

Jambiyas

Saudi-Yemeni war. Land in the San'a basin, for example, is divided between seven tribes. Five of these tribes (Arhab, Bani Bahlul, Bani al-Harith, Bani Hushayh and Bani Matar) belong to the Bakils and two (Hamdan and Sanhan) are Hashid tribes. These tribal units still have such influence in Yemen that no cabinet can be formed without balancing tribal representation.

While the tribal structure is strong in the northern parts of the Yemen, the role of tribes gradually diminishes as you move southwards. In the Hujjariya area south of Ta'izz, where most of the population are Shafa'is, tribal ties are very weak and mobility is high; many people have moved to other parts of the country to become merchants or professionals. In the former PDRY, where the stated goal of the government was to diminish the power of local sheikhs, tribes are smaller and even more fragmented.

Social Classes
In traditional Yemeni society, the religious elite has formed the highest social classes. The *sayyid* class (plural in Arabic: *sada*), direct descendants of the Prophet Muhammad, were at the top of Zaydi society and are highly respected to this day. The *qadhi* group (plural *qudha*), legal specialists who inherited their position without being sada, form another elite group and are respected for their literacy.

At the lowest level of Yemeni society are those people called *akhdam* (singular *khadim*). They can be seen in the cities sweeping streets, cleaning public baths and performing other jobs regarded as menial. A little higher on the social ladder have been the slaves (brought from Ethiopia to the Tihama) and their descendants, called *abid*. These dark-skinned people were often treated as family members, despite the low status of the work they performed.

Most Yemenis fall somewhere between these two extremes – *qabili* (tribespeople) in northern Zaydi terminology, or *'arab* or *ra'aya* in the southern Shafa'i parts of the country. These people, mostly farmers or landowners, take pride in their family connections.

Below this class but above the akhdam are those people of uncertain genealogy and those who perform odd jobs, such as barbers or artisans. They go by many names, such as *nuqqas, bani khums* or *jazr* (butcher), which describe their suspect origins or low-status occupations.

In recent years, this traditional structure has started to break down. As money became a central part of Yemeni daily life during the 1970s, occupations once seen as lowly came to command more respect and, today, Yemenis are more willing to break the social barriers. Although it is still rare for a sayyid to open a restaurant, this is no longer impossible in bigger towns. The rising educational level of the population is also likely to contribute to these changes, since literacy is no longer restricted to the sayyid and qadhi classes. However, marital restrictions still prevail. It will take a long time for the traditional class system to be completely eradicated from Yemeni society, if it ever is.

ARCHITECTURE
Yemeni architecture is unique. Houses are built from local materials: mud, brick and reed on the plains, stone in the mountains. Human settlement here always displays a fantastic harmony with the natural surroundings. Buildings from the mightiest tower houses to the tiniest shacks seem to form part of a great unified plan, as if the Yemenis had an instinctive understanding of the art of building.

Tihama
In the Tihama, houses are low; the only structures of considerable height are the minarets of mosques. Building materials and styles vary from region to region. The most common type of house in the countryside is the reed hut – a round or rectangular house with one room and a sharply topped roof. The appearance of a village of round reed huts is astonishingly African, suggesting links across the Red Sea.

The reed huts are built of reeds, sticks and

Bab al-Yaman, San'a

palm woods, the walls are often covered with a smooth layer of mud and reeds are left visible on the roof. The housing compound of a single family may consist of several one-room huts. Despite the primitive appearance of such dwellings, their interiors are decorated imaginatively and treated with great care.

The larger villages and towns have houses built of brick. The buildings are still low – one or two storeys – and, in larger towns, may extend into many rooms and courtyards. Decorations on the outer walls include unfinished patterns of protruding bricks or elaborate plastered ornaments. Often, the most beautiful decorations face the inner court, with the view from the streets revealing little of the owner's wealth. The most beautiful examples of such houses can be found in the region of Zabid. Brick houses can also be found further to the north, in the town of al-Qanawis.

A third type of Tihami house is the so-called Red Sea house, a townhouse-style building that reflects foreign influence. These multistoreyed houses can be found in

al-Hudayda and, to a lesser extent, in al-Makha in the south and al-Luhayya in the north. Turkish windows and balconies are characteristic of Red Sea houses.

Highlands

In the highlands, the most commonly seen dwelling is the tower house. These buildings are made of stone, brick or mud, depending on which material is locally available, and embody the architectural style that most foreign visitors to Yemen remember for the rest of their lives. It has been said that Yemen was where skyscrapers were invented and that all Yemenis are architects. There is certainly something very special in the way mountain Yemenis build their houses. The four to six-storey towers are imposing, even more so when you realise that houses here have been built this way since time immemorial.

Each tower house is home to one family, with several generations living under the same roof. Various storeys are reserved for different purposes; the bottom floor is for animals and bulk storage while the top floor, often a small attic on the roof of the house, is the most highly valued in the whole house – called the *mafraj*, it is where the owner meets guests. The intermediate storeys contain the living rooms, the women's room, kitchens, bathrooms and the *diwan* (a large room reserved for celebrations).

Mountains In the western and southern mountains, stone is the main building material. Building facades are differently decorated in each region; an expert in Yemeni architecture can identify the village from a house's facade.

Although the outer walls may show mere stone to the streets, the inner walls are often plastered with mud and finished with white gypsum, giving the rooms a pleasant appearance. Often, the plaster is extended outside from the window openings; the windows are generally the most decorative detail of the house, with an elaborate plaster-and-glass fretwork called *takhrim* giving them an air of prestige. The window panes have traditionally been constructed from pieces of alabaster; today, glass of different colours is used.

High Plateaus & Valleys On the central plateaus and by the wadis in the Shabwa and Hadhramawt governorates, houses are built of mud or brick, often used with stone. San'a is a brilliant example of a town in which various techniques have been combined to achieve a most pleasing result: the first couple of storeys laid in stone and the upper storeys built of brick, with elaborate decorations.

In Rada' and Sa'da, you will see mud houses built using *zabur* technique. The walls are made of layers of mud, each layer carefully laid on top of the last and left to dry for a few days before the next layer is laid. The building's stability is ensured by letting the walls lean against each other at the corners, giving the structure its characteristic conical shape. The walls are then carefully finished to give the house a very smooth appearance.

In the wadis of the southern governorates, mud-plastered brick architecture dominates. There are whole villages and towns built exclusively of sun-dried mud bricks: tower houses, palaces, tombs, mosques with their minarets, public wells, everything. In al-Mukalla and the Hadhramawt valley, the decoration of many houses shows Indian and Indonesian (especially Javanese) influence because, according to local tradition, emigrant businesspeople eventually come home to the Yemen, building mosques and houses there.

Imported Styles
Unfortunately, all imported architecture is not to be celebrated. Modern, or post-revolutionary, architecture in both Yemens incorporates imported materials and techniques such as reinforced concrete and cement bricks. Worst of all are the port cities of al-Hudayda and Aden and the new part of al-Mukalla, with the Egyptian block style dominating in the north and the Soviet style in the south. Examples also abound in other big cities like Ta'izz and San'a, and even in Hajja and Sa'da.

Yet, in most parts of the Yemen, few new houses look wholly 'imported' in style. Even walls built with cement blocks usually have a facing made of local stone and something very Yemeni is always apparent in the style of construction and decoration, regardless of foreign influence and technology.

How long traditional building styles will survive is hard to tell. A trend not to be celebrated may, however, be emerging in the form of the worst examples of modern architecture: the schools of the Yemen. Unvarying in style, these stone buildings dot the towns and countryside of the northern provinces in their hundreds as if destined to influence the buildings of the future by shaping the architectural vision of today's young Yemenis.

MUSIC
Yemeni music culture is rich and has longstanding traditions. The most celebrated Yemeni instrument is *al-'ud*, from which the name of the Western lute is said to derive.

Traditional music styles vary greatly from region to region; the feverish rhythms of the Tihama hardly appeal to the dignified 'ud player from San'a. Some Yemeni artists, like the Hadhrami singer Badwi Zubayr, are popular all over the Peninsula.

The best way to obtain popular Yemeni music while in Yemen is to hang around the small cassette stands that abound in the suqs of the Yemen, keep your ears open while the local folks do their business and purchase those recordings you like. A week or two of travelling in Yemen should be enough to help your ears distinguish the most popular hits of the day (even though the rhythmic and melodic conventions differ considerably from those in the West), since radios and cassette recorders generally blare at full volume in taxis and buses. Besides domestic productions, Egyptian, Lebanese and Sudanese music is quite popular in the Yemen.

Some recordings of Yemeni folk music are available in the West. Try, for example, Lyrichord LLST series records 7283 and 7284, *Music from Yemen Arabia*, or 7384, *Music of the Tihama in North Yemen*, and Ethnic Folkways Library P 421, *Music of South Arabia*. Philips 6586040, *UNESCO Collection 'Zaidi & Shafii'*, is a collection of religious songs from San'a, while EMI 3 C-064-18352, *Musical Atlas*, plays you folk music from the Tihama, Sa'da, Hajja, Manakha, San'a, Zabid and Bayt al-Faqih. A French publication is also available: Arabesque 6, *Anthologie Phonographique du Récital Oriental*.

SOCIETY & CUSTOMS

Travel in Yemen calls for some effort; it is certainly not one of those countries in which you can quietly be a spectator of the daily show of local life. Most of the time, you will be the protagonist in that show and the focus of attention. Wherever you go, the Yemenis will show their interest in you by cheering and smiling, greeting you, talking to you and gathering around you. The interest is genuine and thoroughly friendly in tone, so don't make the error of thinking they are only interested in getting something from you.

Generally, this is not the case and, even in the suqs, most traders are not as overly eager to sell their products to you as experience in other Arab countries would suggest.

The Tihami people are accustomed to seeing strangers, being a mix of different races themselves. In fact, in the course of history, they have developed some indifference towards other people when compared to the mountain Yemenis. In the lower Yemen (that is, the southern highlands), you can easily gather a crowd of exhilarated Yemenis around you; all you need to do is ask for a taxi to an unusual destination and, all of a sudden, drivers and passengers will be offering their help.

If you happen to walk near a village school at noon, when the students get out, every child will try to catch a glimpse of you. You soon feel like the queen in a swarm of bees, surrounded by hundreds of small and very active creatures. Everybody is eager to try out the English they have learnt in school (not much) and each expects to be addressed individually. If you have some Arabic greetings at your command, you can easily give them a surprise. Never make the mistake of getting angry with them or they might start throwing stones at you – a common way of treating despised people (like the Yemeni Jews in the past).

As you move further north, people become less open and, in the higher Yemen, they are particularly reserved. Around Sa'da you will still meet many very friendly people but, here, they don't gather around you in such numbers. In the northern highlands, you may even find villages where a stranger is frowned upon and you could have some difficulty finding a place to stay if night falls upon you in a village without an inn. Normally, however, this is not the case and you will find that the legendary Arab hospitality is alive and well.

Dress Code

Yemen is a strict Muslim society, which means that you don't come here for a suntan.

Western women are seen as a 'third sex' and, consequently, are not required to wear veils as Yemeni women do. Nevertheless, it is wise to dress appropriately; you should not make an insult of your appearance or give an improper impression of your sexual availability. Wear loose clothes that reveal nothing above the ankles: long skirts, pants or dresses and tops, preferably with long sleeves. Tops should be long and worn outside pants. Covering your hair might make you feel more comfortable.

Men wearing shorts are not offensive to the Yemenis – merely ridiculous. Long pants and a shirt are recommended. For both sexes, loose clothing and protective headgear also make sense for reasons of climate.

Visiting Mosques

When the YAR was opened to foreign tourism, the mosques were seen as a major attraction. The imams were told to treat tourists well and, in the late 1970s, it was possible to visit many mosques, as long as you took off your shoes.

Unfortunately, this is no longer the case. The foreigners, with their strange behaviour, disturbed those praying in the mosque and the imams soon began to restrict the flow of non-Muslims into the sacred buildings. Today, most Yemeni mosques don't allow non-Muslims to enter at all and, according to Muslim purists, a non-Muslim should not be allowed to visit even the graveyards outside the mosques. Still, a few mosques allow visitors outside prayer times and some historical mosques that are not in active ritual use can also be entered.

If you belong to a tourist group, your entry to a specific mosque may be arranged. A Yemeni friend may also help you get into a mosque. If you show interest in taking a look inside one, you may be able to make friends with somebody if you loiter around the entrance long enough – sometimes, they even fetch a younger man working in the mosque to serve as your guide. On the other hand, your mere presence at the outer door of a mosque may cause such a stir among the believers that you would be wise to leave the scene quietly.

Never rush into a mosque without asking permission. If you are granted entry, take off your shoes. For females, proper dress is crucial: you should not expose your hair or any skin other than your face, hands and ankles. Don't make a fuss in your picture-taking and do not insist on aiming your camera towards those deep in prayer. You may not be allowed into all parts of the mosque, so accept these restrictions. If the imam asks for baksheesh or alms, it is a good idea to oblige.

Qat

Yemen's most popular drug, qat, enjoys quasiofficial status as the national narcotic – the qat plant is even depicted on the one-riyal note. This mild stimulant is used weekly, even daily, by almost every adult Yemeni in the mountainous northern provinces and, according to some sources, trade in qat made up one-third of the economic activity of the YAR in the late 1980s.

In the former PDRY, qat was not as common because low altitudes made that part of the country unsuitable for qat cultivation. Furthermore, consumption of the drug was only allowed on Thursdays and Fridays.

The plant, *Catha edulis*, is a small, evergreen tree or bush and is three to seven metres high when cultivated. It is a hardy plant that needs little care, the main requirement being an adequate supply of water. In favourable circumstances, a qat tree may reach 10 metres; such giants can be seen near Ta'izz on the slopes of Mt Sabir, which gets heavy monsoon rainfall.

Qat prospers only at relatively high altitudes (1500 to 2500 metres). Like coffee, it originated in the mountains of eastern Africa. Nowadays, it occurs naturally in a vast geographical area from South Africa and Madagascar to Afghanistan. It is also cultivated in Kenya, Somalia and Ethiopia but nowhere is it as ubiquitous as in the Yemen.

Yemenis use qat by chewing the fresh leaves. It can also be consumed in other ways – in parts of east Africa, qat is used in tea. Qat is harvested by picking the ends of the branches. These are bound into small bundles to be sold at the market. Only the youngest and freshest leaves are suitable for chewing and, as the leaves wilt within a couple of days of picking, they lose their value very quickly. Qat cannot be dried or otherwise preserved, which means that it must be sold and used by the day after harvesting.

Since qat grows only in the highlands, where communication has traditionally been poor, its use has mainly been restricted to the areas where it is grown. Its cultivation has spread throughout the Yemeni highlands and you can hardly find a village without qat growing nearby. It is reported that qat has replaced coffee in large areas of Yemen because the farmers derive greater profits from it. You can find both growing side by side on the terraces.

Chewing qat is an acquired skill. The leaves themselves are not swallowed; instead, they are pushed against one cheek, where the chewed paste forms a slimy ball that grows steadily as new leaves are added. Maintaining that lump between your teeth and cheek is a complicated trick, as you will find if you try chewing qat. Some kind of anatomical adaptation obviously occurs over many years of chewing: old men's cheeks often appear extraordinarily wrinkled when empty but are capable of holding a wad of qat the size of a tennis ball. Those with the most bulging cheeks are admired most.

The physiological effects of qat have been much studied but, so far, no satisfactory understanding of the drug has been reached. The World Health Organization (WHO) has divided the world's drugs into seven categories; qat forms one of these by itself. Chemical analysis has revealed a plethora of effective compounds in the leaves but it is not clear which of these are the most effective. All that can be said with certainty is that qat is a mild stimulant, it does not have any proven side effects that are hazardous to the health of even a heavy user (though it does cause some constipation) and it is obviously not physically addictive. It *appears* to be at least psychologically addictive when observed by a foreigner conditioned to think all drugs are addictive but research does not confirm this.

Yemenis attribute all kinds of positive effects to qat. Because it is said to increase endurance, qat is often chewed when people are engaged in heavy or monotonous labour, especially when travelling. It is said to help you do without food, drink or sexual relations; on the other hand, it is customary to eat well before chewing qat because it is supposed to enhance the pleasure of drinking and smoking. It is also said to strengthen potency. It certainly helps you stay awake.

Qat is said to stimulate the intellect, raise the spirits and increase mutual understanding and communication. Based on direct observation, I can confirm that it enhances the talkativeness of Yemenis although, after chewing qat for a few hours, the user ends up in an introverted, meditative, almost depressive state of mind. Mystics tend to believe that qat intensifies their communication with God.

The most important feature of qat is that it is, above all, a social drug – you rarely chew it alone. Most qat is chewed at qat parties. These take place in the afternoons in the mafraj of Yemeni houses. The fact that the streets of a Yemeni town are almost deserted in the afternoons does not mean that the locals are having a siesta; rather, it reflects the widespread popularity of qat parties. Every male Yemeni has to attend such parties at least once a week; those who can afford it attend daily. A man who avoids these parties will soon be regarded as some kind of freak, a voluntary social outcast, and it is agreed that something is wrong with him.

Qat parties are not planned days ahead; like everything in the Yemen, they happen spontaneously. In the morning, men meet each other in the suqs, mosques and elsewhere, exchange news and find out where each one is going to chew qat that day. Everyone offers their house for this purpose in turn and each man attends the qat parties of those social circles with which he wishes to be associated.

Qat is not cheap. A *rubta*, or small bundle of six or 10 qat branches containing enough leaves for a typical three to four-hour chewing session, may cost anything from YR 20 to YR 150 (typically YR 40 to YR 60) depending on supply and demand, the season, the quality of the qat and the general income level of customers in that particular suq. This is expensive in a country where an unskilled labourer may earn YR 60 to YR 80 a day and a skilled worker may earn only double that.

A Yemeni may chew one rubta once a week or two rubtas every day; heavy users who chew qat in the mornings while working and in the evenings after qat parties may chew as much as four or six rubtas a day. When asked how much they chew, a Yemeni often tells you how much they spend on qat in a week. Surveys show that most Yemenis chewing qat regularly spend between one-quarter and one-half of their total income on it. Those on meagre incomes buy cheaper qat in order to chew more often, while those enjoying large incomes display their wealth by buying the most expensive qat. It is absolutely essential that a person buy their own daily qat supply – this is a kind of basic status symbol in Yemen and continuously measures the income standard in a very public way.

Even if you're not invited to a qat party (or if you don't dare accept an invitation), you will have ample opportunities to observe qat chewing. Almost any gathering of Yemenis between 2 and 6 pm tends to become an occasion for chewing qat, be it a bus trip or a football match. Taxi drivers chew qat while driving, shopkeepers have bulging cheeks in the early evenings, men walking in the streets chew it – you can't avoid encountering qat in the Yemen. Women also chew qat, though not as visibly.

You will frequently be asked whether or not you have chewed qat. Your answer will reveal more about you than you might think. If you haven't chewed qat, you haven't been in the country for long or, if you have stayed for a while, you are willing to maintain your foreigner's status and are not prepared to mingle with the Yemenis. If you have chewed qat, you obviously have some

Yemeni friends with whom you have been chewing and you will be given much more respect.

Often, you will be offered qat. The Yemenis consider it courteous to offer a branch of qat to the stranger next to them in a taxi, for example. If you accept it, you will be at the very centre of exhilarated attention. Don't be embarrassed; they are not making a fool of you. The bulging cheek of a Yemeni arouses similar admiring reactions. You are not likely to be offered a whole cheek-full of qat. If you are invited to chew with somebody and you accept the invitation, it's wise to buy your own.

RELIGION

The state religion of Yemen is Islam. Yemen was one of the very first regions to join the Islamic revolution, with the local Persian rulers converting to the new religion as early as the year 6 AH (Anno Hijra) – that is, 628 AD. According to official sources, all Yemenis today profess the religion of Islam, and this certainly appears very much true.

A small but important Jewish minority existed in the country through the first 14 Islamic centuries. During the years 1948 to 1950, the newly established state of Israel organised operation 'Magic Carpet', a major airlift from Aden through which some 50,000 Yemeni Jews emigrated to Israel, leaving only a few hundred behind. Most of them are today scattered around the Yemen, with the biggest concentration in a village near Sa'da. There are also small Christian and Hindu communities in Aden.

Islam

The Islamic faith is based on the believer's total submission to God and this principle is a very visible part of the daily life of every Muslim. In fact, in Arabic *islam* means 'submitting' and a *muslim* is a 'submitter' to God. The faithful observe the five so-called pillars of Islam: the creed, performance of prayer, giving of alms, observance of fasting and performance of pilgrimage.

There is almost a sixth pillar: *jihad*, which means both 'holy war' and 'striving in the way of God'. The concept of jihad has been much disputed and misunderstood by Muslims and non-Muslims alike. It may just as easily be interpreted as meaning a holy war against the godless, the unbelievers, as meaning an internal struggle against man's basic unholy instincts. While the latter interpretation is much preferred today, there will always be those who use the word to encourage war and disorder. It is for this reason that Islam has gained a reputation, in the eyes of many Westerners, as a dangerous religion with fanatical followers. However, in its essence Islam is as peaceful a religion as any.

The Creed The core of Islamic belief is expressed in beautiful calligraphy on the flag of Saudi Arabia: 'There is no God but God and Muhammad is the Prophet of God.' Anybody who utters this phrase in the presence of two reliable witnesses may be regarded as a Muslim. We have heard men walking the streets of small Yemeni villages recite this testimony to no-one in particular.

Muslims also believe in the angels who brought God's messages to humans (it was the archangel Gabriel who communicated the Koran to Muhammad), in the prophets who received these messages, in the books in which the prophets expressed these revelations, and in the last day of judgement. The Koran mentions 28 prophets, of whom Muhammad was the last and the one who received the final revelation from God – there will be no more prophets. This makes the Koran the last of the books, towards which the revelations of earlier prophets progress. The day of judgement will be announced by the archangel Asrafil blowing a trumpet and, at that time, all people will be summoned to either paradise or hell, according to whether they have struggled along God's path or abandoned it.

Islam shares many holy men and scriptures with Judaism and Christianity. Twenty-one of the 28 Islamic prophets are also mentioned in the Bible, and Adam, Noah, Abraham, David, Jacob, Joseph, Job, Moses and Jesus are particularly honoured, although the divinity of Jesus is strictly denied. The Koran also recognises the scriptures of Abraham, the Torah of Moses, the Psalms of David and the Gospel of Jesus as God's revelation.

Prayer The ritual of prayer is an essential part of a believer's daily life. Every Muslim should pray at least five times a day: at sunrise, noon, late afternoon, sunset and night. Five times a day, the muezzin (from Arabic *muwadhdhin*) calls believers to the mosque for prayer. It is perfectly permissible to pray at home or elsewhere; only the Friday noon prayer should be conducted in the mosque. It is preferred that women pray at home and only a few mosques are designated for women.

The act of praying involves a series of predefined movements of the body and the recital of prayers and passages of Koran, all designed to express the believer's absolute humility and God's sovereignty. First, believers wash themselves to show their will to purify themselves – there are fountains or ablution pools in mosques for this purpose. Then, they go to the place of prayer, face Mecca (the proper orientation is indicated by the alignment of the mosque) and perform one or more *rakats* (cycles of prayer), during which they read certain passages of the Koran, pray, bow and prostrate themselves. There is a different series for each of the day's five prayer times.

Alms A Muslim should pay one-fortieth of their annual income to the poor as *zakat*, or alms. To the believer, this institution is as essential as prayer. The practice of giving alms reflects both the need to 'purify' earthly wealth and the individual's willingness to demonstrate social responsibility.

The giving of alms may once have been an act of a more individual nature than it is today, when the institution has developed along lines very similar to those used by Western welfare states in taking care of their poor. In the Yemen, as in other Arabic countries, a special Ministry of Waqfs and Religious Guidance controls the distribution of religious charitable endowments.

Fasting The ninth month of the lunar year, Ramadan, is the month of fasting. During Ramadan, Muslims abstain from eating, drinking, smoking and sexual intercourse between sunrise and sunset. Extra prayers and recitations of the Koran are encouraged, since the purpose of fasting is to bring people closer to God.

The considerable effort needed to fulfil this religious requirement greatly contributes to each individual's sense of belonging to the Muslim community – everybody shares this experience at the same time. Fasting also has a great influence on the daily routines of any predominantly Muslim country because all daily activities are, of necessity, kept to the lowest possible level. Ramadan is not a detested month, though. In fact, Muslims love it; fasting during the daylight hours gives them a reason to feast in the dark. Nights are lively, joyous occasions and many people stay awake all night, leaving sleep for the afternoons.

Pilgrimage Every Muslim who can afford to do so should make the pilgrimage to the holiest of cities, Mecca, at least once in their lifetime. The reward is considerable: the forgiving of all past sins. The *hajj* pilgrimage takes place every year during Dhul-Hijja, the last month of the Muslim calendar. Pilgrimages can also be made at other times of the year.

Since Yemen shares a border with Saudi Arabia, a very high percentage of Yemenis perform this ceremonial journey. Of the 1.6 million hajj pilgrims who enter Saudi Arabia each year, some 7% to 8% are Yemenis. This figure does not include the many Yemenis who work in Saudi Arabia and perform the pilgrimage while there.

LANGUAGE

Arabic is the language spoken in the Yemen. Radio broadcasts and daily newspapers are in Arabic, which is the official language. The exception is the evening TV news, which is in English. Having some Arabic at your command makes all the difference. Your trip will certainly be much more enjoyable if you don't have to deal with problems in communicating.

Coping without Arabic

Many Yemenis speak a non-Arabic language. We encountered a few old men who spoke excellent Italian. The explanation: in the 1930s, Mussolini made Abyssinia (today's Ethiopia) a colony of Italy. These Italian speakers came to Yemen from Eritrea. Migration still occurs from various African countries, spreading African languages which will probably not be familiar to you.

Some Yemenis speak Russian because the Soviet Union has played a major role in developing the basic infrastructure (and the military) in both parts of the country since the revolutions. In the southern governorates, Russian was the most important non-Arabic language during the 23 years of Communist rule and, in the Tihama region, you can still see road signs written in the Cyrillic alphabet. The People's Republic of China also gave generous aid in the form of work brigades, but we haven't observed the Yemenis' ability to speak Chinese.

Today, English is the most important non-Arabic language. It is widely understood by older Yemenis in the southern governorates because of the region's colonial past. After the revolution and the civil war, the new government of the YAR recognised the need for education in general and knowledge of English in particular. So, even in the most remote mountain villages, you'll quickly be surrounded by a group of kids eager to brush up on their English. The schooling programme is still young, however, and you'll soon learn to ignore the 'Hello-what's-err-name' – a question that seems to exhaust their entire English vocabulary. Other common greetings, used synonymously, are 'how are you', 'I love you', 'no friend', 'thank you' and 'I'm sorry'.

However, things are improving, albeit slowly. You can already get along fairly comfortably in San'a and Aden using just English. Compare this to the mid-1980s, when all San'a's street signs were in Arabic and you couldn't get a taxi from the centre of San'a to the airport if you didn't know that airport should be pronounced 'mata:r', with very dark a's (pronounced at the back of the mouth).

If you get really stuck, say in a government office in a town of reasonable size, the staff will usually manage to fetch a fairly able interpreter within 30 minutes or so. Don't expect this to happen in remote mountain villages, though.

Exactly why the younger generation does not speak English better is hard to tell. Certainly, it is not for want of trying. We have been shown exercise books from advanced classes: the students solve impressive grammatical drills with little difficulty. However, only a small fraction of what is learnt is actually applied to the spoken language. This is due partly to the scant opportunities for practice and partly to the weak links between the written and spoken language of their mother tongue. To appreciate this fact, we must look briefly at the history of the Arabic language.

Classical Arabic

The holy book of Islam, the Koran, was dictated to Muhammad by Allah (God) in the early 7th century AD – the literal meaning of 'Koran' is 'recitation'. The Koran was dictated in the language of Muhammad which, at that time, was used only in parts of the Arabian Peninsula. It was then mainly a spoken language; the earliest known written examples date from the previous century. The Koran was written down around the time of the Prophet's death and, by the end of the Umayyad Caliphate in 750 AD, differing versions had disappeared and the text had found its final form.

The Koran is the word of Allah and is thus final; not a dot can be changed. During the first centuries of its existence, Islam spread rapidly throughout the Middle East and North Africa and, with it, the language of the Koran, previously unknown to the new converts. To prevent Allah's word from foreign influences (which were threatening to force the language into a process of evolution), the Islamic scholars codified Arabic by introducing precise grammatical and lexical rules consistent with the usage in the Koran. The result of this work is known as 'classical Arabic', the language used by early Islamic poets and writers. It is still in active ceremonial use and is taught in the Koran schools.

Colloquial Arabic

With the written form of the language frozen, only spoken Arabic could evolve. Across a vast geographical area and over more than 1000 years, the evolution led to a wide collection of colloquial dialects. The decline of Arab civilisation in the colonial era (from the 15th to the 19th centuries AD) led to the unforeseen isolation of Arab people from one another, speeding up the differentiation of various dialects. In the 20th century, pan-Arab ideals and modern communications have had the opposite effect.

While French and Italian developed from Latin over a similar period of time into two distinct languages, the dialects of Arabic cannot be classified as separate languages, a fact largely attributable to the influence of the Koran. Yet, this does not mean that the dialects are always mutually intelligible. While a Saudi sheikh may readily understand the appeals of an Egyptian beggar, a Yemeni farmer might have serious difficulties bargaining in a Moroccan marketplace.

There are dozens of Arabic phrasebooks on the market, most of which are of questionable value in the Yemen, since they describe a different dialect. With a phrasebook of Maghrebi, Egyptian, Levantine or Iraqi Arabic, you can probably get your questions understood. However, they will not help you much in understanding the answers. Worse still, the books may teach you Modern Standard Arabic (discussed later in this chapter).

To my knowledge, there is no Yemeni Arabic phrasebook but any book that concentrates on Peninsular Arabic should do the job. If you are serious about the language, there is a 10,000-word Yemeni Arabic-

German-English dictionary: *Jemenitische Wörterbuch* by Jeffrey Deboo (Verlag Otto Harassowitz, 1989).

There is considerable variation between dialects in different parts of the Arabian Peninsula. Nevertheless, the inhabitants of this area usually understand each other and this situation improves all the time because of better communication and increased economic activity. There are even different dialects within the Yemen; the Sumarra Pass is a linguistic watershed often mentioned in treatises on this subject. In practical terms, this means that, even if you are able to get your message across, you may have difficulties understanding what you are told or asked.

Modern Standard Arabic

The spoken forms of Arabic never found their way onto paper. The language of the Koran was so highly appreciated that colloquial dialects were considered a sign of linguistic degeneration and not worthy of being written down. This attitude still prevails.

On the other hand, the vocabulary and idioms of classical Arabic reflect the traditional tribal Bedouin society; a more suitable means was needed to convey information and ideas in the modern world of mass media, international communications, politics and advertising. Over the past 100 years, a new form of Arabic has emerged – Modern Standard Arabic. This 'streamlined' version of classical Arabic is capable of expressing modern concepts in new words and idioms.

Modern Standard Arabic is taught alongside classical Arabic in all Arabic countries and is understood by every educated Arab. It is the language children learn to read and write. It is used in all 'serious' communication, from formal speeches to novels, from films to legal documents. It is also a useful means by which two Arabs from different countries can speak with each other, whatever the topic of conversation. Moreover, it is the language Westerners are generally taught in Arabic courses all over the world –

for most students, it is quite a shock to realise how far it really is from the spoken forms of the Arabic language.

Modern Standard Arabic was created when Arab people started to free themselves of colonial rule and needed not just a tool to communicate with each other but also a symbol of Arab unity. Thus, the language contains very few words borrowed from Western languages; new words are derived from old Arabic roots. This is probably one of the reasons that so few Westerners actually learn Arabic – there are no familiar words with which to start.

Alphabet & Transliteration

The Arabic script is cursive, like English longhand, and is written from right to left. The shape of a letter depends on its position in the word and most letters assume four different shapes. There are no capital letters and only one set of type is used; instead, there is a rich variety of calligraphic styles ranging from the simple (for taking quick notes with a ballpoint pen) to the very decorative (for ornamental use).

The alphabet has 28 consonant characters, 18 of which represent sounds also used in English, while the rest will sound unfamiliar to native English speakers. Three of the consonants are semivowels and these can represent either consonants, long vowels or diphthongs. Short vowels are never written. There is considerable variation in the pronunciation of vowels in different areas and pronunciation variants also occur with some consonants.

Transliterating Arabic into Latin script is an inherently difficult problem to which a final solution has not yet been found. There are a couple of 'scientific' systems as well as a plethora of nonscientific systems in use today. I own half a dozen books about the language and each uses a different method of transliteration. One consequence of all this is that you will see Arabic names written in various ways in Western newspapers and on maps.

Although your ear will not distinguish the

There are four vowel sounds in Arabic not represented in the alphabet:

'		glottal stop, like the non-voice before *Oh, Lord!*
a		as in *hat*, or as in *hut* (with emphatics)
i		as in *hit*
u		as in *put*

The alphabet itself consists of 28 consonants:

Arabic	Name of Letter	Transliteration Exact	Informal	Pronunciation
١	'alif	a:	a	as in *man* but longer
ب	ba:'	b	b	as in *big*
ت	ta:'	t	t	as in *tongue*
ث	tha:'	th	th	as in *thin*
ج	ji:m	j	j	as in *jam*; or (more common) like *g* in *go*
ح	Ha:'	H	h	strong *h* from back of throat, like blowing on spectacles to clean them
خ	kha:'	kh	kh	like *ch* in Scottish *loch* or German *achtung*
د	da:l	d	d	as in *dim*
ذ	dha:l	dh	dh	like *th* in *this*
ر	ra:'	r	r	prolonged *r* with quick taps of tongue against upper gum; as in Spanish *caro*
ز	za:y	z	z	as in *zip*
س	si:n	s	s	as in *sock*
ش	shi:n	sh	sh	as in *shoe*
ص	sa:d	**s**	s	emphatic *s*; a bit like in *sum*
ض	da:d	**d**	d	emphatic *d*; a bit like in *dumb*
ط	ta:'	**t**	t	emphatic *t*; a bit like in *tar*
ظ	za:'	**z**	dh	emphatic *dh*; a bit like *z* in *czar*
ع	'ayn	'	'	nothing like this in English; gag muscles at back of throat for voice like when puking; often *a* as in *but* is close
غ	ghayn	gh	gh	Parisian *r*
ف	fa:'	f	f	as in *fat*
ق	qa:f	q	q	like *k* but darker, further back in throat; or *g* as in *go* (common in Yemen)
ك	ka:f	k	k	as in *king*
ل	la:m	l	l	as in *lamb*
م	mi:m	m	m	as in *man*
ن	nu:n	n	n	as in *name*
ه	ha:'	h	h	as in *ham*
و	wa:w	w	w	as in *wet*; or
		u:	u	long *u* as in *mood*; or
		aw	aw	diphthong as in *how*
ى	ya:'	y	y	as in *yes*; or

emphatic consonants from their ordinary counterparts, they audibly affect the nearby vowels, making them darker (ie they are pronounced at the back of the mouth). Thus, *ay* is pronounced as in 'why' if there is an emphatic present in the word but is otherwise pronounced more as in 'way' (though not quite). With the exceptions of 'ayn and ghayn, other sounds should be utterable for a native speaker of the English language.

In this book, I will use the informal notation for normal text because it's easier to read but I will also present an exact pronunciation and transliterations of the geographical names. For many names, more than one transliteration is in common use; I will list some of them. For example, in the chapter on the capital of the Yemen, you will see San'a (**s**an'a; Sana, Sanaa). Within the brackets, the exact pronunciation is given first, followed by one or more alternative spellings.

Phrases

Usually, I oppose phrase lists as they are of very limited use – the selections often indicate a perverse sense of humour, you can't pronounce them anyway and, even if you succeed, you can seldom grasp the answer.

In Arabic, however, a phrase list is useful because the behaviour of the Arabs is highly ritualised and everyday conversation consists of some 50 to 100 very common phrases. If you know them well, you should get by quite smoothly. You should also know the numerals because you'll get much better prices if you can bargain in Arabic. Unfortunately, the numerals are among the most difficult words for a Westerner to pronounce.

The following phrase list gives you about 40 common phrases in colloquial Yemeni Arabic. (You can find very different phrase lists in other books.) I have tried to keep the phrases as short as possible so that they will be easy for you to pronounce and remember.

Greetings & Civilities

Hello. (greeting)
  is-sala:mu 'alaykum

Hello. (response)
  wa 'alaykum is-sala:m

Good morning.
  *s**aba:H il-khayr*

Good morning. (response)
  *s**aba:H in-nu:r*

Good evening.
  masa:' il-khayr

Good evening. (response)
  masa:' in-nur

How are you? (to man)
  kayf Ha:lak

How are you? (to woman)
  kayf Ha:lik

How are you? (to group)
  kayf Ha:lkum

Fine, thanks. (response)
  il-Hamdu li-lla:h or
  bi-khayr il-Hamdu li-lla:h or
  il-Hamdu li-lla:h bi-khayr

And you? (to man/woman/group)
  wa inta/inti/intkum?

Thank you.
  shukran

You're welcome .(response)
  'afwan

Please. (to man/woman)
  min fadl-ak/fadl-ik

Would you please tell me ....
  mumkin tiqu:l-li ....

Goodbye.
  ma'a s-sala:ma

Small Talk

Do you speak Arabic?
  titkallam 'arabi?

Yes.
  aywa/na'am

No.
  la:

A little.
  shwayya

What?
  aysh?

What's your name? (to man/woman)
  aysh ismak/ismik?

My name is Muhammad/Maureen.
  ismi muHammad/maureen

Where are you from? (to man/woman/group)
min wayn inta/inti/intkum?
Where are you from?
inta/inti/intkum min wayn?
I'm from the USA/Australia.
ana min amri:ka/ustura:liya
We're from the UK.
iHna min brita:niya
He's from France/Finland.
huwa min faransa:/finlanda:
She's from Germany.
hiya min alma:niya
He's my son/brother/father/husband.
huwa waladi/akhi/abi/zawgi
She's my daughter/sister/mother/wife.
hiya binti/ukhti/ummi/zawgati
OK. (good, acceptable)
tammam/kwayyis/tayyib
OK. (finished, understood)
khala:s

How do you like the Yemen?
kayf al-yaman?
Yemen is OK/a beautiful country
al-yaman tammam/bilad jami:l
I don't understand.
mush fahim
Never mind.
ma'laysh
I don't have a pen.
ma: fi: qalam
I want to take a photo/have a photo taken.
mumkin su:ra

Accommodation
Is there a hotel here?
fi funduq hina:?
Where?
wayn?
Is this house a hotel?
ha:dha l-bayt funduq?
Do you have a free bed in the dorm?
fi: takht/kursi?
Do you have a free room?
fi: ghurfa?
Is there a bathroom?
fi: Hamma:m?
I want to see the room first.
mumkin ashu:f al-ghurfa

Is there hot water?
fi: ma:i Ha:rr?
It's not good, the water is cold.
mush tammam, ma:i ba:rid
How much is this?
bi-ka:m ha:dha?

Getting Around
Where is the bus office?
wayn al-maktab al-ba:sa:t?
How much is it to al-Hudayda?
ka:m riyal ila: l-Hudayda?
How many km to the airport?
ka:m ki:lu ila: l-matar?
Two tickets to Sa'da please.
tadhkirayn ila: sa'da, min fadlak
Please give me a ticket to al-Mukalla.
mumkin tadhkira ila: l-mukalla
Does this bus go to Ta'izz?
ha:dha: l-ba:s ila: ta'izz?
Does this taxi go to Ibb?
ha:dha: t-taksi ila: 'ibb?

When?
mata?
Now.
ha:lHi:n/da:lHi:n
In half an hour.
ba'd nuss sa:'a
In an hour.
ba'd sa:'a
In a couple of hours.
ba'd sa:'atayn
Tomorrow.
bukra
Let's go.
yalla

At the Check Point
Your papers, please.
waraka
Your passport, please.
jawa:z/ba:sbu:r
Your tour permit, please.
tasri:H

Food
We'd like two glasses of tea, please.
mumkin ithnayn sha'i

I'd like to see (what's) in the kitchen, please.
mumkin ashu:f fi: l-matbakh
I'd like a fork and knife, please.
mumkin shawka wa sikki:n

restaurant
mat'am
traditional tea
sha'i talqi:m
teabag
sha'i libtun
tea without milk
sha'i aHmar
tea with milk
sha'i ma' Hali:b
sugar
sukkar
coffee
qahwa
water
ma:'i/muya
cold drink
ba:rid
beef
laHam baqari
mutton
ghanami
chicken
dija:j/tiqayq
fish
samak
liver
kibda
kidney
kila:wi
brains
mukh
potatoes
bata:ta
rice
ru:z
bread
khubz
salt
milH
pepper
filfil
mustard
khardal

Shopping

Do you have ...?
fi: 'ind-kum ...?
 oranges
  burtuqa:li
 grapes
  'anab
 bananas
  mawz
 cigarettes
  saja:yir
 matches
  kabri:t
 a loaf of bread
  Habbat khubz
 two loaves of bread
  Habbatayn khubz
 a bottle of water
  shi:shat ma:'i
 two bottles of water
  shi:shatayn ma:'i

Yes, we do have...
fi:...
No, we don't have...
ma: fi:...
money
flu:s
expensive
gha:li
cheap
rakhi:s

Here are some common prices:

YR 1
wa:Hid riyal
YR 1½
riyal wa nuss
YR 2
riyalayn
YR 2½
riyalayn wa nuss

Some Useful Phrases

Where is the post office?
wayn maktab al-bari:d?
Where is the pharmacy/hospital?
wayn saydali:ya/mustashfa

Where is the police station?
wayn maktab ash-shurta?
Where is the tourist office?
wayn maktab as-siya:Ha?
Is it far from/near here?
ba'i:d/qari:b min hina?
I want to speak with the manager, please.
mumkin atkallam ma'al-mudi:r

Numbers

The clock dial is a good way to become familiar with the Arabic numbers. The term 'Arabic numbers' generally refers to the positional number system, *not* to the symbols used in Western countries. Don't let the visual similarity of some Western and Arabic number symbols confuse you. Pay special attention to the order of the words in numbers from 21 to 99.

This is how the numerals read:

0	*sifr*
1	*wa:Hid*
2	*ithnayn*
3	*thala:tha*
4	*arba'a*
5	*khamsa*
6	*sitta*
7	*saba'a*
8	*thama:niya*
9	*tisa'a*
10	*'ashra*
11	*Hida'sh*
12	*ithna'sh*
13	*thala:ta'sh*
14	*arba'ta'sh*
15	*khamsta'sh*
16	*sitta'sh*
17	*saba'ta'sh*
18	*thamanta'sh*
19	*tisa'ta'sh*
20	*'ashri:n*
21	*wa:Hid wa 'ashri:n*
22	*ithnayn wa 'ashri:n*
30	*thala:thi:n*
40	*arba'i:n*
50	*khamsi:n*
60	*sitti:n*
70	*sab'i:n*
80	*thama:ni:n*
90	*tis'i:n*
100	*miya*
200	*miyatayn*
300	*thala:thmiya*
400	*arba'miya*
1000	*alf*
2000	*alfayn*
3000	*thala:that a:la:f*
6666	*sittat a:la:f wa sittmiya wa sitta wa sitti:n*

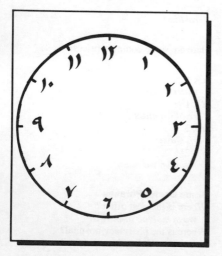

Body Language

The Arabs are famous for being able to communicate most complex ideas through gestures, both standard and improvised. The Yemenis are no exception. Body language tends to be universal and you should have no problems understanding or speaking it yourself, although there are some important differences. The Western 'OK' sign of thumb touching forefinger in a circle, for example, is obscene, referring to a woman's vagina. Familiar gestures include the biker's 'thumb's up' signal, a universal expression of agreement or support, and the Western 'up yours' gesture, a severe insult in the Yemen, as elsewhere.

To beckon someone, you should put the

fingers of your right hand together, hold the hand downwards and motion towards yourself.

'No' can be expressed by raising both eyebrows. Blinking with both eyes simultaneously means 'yes'. If you hold the thumb and forefinger of the right hand stretched out at right angles to each other with the other fingers curled into the palm, facing the speaker, then wave the whole hand back and forth a couple of times, it conveys a general interrogative sense which applies to a wealth of situations.

Facts for the Visitor

VISAS & EMBASSIES

Everybody needs a visa to enter Yemen and it is easy to get one. Any Yemeni consulate will issue you an entry visa as long as there is enough room in your passport (one blank page will be needed) and you are not an enemy of Yemen – a citizen of Israel or South Africa. If one of these countries has ever granted you a visa, you can forget about your trip to Arabia Felix – at least until you've acquired a new passport.

The entry fees vary from embassy to embassy but are generally about US$30 for citizens of the country where the embassy is located, and twice or thrice that for other applicants. The period covered by an entry visa also varies. They may be valid from one to three months, with visas issued by far-off embassies tending to be valid longer.

The maximum duration of stay is written in the entry visa. This is not definitive, however. The actual date by which you have to either exit the country or apply for an extension will be specified in the 'residence' visa (see below) which you get upon entry into the Yemen, so don't let the markings in your entry visa affect your plans in any way.

Entry Visa

The visa application forms must be completed in triplicate (or in quadruplicate at some embassies), so you will need three (or four) photographs.

The form asks you the customary questions about your person and passport. For your religion, it is perfectly safe to write 'Christian' – Arabs think that Christians believe in the same God they do but are incompletely informed because they haven't received the message of Muhammad.

Traditionally, the same applies for Jews but, given the present world political situation, I would not proclaim myself to be a Jew. Yemen sees the Palestinian question as the pivot of its Arab policy and an active PLO faction has been based in the country since Israel ousted the organisation from Lebanon in 1983. Other religions are probably safe but stating 'none' might create a stir among the highly religious Yemenis.

If you apply for a tourist visa, the purpose of the visit will obviously be 'sightseeing' or simply 'tourism'. In this case, a return air ticket is needed to prove that you will only be in the country temporarily. Since prospective travellers may be unwilling to buy a ticket before getting the visa, this is not a hard and fast rule in practice, at least when you are dealing with an embassy in the Western world. They are probably stricter on this point in those places, like eastern Africa, where flocks of people are trying to emigrate to countries with more promising economic futures.

In giving details of your profession, I don't recommend that journalists say so unless invited for an official visit; otherwise, the trip might turn official anyway! If you're travelling on business, you will need a reference in Yemen – a letter from the Yemeni company or organisation with which you are dealing. The letter must state, in detail, the reasons for your trip and the name and address of the Yemeni referee.

Residence Visa

Residence visas are issued automatically when you arrive at the San'a International Airport. I'm not quite sure if this happens at other border stations, too. If you arrive in Yemen by land or by sea, you'd better check the stamps in your passport. The residence visa is a triangular stamp, usually placed on the same page in your passport as the entry visa.

If you haven't got the triangular stamp and you plan to stay in the country for more than seven days, you will have to register at the Immigration Office in San'a, Ta'izz or al-Hudayda, or at the Foreigners' Central Registration Office in Crater, Aden, within seven days of arrival.

The length of time you are entitled to stay in Yemen will be written in your residence visa. For tourists, this period is usually one month, regardless of what your entry visa says. The dates will be written in Arabic numerals only so, if you have difficulties deciphering the dates, ask any English-speaking Yemeni to read them to you – they will be only too eager to help and will probably use the opportunity to study the details of your strange passport thoroughly!

Visa Extensions

If you need to stay more than a month in the Yemen, you can get two-week extensions of your residence visa from the Immigration Office of the Ministry of Interior at no cost. There are immigration offices in San'a, Ta'izz, al-Hudayda and Aden (see the maps of those cities).

Re-Entry Visa

If you are working in the Yemen, re-entry visas are granted for short-term leaves. You can get your re-entry visa from the Immigration office.

For tourists, there are no such arrangements so, if you decide to visit Djibouti, Somalia or some other nearby destination (relatively cheap from San'a or Aden), you will need a new entry visa from that place. It might be best to plan your trip so that you arrive in Yemen once only.

Vaccination Certificate

You will need international vaccination certificates for cholera and yellow fever if you come from or through an infected area (getting these vaccinations is a good idea anyway). Some embassies are still using old application forms which require a smallpox certificate too, despite the fact that the Yemens dropped this requirement in 1980 after the WHO officially declared the disease eradicated from the globe. Seemingly, some of the embassies have not been informed! Visitors flying in directly from Western

Europe no longer need any vaccination certificates.

Yemeni Embassies

Yemen has embassies in most of the Arab countries, as well as in many European, African and Asian countries and the USA – apply for the visa at the embassy most convenient for you. If it is difficult for you to get to a Yemeni embassy, you can apply for your visa by post; just order the application forms and you'll receive further instructions in a week or two. Embassies in Western capitals have application forms in Arabic as well as in relevant Western languages. We used London twice and found the method reliable and reasonably fast, although the obligatory use of registered mail when sending passports and cheques adds somewhat to the cost.

If your country's postal service is unreliable or you are not on a tight budget, you could plan your route to Yemen to include a few days stop in some nearby capital. Better still, if you include the visit to Yemen in your grand tour of north-east Africa or the Middle East, you can get your Yemeni visa in almost any capital city en route. The visas usually take 48 hours to issue. The Yemenis are sometimes flexible – once we got visas from Djibouti the next day – but, sometimes, they are definitely not, so don't count heavily on this. Most Yemeni embassies are only open in the mornings and close at noon.

It is difficult to list the Yemen's embassies worldwide since, following the unification of the YAR and the PDRY, the number of embassies in any given country will be reduced to one and we do not yet know which one will go. Here, however, are the addresses of embassies of the former YAR in non-Arab countries.

Canada
    Suite 500, 56 Sparks St, Ottawa, Ontario, K1P 5A9 (☎ (613) 2306136)
China
    4 Dong Chi Men Wai St, Beijing (☎ 523346, 523991, 523748)
Czechoslovakia
    Washingtonova 17, 12522 Prague 1 (☎ (2) 222411)

Djibouti
  Plateau du Marabout, 127/4 Ahmad Ibrahim Building, PO Box 1913, Djibouti (☎ 352975/6)
Ethiopia
  Role International Rd, PO Box 664, Addis Ababa (☎ 181260/5)
France
  21 Ave Charles Floquet, 75007 Paris (☎ (1) 43066622)
Germany
  Adenauerallee 77, 5300 Bonn (☎ (228) 220273, 220451, 261490/9)
  Waldstrasse 15, 1110 Berlin (☎ 4800391)
India
  B-55, Pashami Marg, Vasant Vihar, New Delhi 110057 (☎ (11) 674064, 674743, 674472, 674124, 674391)
Italy
  Via Verona 3, Int 4-00161, Rome (☎ (06) 4271018, 4270811, 4270281)
Japan
  12-24, Nishi, Azabu, 4, Ohome, Minato-Ku (1106), Tokyo (☎ 4997151/2)
Netherlands
  Surinamestraat 9, 2585 GC The Hague (☎ (070) 653936/7, telex 33290)
Pakistan
  H No 46, St 12, F, 6/3, PO Box 1523, Islamabad (☎ (51) 821146/7, 828441)
Somalia
  Martyr Mahmoud Harbi St, PO Box 264, Mogadishu (☎ 80038, 80310, 38016)
Switzerland
  Kistlerweg 2, 3006 Bern (☎ (031) 444885)
UK
  41 South St, London W1 (☎ 4914003, 6299905/6/7/8)
USA
  Suite 860, Watergate Six Hundred, 600 New Hampshire Ave NW, Washington, DC 20037 (☎ (202) 9654760/1, 8654781)
  United Nations, 8th floor, 747 3rd Ave, New York, NY 10017 (☎ (212) 3551730/1)
USSR
  2 Neopalimovskij Per 6, Moscow (☎ 2461814, 2464427, 2461554)

You will also find embassies of Yemen in the capital cities of all Arab countries except Bahrain and Oman. Use a taxi and apply for your visa in person – if you choose this option, you're probably proficient enough to get by in the Arabic world without further advice.

Foreign Embassies in the Yemen

This list gives you the addresses of some non-Arab diplomatic representations in San'a:

China
  Az-Zubayri St (☎ 275337)
Czechoslovakia
  As-Safiya al-Gharbia al-Junubiya (☎ 247946)
Djibouti
  Southern Ring Rd (☎ 247791)
Ethiopia
  Hadda Rd (☎ 208833)
France
  Al-Bawniya Area (☎ 73169, 275995)
Germany
  Rd No 22, Hs No 9-49 (☎ 216756/7)
Hungary
  As-Safiya, St 5, Hs 9 (☎ 248147)
India
  Az-Zubayri, St 8, Bldg 6 (☎ 241980)
Italy
  St 29, Bldg 5 (near Muhammad 'Ali ash-Shawkani St) (☎ 78846, 73409)
Japan
  Ring Rd as-Safiya al-Gharbiya (☎ 207536, 79930)
Netherlands
  Hadda St (after Ring Rd) (☎ 215626/7/8)
Pakistan
  Ring Rd (near Hadda St) (☎ 248813/4, 248866)
Somalia
  Hadda St (☎ 208864)
UK
  al-Hamadani St (☎ 215630/1/2/3)
USA
  Sa'wan St (☎ 238842/52)
USSR
  26th September St (☎ 78272, 203142)

IMMIGRATION & CUSTOMS

These days, the immigration process in Yemen is no more cumbersome than that in any other country. Most tourists arrive in Yemen through the San'a International Airport, although Aden's facilities are more modern and the capacity of its airport is greater.

You must first fill in the blue arrival card. This will have been handed to you on the plane if you flew Yemen Airways; otherwise, you can pick one up in the arrival hall. The arrival card is in two parts, each with irritatingly identical questions. Fill it in with patience – you will find most of the answers in your passport.

Don't forget to supply your address in the

Yemen; if you don't, you will be asked for it. The Yemeni immigration officers don't quite realise that someone could enter the country as a tourist without prebooked hotel reservations, so choose a hotel in San'a and use it as your address. This is just a formality and nobody will be interested in it afterwards – the form just has to be completed.

The card is then handed, with your passport, to the immigration officer, who will stamp into it the entry date and residence visa.

After passport control, you wait for your luggage and can take the opportunity to admire the imaginative packing methods of local folks returning from abroad with their belongings. The customs procedures tend to be time-consuming because every bag and pack must be opened, be it closed by locks, ropes or seals. Strangely, however, their contents are usually inspected in a most casual way. If possible, choose a queue containing only foreigners – the one Yemeni standing ahead of you with only a small attaché case is probably holding the place for his two wives and four brothers, who'll carry the 20 or 30 pieces of their luggage!

Also, don't try to get your handbag past the examination – at the exit, there will be an armed guard who's not going to let you pass with an unmarked bag. By the way, this 'guards watching guards' method is a typical Yemeni phenomenon and you will encounter it many times during your stay. Just ask the inspector to mark every piece of your luggage even if they don't look into all of them.

Yemen's customs regulations are discretionary for most articles; in fact, when we asked about them on our first visit to the country, we were simply told that they are 'as anywhere else' – no need to explain that further!

Imports

You are allowed to bring in 200 cigarettes, 50 cigars or 250 grams of pipe tobacco into the Yemen. Alcoholic beverages are prohibited within the country but non-Muslims can bring in one litre. Women are allowed to have 'reasonable' quantities of cosmetics and jewels with them. If you come by land, you are permitted to have 50 litres of gasoline for your car.

Pornographic material is prohibited, of course, in this Islamic country. Your magazines may be examined and video cassettes seized for closer inspection (you can reclaim them a few days later at the Ministry of Information or the immigration office).

Computers (even electronic typewriters) are likely to cause you some trouble. Don't bring one unless it's absolutely essential and be prepared to negotiate about it for weeks.

Other regulations are not likely to affect the average tourist. You are allowed to bring in gifts not exceeding US$25 in value, domestic animals holding international health certificates, and so on. If you are a businessperson, you are allowed to bring samples of your products as well as brochures and other promotions aids, provided you take them out with you when you leave the country.

Exports

You are permitted to export anything you have been able to purchase in the Yemen. This doesn't include, of course, items of historical value – you can't take with you the nice marble capital you found lying in the sands near the Ma'rib Dam. Officially, all articles more than 40 years old belong to the national heritage and cannot be exported without permission from the General Tourism Corporation. Don't be alarmed, though, because the silverware you bought in the suqs is probably not as old as you imagine...

TOUR PERMITS

The final piece of Yemeni bureaucracy with which you should be familiar is the tour permit; you must have this in order to travel within the Yemen.

To appreciate the importance of the tour permit, you need to understand that, while Yemen is a country of free enterprise, it is also run by a military government and civil rights here do not reflect the same concept of personal freedom found in most Western countries. Yemenis themselves are now able to travel fairly freely in their own country, though they are obliged to carry their ID cards. However, foreigners living in Yemen have permanent access only to certain areas. To visit other villages or towns, they must get specific permission from the authorities. If you work as a teacher in Bayt al-Faqih, for example, you might be entitled to visit al-Hudayda once a week but, to visit any other place, you would need special permission.

The control system is impressive – there are roadblocks around every major town and along every traversable road, permanently occupied by a handful of soldiers. All travellers must stop at these checkpoints and their identity cards may be examined if they are not familiar with the soldiers. Foreigners always have to show their passports and explain where they are going and why. Very often (but not always) they are asked to show their tour permits.

The system is not just to check people; sometimes, bags are also inspected. The belongings of locals get checked as often as those of foreigners. Exactly what they are looking for is hard to tell but the effect is that, if you have been able to smuggle anything in, you haven't made it yet. In the Tihama, foreigners are often suspected of carrying alcoholic drinks because the al-Makha port is especially notorious for booze smuggling.

Control tends to vary depending on the checkpoint and the person in charge. The time of day is also a factor: you are less likely to be checked thoroughly in the afternoons when the soldiers are busy chewing qat. On the other hand, if you drive through San'a in the middle of the night, you will be inspected at all major crossroads and stopped by every soldier and police officer en route.

Note that these comments apply to conditions in the northern part of the country before and shortly after the unification. In the former PDRY, tourists were only allowed to travel in groups and the tour guides handled the details. In 1990, individual travel became legal in the southern governorates, too, but the tour permit system was not in effect there when we visited. It is not clear what the regulation will be in the unified Yemen. Tour permits will either be required throughout the country or be scrapped altogether – we heard both predictions when we asked about the plans.

Obtaining Permits

Tourists can readily get permits to travel in most parts of the country. The authority concerned is the General Tourist Corporation (sometimes spelt Cooperation), a government organisation headquartered in San'a and with branch offices in al-Hudayda and Aden. No fees are charged for the permits.

The San'a office is the one you will probably visit because San'a is the most likely point of entry and because this office can grant permits to all northern provinces as well as to Aden. Other branch offices handle their own provinces and only grant you access to San'a if you have arrived in some other port or have lost your permit. If you do lose your permit, there are also branch offices in Ibb and Ta'izz. The San'a office is conveniently located by Tahrir Square. The staff speak English and, as usual, business hours are in the mornings. For the southern governorates, the Aden office in at-Tawahi will handle the permits, should these become obligatory.

Tour permits are applied for in person and the officer prepares them on the spot. You will need to show your passport first; if you are part of a group, you will get a single form with everyone's names and passport details written down on it. After that, you will be asked about your travel plans. It is essential to have done some planning beforehand so that you can name the towns and villages you want to visit.

However, your list should not be too long because there is not much space on the form and the officer might become nervous. Don't list too many small villages you found on some strange map from abroad – it is better if the officer knows the places you name. It is also a very good idea to point out the places on a map while explaining your route – you might well use the maps in this book for this purpose.

Recommended areas for tourists include all the towns and villages along the main asphalted roads from San'a to Sa'da, Hajja, Rada', Ta'izz, al-Makha and al-Hudayda as well as a few other remarkable sites, including Shibam, Thilla, at-Tawila, al-Mahwit, Hammam 'Ali, Hammam Damt and al-Khawkha. This list is standard; you may get these if you haven't prepared any plan at all and leave the decision to the officer. It is, of course, better to know what you want and, if you have any specific plans, you should make them known now.

Make sure to mention all the towns and villages you want to stop at, even if they lie along the main routes. Manakha, for example, is a few km off the San'a to al-Hudayda road and so needs to be mentioned specifically. The first time we tried to visit Bayt al-Faqih, we were turned away by an exceptionally zealous policeman because the village was not on our list, although every other conceivable Tihamese locality was included.

Once you have the permit, get plenty of photocopies of it because the staff at some checkpoints may take your papers instead of just looking at them. They have to keep a record of the who foreigners pass by and, for this, they need your name and passport number.

The Arabic word for tour permit is *tasrih* (properly transcribed as tasri:H) but you may simply be asked for *waraqa*, or paper. By waraqa, they may also mean your passport *(jawa:z* or *ba:sbu:r)* . In any case, never give away your original tour permit!

Some people living in Yemen actually advise against showing your passport at the checkpoint; instead, they suggest making copies of your passport, too – the pages with your photo and visa. You can always tell them your passport is in San'a.

There are photocopy machines in almost every photo studio in San'a (and in other cities, too). One convenient studio is by the narrow shopping alley that leads from the park in front of the General Tourist Corpora-

tion to Gamal Abdul Nasser St. If you order 10 or more copies, they should not cost you more than YR 2 each. The Arabic word for 'copy' is *sura* (or su:ra); the same word is used for a photo or picture.

Off-Limit Areas

You may not get permission to visit all the places you name. Border areas are definitely off limits. Some other places may also be temporarily forbidden. It seems that the limits of the tourist area vary according to when and from whom you apply for the permit. You may be denied permission to visit a specific village because the officer thinks there is nothing of interest there and is courteously saving you the trouble and disappointment. Some areas may not be recommended because they are in a state of relative economic and cultural backwardness; the Yemenis clearly suffer from a severe inferiority complex and continually compare their living standards with those of neighbouring oil-rich countries.

On the other hand, most of the border areas are off limits for reasons that can be easily understood: the desert borders are not clearly defined and border disputes have been all too common in this part of the world throughout the 20th century. Recent oil discoveries in the central deserts and the deterioration of the Saudi-Yemeni relationship have certainly exacerbated this problem. Indeed, we have found that getting extensive tour permits has gradually become more and more difficult since 1984.

One reason for this is that certain areas, especially in the northernmost part of the country, are not under complete government control. Moreover, the influx of tourists in the late 1980s has caused the inhabitants of some much-visited mountain villages to grow surly towards Western visitors. Of course, the Yemeni government is not willing to let tourists wander in areas where they are not absolutely safe. You might feel that this is overly protective but there have been some nasty incidents.

As matters stood in 1990, the General Tourist Corporation in San'a was not granting permission to individual travellers to visit places like the Shihara mountain, Ma'rib and Baraqish; you could still make the visit through a local tour operator, who would provide you with a local guide. Other places, such as Sirwah and Suq al-'Inan, were completely off limits.

What happens if you do travel in off-limits areas? This depends on where you try to go. In some areas, you might get through because of loose controls; if the officers at a checkpoint have seen few foreigners, it might not even occur to them that you should have any documents other than your passport, or they might not bother to read your tour permit.

On the other hand, if they notice that you don't have a permit, you are certainly not going to get through. However, if you behave yourself, they are not going to put you in jail, either; you will just have to turn back. If you have a good command of Arabic or there

happens to be someone around who speaks good English, you might try explaining what you want but this is generally useless. We have seen Arabs being forced to leave the bus – you can't visit even a well-established tourist site without the necessary permission. *Don't* make the mistake of offering money to the soldiers – they won't accept it.

MONEY
Before the unification in 1990, both Yemens had currencies of their own: the riyal in the YAR and the dinar in the PDRY. At the time of writing, both currencies are legal tender throughout the Yemen, though it is much more common to see riyals used in the southern part of the country than dinars in the north. The government has not yet disclosed details of the monetary union but my guess is that the riyal will be adopted as the official currency, with the dinar continuing to circulate in the south for a couple of years.

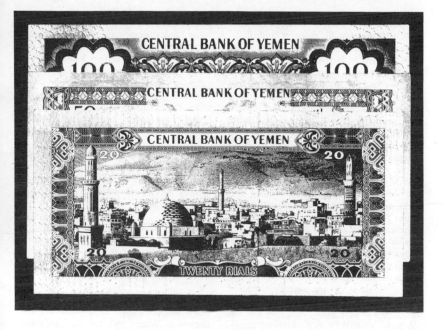

The riyal (denoted in this book by the abbreviation YR) is divided into 100 fils. The minimum pricing unit these days is YR 1 and the coins of 25 fils and 50 fils are being taken out of circulation. There is both a coin and a banknote worth YR 1 and banknotes of 5, 10, 20, 50 and 100 riyals. The notes are easily distinguished since they are bilingual; values are printed in Arabic on one side and in English on the other. You soon learn to recognise them by their colours. The coin values are shown only in Arabic.

The dinar (YD) is divided into 20 shillings or 1000 fils, so that a shilling is worth 50 fils. The shilling, or dirham as it is officially called, is a unit used in speech for convenience; the coins and banknotes always show their value in fils and dinars. The 5, 10 and 25 fils coins are worthless on their own and are falling into disuse. The 50, 100 and 250 fils coins are common and are referred to as 1, 2 and 5 shillings respectively. There are 250 and 500 fils banknotes as well as

banknotes worth 1 and 5 dinars; the latter are often referred to as 20 and 100 shilling notes.

The exchange rates at the time of writing were:

US$1	=	YR 12
US$1	=	YD 0.420
YD 1	=	YR 28
YR 1	=	YD 0.035

Changing Money

You can't buy Yemeni riyals abroad but all major Western currencies are accepted in the Yemen. The problem is where to change them on arrival. There is an exchange counter in the arrival hall of the San'a International Airport, before passport control, but it seems to be irregularly staffed. You will find a couple of other bank offices at the San'a airport. These are open only from 8 am to noon and, in practice, perhaps from 9 to 11 am. Quite possibly, they never open at all.

In Aden, there is a branch office of the state bank after you pass the passport control.

You will need local money to get away from the airport. If you arrive during business hours (that is, 8 am to 1 pm), you could get a taxi and ask the driver to take you to a bank first. Another alternative is to change money with an airport worker, local passenger, anybody. If you offer a profitable enough bargain, any Yemeni will be eager to do some banking with you – if they don't happen to have the money, they'll borrow it – so it might be a good idea to carry about US$20 worth of small notes when entering the Yemen.

All major world currencies are recognised in the Yemen. As only Yemeni (and Saudi) currency can be used in daily transactions, you have to exchange your money for local currency. You will also have no problems changing US dollars, British pounds, French francs or German marks. On the other hand, it is difficult to change minor currencies; even the francs of nearby Djibouti are exchanged at very poor rates, if at all. The US dollar is recommended – despite periodic weaknesses in the US dollar, the exchange rate seems to be steadily improving. US$100 bills will get you somewhat better rates than smaller denominations.

Moneychangers You can change your money either in commercial banks or with moneychangers in the suqs of larger cities. The moneychangers offer rates some 15% better than the banks but using them is not exactly legal. Until the mid-1980s, authorised moneychangers operated from small offices in the city centres in the YAR. However, their operations were outlawed by the government in early 1988.

Banks If you use a bank, choose an international one such as Bank Indo-Suez; they are usually the most flexible and English is more likely to be spoken. As recently as the mid-1980s, the domestic banks used very complex and time-consuming bureaucratic routines when changing money but, these days, the process has been streamlined a lot

and you should have few problems. Still, some bank offices may not offer exchange services at all. Banks are open from 8 or 9 am until noon in the former YAR, from 7.30 am to 12.30 pm in the former PDRY.

Hotels Bigger hotels also change money, at official rates. In the south, this applies to all hotels of the former state-controlled tourism company.

In smaller towns, you will probably not be able to change any money at all. In fact, you should not count on being able to change money anywhere outside the Yemen's biggest cities.

Travellers' Cheques
You can now change travellers' cheques in most banks. Stick to major worldwide companies, though, if you decide to use travellers' cheques.

Credit Cards
For a budget traveller, credit cards are quite useless in Yemen and, for everybody else, they are of limited use as they are only accepted in a few five-star hotels. American Express is about the only recognised card.

Carrying Cash
I recommend that you use cash instead of travellers' cheques and credit cards as it is easier to handle and relatively safe to carry around – if there is a country left in the world where crime is rare, it must be the Yemen.

Theft is restrained here by a set of values that have remained beyond question for 1400 years. It is not because Shari'a, the Islamic law, orders the right hand of a thief to be cut off – it is because theft is virtually nonexistent in this culture. If you drop your wallet in the suqs it will probably be handed back to you. You will see locals walking in the streets counting thick bundles of banknotes in their hands; similar behaviour in a Western capital would probably provoke an act of street violence. Foreigners may have no such qualms, however, so keep an eye on your fellow travellers.

Of course, reasonable precautions are advisable. Carrying most of your cash in a money belt under your clothing should be enough. Many Yemenis have travelled abroad a lot since the revolution and some might have begun to think that stealing from a non-Muslim is not so bad after all, since non-Muslims steal from one another routinely. Certainly, overcharging for services is not seen as robbery, so don't boast of your wealth.

Costs

Is Yemen cheap or expensive? This depends on what you are after. If you conform to the traditional Yemeni lifestyle, you can travel cheaply here, but if you continue enjoying French fries, beer and private bathrooms with hot water, you will find that it was only the flight ticket that was cheap. If you try something in between, you will probably find that Yemen is definitely not cheap but nor is it unbearably expensive.

Yemen ranks among the poorest 40 countries in the world if measured by the per capita gross national product. This means that people have to be able to meet their daily needs using little money. Basic food is cheap, for example. A glass of tea or a loaf of bread costs YR 1 and you can have a simple but nourishing dinner in a street-level San'a restaurant for YR 20. A live chicken sells for YR 20 in the market but the bill for a grilled one in a restaurant is YR 40.

As for hotels, you'll find everything from absolutely basic inns at YR 5 per night to Western-style five-star deluxe hotels charging YR 2000 a night. Transport, your third main expense, is not overwhelmingly expensive as long as you don't hire a car for your personal use. The longest bus hauls take four hours and cost YR 90 in the former YAR, 12 hours and YD 5 in the former PDRY. A service taxi may charge YR 100 for the same distance.

On the other hand, luxury import items are expensive because the riyal has been effectively devaluating against Western currencies in recent years. Luxury goods are readily available, however, since about every fifth Yemeni was working abroad in the early 1980s, effectively spreading the word about the fruits of modern technology.

Tipping

This questionable practice simply doesn't exist in Yemen and you would be wise not to introduce or encourage it. Service is included in restaurant and hotel prices. Fares for taxis and other such financial arrangements are best negotiated in advance.

Bargaining

Contrary to what you might expect, Yemen is not a place where time-consuming bargaining is the rule. Grocery prices are always fixed and, even in the suqs, bargaining is rare, often impossible. This doesn't mean you should pay whatever you are asked. Use your judgement and compare the prices offered by different traders; if you have the time and opportunity, check prices in different suqs. You will also find a few things that are unique to each suq.

When a trader quotes a price, it is often final (or close to it). It may not be the same price that would be asked of a fellow Yemeni and it probably includes a 'foreigner's tax'. However, it is final in the sense that it is your price and, because you seem able to afford it, you won't be offered a lower one.

PLANNING YOUR TRIP

It pays to plan your visit to Yemen beforehand. Take at least a cursory look through this book and decide which places you want to see and in what order. However, leave room for improvisation. One of the most fascinating aspects of Yemen is that you may run across curious things that are not documented anywhere. You might walk to a small village not drawn on any map and local residents will take your hand and lead you to some astonishingly well-preserved pre-Islamic structures or strange geological formations. I won't guarantee that this will happen to you but it has happened to us.

Itineraries

The number of asphalted roads in Yemen is

increasing rapidly but the lack of road connections will still have a big effect on your touring plan. For example, the only useful route from Ibb to Zabid is via Ta'izz – there are alternatives but they are either impractical or off limits.

Most visitors traverse the big triangle between San'a, Ta'izz and al-Hudayda. This takes at least a week but, depending on your means of transport, how many towns you visit en route and what kind of accommodation you find acceptable, may take much longer. Sa'da and Shihara can be visited on one trip from San'a. Even if you hire a private taxi for the trip, you'd better allocate at least four days to visit these two towns.

A visit to Hadhramawt from San'a will take at least two weeks if you are using ground transport. You have to go to Aden first, from there to al-Mukalla and, finally, to Say'un in Hadhramawt, and take the same route back – making the trip as long aas one from Amsterdam to Istanbul, or Stockhol to Rome! The trip takes at least five days in one direction, with every other day spent in buses or taxis, so flying in the other direction is worth considering if it fits into your budget.

Due to San'a's range of accommodation, visitors like to use the city as a base for excursions. Ma'rib is one of the places visited by most tourists (too) hurriedly; they leave San'a early in the morning, sit in the car most of the day and return late in the evening. There are excellent roads from San'a to Hajja, Shibam, Thilla, at-Tawila, al-Mahwit and Manakha, and any of these towns can be comfortably visited in one or two days. On the other hand, these towns lie in the mountain area which is best suited to trekking; you could spend weeks walking and hitchhiking along the dirt roads from town to town.

Weekly Markets

When planning your trip, you should take into consideration the system of weekly markets. While large cities like San'a, Ta'izz and al-Hudayda have suqs that are open every day, the smaller villages conduct business one day a week only. Farmers and craftspeople from the neighbourhood gather at these weekly markets to sell their products, making the suqs colourful social events. The system thus clearly serves not only commerce but also the purpose of passing information (and time).

Market day differs from village to village and it pays to visit at least some of them. If you visit the Tihama, you should try to see Bayt al-Faqih's Friday market, which has been deservedly famous for hundreds of years. Some villages have few permanent inhabitants and, consequently, are almost dead except on market day; examples are Suq at-Talh near Sa'da and Suq al-Khamis in the northern Tihama. In other villages, the market may be quite small but still creates a clearly different atmosphere to other days of the week.

Weekly markets are very common in the northern part of Yemen and in the Lahej and Abyan Governorates in the south. The system is known in most Arab countries but nowhere else has it gained such widespread acceptance. This ancient practice was documented by the Danish explorer Carsten Niebuhr in the 18th century, who commented on the extraordinarily large number of markets. And they show no signs of dying out – recent counts show that the introduction of permanent roadside markets by the main asphalted highways and of Western-style supermarkets in the cities has had no impact on the number of weekly market sites.

The Time Factor

If you make firm day by day plans, they have no chance of being realised completely. There are 1001 details that can go wrong; Murphy's Law says that they will go wrong and you'd better believe it.

The most obvious thing that can go wrong is your schedule. Everything takes more time in southern Arabia than it would in your home country. The bus that leaves at 7 am will actually leave an hour later (or half an hour earlier, causing you to miss it!), 200 km in a taxi will take five hours (because of lunch, prayers and checkpoints on the road) and buying a bottle of Coke takes half an hour (you only have 50 riyal notes and the shopkeeper has no change).

This is all the more frustrating when there are things you have to do at certain times. Banks and government offices are open only in the morning; everything is closed in the afternoon. You will also want to visit certain places on certain days because of the system of weekly markets. The best advice is to allow plenty of time and make your schedule flexible enough to accommodate the inevitable delays.

Length of Stay By now, you should have some idea of how long to stay in the Yemen. Staying one week will probably turn out to be very expensive because you will want to come back and see what you missed. If you maintain a frenzied pace and use expensive private taxis every now and then, two weeks will give you enough time to see most (but definitely not all) of the historical towns in the northern part of the country, though you'd need another couple of weeks for the southern governorates. The most extensive organised tours in Yemen take two weeks and cost more than US$1000 per person (not including flights to and from the Yemen). A three or four-week visit is good for an independent traveller; you'll have ample time to visit all the famous sites, you can wander around in the mountains (a must in the Yemen, even if hiking is not your cup of tea) and you have a chance to change your plans if you find something you didn't expect.

The Weather Factor
There is no ideal season to visit Yemen because climatic conditions vary so greatly between regions. The Yemenis themselves, in their inimitably optimistic way, recommend that you visit the country 'any time'. This is sound advice because, at all times, some region is sure to be at its best.

If you have more than a passing interest in the Tihama region or are planning to visit Aden and Hadhramawt, summer is certainly the season to avoid. The Arabian Peninsula is said to be one of the most hostile places on earth to human habitation and you'll really believe this if you visit the coastal areas of Yemen in summer. The air is extremely humid and hot, there is no rain and the wind keeps carrying sand everywhere, particularly under your clothes.

If you visit the Tihama in December, you may still think the air extremely humid and hot, and the windblown sand just as much of a problem. However, rest assured that it's worse in July. The coastal areas are always hot and, even during the rainy seasons, the sands are seldom wet enough to resist the wind. This makes things very dusty. The Hadhramawt valley has more pleasant temperatures and dry air in the winter.

In contrast, the highlands can get quite cold in winter. From late November to early January, San'a has nightly frosts and, in the mountains, it is chilly indeed. Even in October and February, you will need some warm clothes in the early mornings and after sunset.

May to early August is dry and hot everywhere and you probably won't need heavy clothing, even if you plan to do extensive trekking in the highest mountain areas at this time. (As a rough guide, the temperature goes down by more than 0.5°C but less than 1°C for every 100 metres you climb.) There are no clouds, the sun shines from 5 am to 6.30 pm and the weather may turn out to be unbearably hot. You soon learn why the Yemenis offer no services in the afternoons; your own level of activity will also peak in the mornings and evenings.

In addition to temperature, there is another factor to consider: water. The dry seasons are really dry; from late October to early February and from May to June, there are perhaps three rainfalls in San'a and, though it may rain throughout the summer in the Ibb region, most of the country is parched for at least eight months of the year.

If architecture is higher on your list of priorities than nature, this may sound all right. However, as most of the roads and streets in Yemen are not asphalted, heavy traffic and turbulent winds continually raise huge clouds of dust. You will be all too happy to have a shower several times a day. Another drawback is that, during the dry winter months (almost half of the year), most of the fields lie barren. Half the trees have dropped their leaves and those trees that do have foliage left are so brown with dust that you might not even notice. You simply won't understand how Yemen earned the epithet 'the Green Land of Arabia'. Worse still, your friends back home will not appreciate your unique photos of the extraordinary mud architecture in the Dhamar basin if they can't distinguish the brown houses from the brown fields.

The rainy seasons – the lighter one in March-April and the heavier one in August-September – offer pleasant temperatures of 20°C to 30°C in the high plateau areas and, even in the mountains, you won't need heavy clothing. However, what is dust during the dry season becomes mud when it rains. You may find that small dirt roads along the wadis – plenty of them around here! – are untraversable, even with a 4WD vehicle, so you'd best stick to the main roads.

Trekking can also be anything but enjoyable when you encounter a torrent delivering 10 cm of water in just a couple of hours. It is easy to get caught by a rainstorm because the mornings are often deceptively bright and warm, and the clouds don't gather until the afternoon. Heavy mountain rains can be extremely dangerous to trekkers because the cascading water carries rocks the size of small cars down the slopes. And, of course, you won't be able to see the mountains because of the clouds!

The temperatures are highly dependent on the continuity of sunshine, too; a cloud obscuring the sun may drop the temperature by a dozen degrees in a few minutes. So, if you plan to do extensive trekking in the rainy season, you will need light, warm, windproof and water-resistant clothes and boots. The worst rainfalls occur in the Ibb province and in the western mountains – some of the best areas for trekking.

The periods just after the rainy seasons April-May and September-October – are ideal for trekking. The roads are drying fast,

there is plenty of water flowing in bigger wadis and even unirrigated fields and groves are green, yielding their harvest. Nevertheless, the rains are a sight in themselves so, if you want to see as many faces of Yemen as possible in a few weeks, it is worth considering March- April or September as the time of your visit. On average, the country is usually very good then, though you do run the risk of your trip falling in an exceptionally wet year.

WHAT TO BRING

When packing for your trip to the Yemen, be selective. The less weight you take with you, the happier you will be. You will not stay in the same hotel all the time so, even if you're not planning a hiking holiday, be prepared to carry your things around. Yemen today is quite a modern country and, with a few exceptions, you will be able to buy any commodities you might need, so why carry everything all the way?

In the supermarkets of the Yemen's bigger cities, you can buy all the little things you need for personal hygiene, from tissues to toothpaste and toilet paper (and, nowadays, even sanitary napkins and tampons). Don't expect to find these items in smaller villages, though.

Bring supplies of medicine for minor ailments: Band-aids and iodine for small wounds, charcoal and salt tablets, painkillers and so on. If you travel in winter, it is advisable to bring some eardrops and medicine for colds. Vitamin tablets are also worth considering if your stay is not a very short one; given the hygienic conditions, you can't get vitamins in the normal way from fresh vegetables (you shouldn't eat those). If you have a chronic ailment requiring special treatment, bring whatever is needed with you.

Yemeni towns are loaded with pharmacies that stock all the wonders of modern medicine, even those banned in the Western world because of harmful (even lethal) side effects. No prescriptions are asked for; in fact, the pharmacy staff often have to do the doctor's job when customers drop in to discuss their

Top: View over Sa'na
Left: House in Sa'na
Right: Two men from Manakha

Top: A highland village near al-Mahwit
Left: Children of the Bani Matar tribe, Bayt Baws
Right: Street market in Shibam, Kawkaban fortress on top of the hill

problems and ask for solutions. Often, the customer is offered half a dozen alternatives. If you are a doctor and know your medicines, you can probably find one for any curable disease. However, if you are looking for a particular medicine, don't count on finding it. The pharmacy you happen to choose might not have that particular preparation in stock or you might not Arabicise your pronunciation sufficiently to be understood.

It's also a good idea to bring a flashlight with you; when night falls, Yemeni towns and villages are lit dimly, if at all.

BUSINESS HOURS & HOLIDAYS

Government offices and banks are open from 8 or 9 am to about noon or 1 pm and are closed in the afternoon. Post offices in the northern provinces are an exception; they are also open from 4 to 8 pm. Of course, this applies only on weekdays (Saturday to Thursday); on Fridays and other holidays, the offices stay closed and on Thursday they tend to open half-day.

The private sector has more flexible hours of business and most shops and restaurants are open mornings and evenings, closing for a few hours in the early afternoon for qat time. The exact schedule varies according to the day of the week, the district and the individual entrepreneur.

The Calendar

An essential consideration when timing your trip to Yemen is the Muslim calendar, which is used alongside the Gregorian calendar familiar to Westerners. All religious feasts are celebrated within the framework of the Muslim calendar, while secular authorities arrange their activities according to the Christian system.

The Muslim year is based on the lunar cycle and is divided into 12 lunar months, each with 29 or 30 days. Accordingly, the Muslim year is 10 or 11 days shorter than the Christian (solar) year. The Muslim festivals thus gradually move through the Christian year, completing a full cycle every 33 years or so.

When planning your trip to the Yemen,

you should take note of what month Ramadan occurs in that year. Visiting a strongly Muslim country like Yemen during Ramadan can be a trying experience unless you are a frequent traveller in the Arab countries and know what you're doing.

The Muslims' rules of abstinence may be quite hard to observe, especially the one forbidding drinking during daylight hours (even if Ramadan falls during a hot summer month). As a non-Muslim, you may drink and eat whenever you wish, provided you don't do it under the eyes of the believers – do it only in your hotel room.

Given the afternoon temperatures (even in winter), people's activity level is extremely low during Ramadan. Many shops are closed, banks and government offices have even shorter opening hours than usual, bus timetables have fewer entries and it is difficult to get a taxi during the day. Every kind of business is at a standstill.

The first four days of the Shawwal month immediately following Ramadan mark the 'Id al-Fitr festival of breaking the fast. Another major holiday is the 'Id al-Adha, or 'Feast of Sacrifice'. It begins on the 10th of the Hajj, the month of pilgrimage, and celebrations continue for up to six days. Do not count on getting any weekday business done on these days.

Muslim Holidays

The dates of Muslim holidays up to the year 2000 are listed in the table on the next page.

If you compare these dates with those given by other sources, you may find that these are consistently one day later. The explanation is that, according to the Muslim calendar, a day begins at sunset, while in the Christian calendar, a day begins at midnight. The Muslim dates given here correspond to the morning according to the Gregorian calendar, as most of your daily activities are likely to happen within that part of the 24-hour cycle.

Note that Muslim and Christian calendars are used side by side in the Yemen. (In the former PDRY only the Christian calendar was in official use.)

Table of Holidays

Hijra Year	New Year	Prophet's Birthday	Ramadan Begins	'Id al-Fitr	'Id al-Adha
1411	24.07.90	02.10.90	17.03.91	17.04.91	23.06.91
1412	13.07.91	21.09.91	05.03.92	05.04.92	11.06.92
1413	02.07.92	10.09.92	23.02.93	26.03.93	01.06.93
1414	21.06.93	30.08.93	12.02.94	15.03.94	21.05.94
1415	10.06.94	19.08.94	01.02.95	04.03.95	10.05.95
1416	31.05.95	09.08.95	22.01.96	22.02.96	29.04.96
1417	19.05.96	28.07.96	10.01.97	10.02.97	18.04.97
1418	09.05.97	18.07.97	31.12.98	31.01.98	08.04.98
1419	28.04.98	07.07.98	20.12.99	20.01.99	28.03.99
1420	17.04.99	26.06.99	09.12.99		

Secular Holidays

The dates of these holidays are set according to the Christian calendar:

May
  Labor Day (1st)
  Day of National Unity (22nd)
September
  Revolution Day (26th)
October
  National Day (14th)
November
  Independence Day (30th)

The two Yemens observed each others' national days before unification and now both days are national holidays in the unified country.

You should also take into account that if a holiday falls on a Wednesday or a Sunday, the Yemenis eagerly take the opportunity to enjoy a 'long weekend' (from Wednesday to Friday or from Friday to Sunday). This means that most shops will be closed for these three days.

TIME

Yemeni time is three hours ahead of Greenwich Mean Time. No daylight savings system is applied in summer. When it's noon in San'a or Aden, the time elsewhere is:

City	Time
Paris, Rome	10 am
London	9 am
New York	4 am
Los Angeles	1 am
Perth, Hong Kong	6 pm
Sydney	8 pm
Auckland	10 pm

ELECTRICITY

The electricity voltage is around 220 volts, 50 cycle. To use electricity in hotels, you need the appropriate plugs; an isolated screwdriver will be a great help (the hotel staff will gladly lend you one and may even assist you in using it).

BOOKS & MAPS

A surprising number of books about Yemen have been written by Westerners in the last 25 years or so. There are also quite a few volumes from earlier times. Many of those books were printed once only, are difficult to find and are limited in coverage. The many academic studies and project reports may be rich in information but are often poor in readability. Most of the published books are about the YAR. They may not be among those you find on the shelves of your local bookstore, though. If you plan to buy books about the Yemen, you have two practical alternatives: buy them either before or after your trip. Don't count on finding any in Yemen itself.

In fact, in Yemen you can hardly find anything printed in Western countries except *Time* and *Newsweek* magazines. Although there are plenty of bookstores in San'a and quite a few in Ta'izz, al-Hudayda, Aden and al-Mukalla, their selections are almost exclusively in Arabic. If you need some reading to help you fall asleep at night, you'd better take your favourite paperbacks with you.

General Reading

The ultimate work on any aspect of Yemen is the fabulous *San'a – an Arabic Islamic City* by Serjeant & Lewcock (1983). The tome, published by Scorpion Press and the World of Islam Festival Trust, is a limited-edition (2000 copies only) luxury volume and contains everything you might ever want to know about Yemen in general and old San'a in particular. I have seen it a few times in London bookstores but have never had the $300 with me!

A more modest volume is Michael Jenner's *Yemen Rediscovered* (Yemen Tourism Company, 1983), a general description of the Yemens. This book has awakened in many people the desire to see Yemen's wonders for themselves. The text is not particularly informative but the book does have many better than average photographs. I recommend this one mainly because it is widely available and has also been published in German and French.

Concept Media have a coffee-table book containing perhaps the most wonderful photographs of the Yemen: *Arabian Moons – Passages in Time Through Yemen* by Pascal & Maria Maréchaux (1987).

Society & People

A recent study of a single but all-embracing aspect of life in Yemen deserves special attention: Shelagh Weir's *Qat in Yemen – Consumption & Social Change*. This lively little book tells you far more about the daily life of today's Yemeni than its title would suggest.

History

The first written information about Yemen dates back to the era of Herodotus. However, a general reader will probably want to start with something less ancient. The absolute classic is Carsten Niebuhr's *Travels Through Arabia & Other Countries in the East* from 1792, a scientific but lively description of the famous Danish expedition's journey to Arabia Felix. A great part of this book describes the Yemen, where the expedition spent a lengthy period from December 1762 to August 1763 – mostly in the Tihama but with visits to Ta'izz and San'a. Unfortunately, it is hard to get your hands on even though it was reprinted in Beirut in 1965 – try academic libraries.

Interesting insights into Yemen of the early 1900s are to be found in Freya Stark's travel books from south Arabia. While Ms Stark's books are definitely habit-forming, I will here only recommend *The Southern Gates of Arabia* (1936), in which she describes her journey to the Hadhramawt. The book has been reprinted several times in the 1980s and is easy to find.

For those interested in the Yemen's more recent history, especially developments immediately before, during and after the revolutions, I highly recommend Fred Halliday's *Arabia without Sultans*, published by Penguin Books in 1974 and since reprinted many times. If you are able to see through the Marxist parlance adopted by the author, this book gives a detailed and quite accurate account of the recent development of the Peninsular countries, with some 180 pages devoted to the Yemens.

Architecture

If architecture is what you're after, Fernando Varanda's *Art of Building in Yemen* (MIT Press, 1982) is outstanding. This hefty volume contains all the photos you are likely to snap in the northern provinces, and then some. The text is full of facts but still very readable and almost every page is illustrated.

Travel Guides

The tradition of guidebooks on Yemen spans only a few years, from the early 1980s. Available in Yemen only is Fritz Piepenburg's 1988 *New Traveller's Guide to Yemen*, a rework of the same author's 1983 pioneering edition. Published by Yemen Tourism Company, it contains a general overview of the region and its history as well as lengthy descriptions of 'major sightseeing tours' in the Yemen. The book covers both the YAR and the PDRY and it might be worth a look.

However, as the book is something of a semiofficial guide to the country, the author is extraordinarily shy in presenting any detailed information on present-day reality in the countries. Because the sightseeing tours described are those offered by Yemen Tourism Company, a lone traveller relying on this book may face some surprises on the road, since the conditions out there are not necessarily the same for groups as for loners. The practical information is in condensed form and is partly out of date.

There are also fully official guidebooks to both countries: *Tourist Guide of Yemen Arab Republic* and *Tourism in Democratic Yemen*. These books mainly offer gorgeous colour plates and are of historical interest only – if you can still find them in the General Tourist Corporation bookstores.

A recent work is APA Publications' 1990 *Yemen* in their Insight Guides series, edited by Joachim Chwaszcza. This work of more than 300 pages by a dozen authors has plenty of excellent photographs of both the old and new Yemen. Written just before unification, the book only grants five text pages to the southern governorates.

Maps

You might want to buy a detailed map of Yemen before starting your trip. However, I'm sorry to inform you that this is impossible. The Michelin road atlases that cover a third of a continent are probably the best maps generally available in the West, so you could plan a rapid tour through the countries in your own car – if you could bring it with

you! For the trekker planning to spend a couple of weeks in the Yemeni mountains, no information about the roads and paths exists on paper – the only source of information is locals speaking wildly differing dialects of Arabic in each village.

The best available map of the northern provinces is probably the *Touristic Map of Yemen Arab Republic*, published by Deutsch-Jemenitische Gesellschaft eV. It is a road map in a 1:1,000,000 scale with contours and 'hints for tourists' such as 'picturesque town', 'hotel, European standard' and so on.

Some maps are available in the Yemen. The General Tourist Corporation sells rather useful street maps of San'a, Ta'izz and al-Hudayda. These show the location of government institutions, hotels and mosques in the early '80s – the only problem is that, often, only the mosques remain in the same places. No maps of the former PDRY are available.

In fact, the Yemeni governments seemed to think that selling maps was like putting weapons into enemy hands. Although extensive cartography is being done and plenty of maps have already been printed, these are not available to the general public. You can see fairly detailed maps of the YAR and of smaller towns in the offices of the General Tourist Corporation or at the Salah Museum in Ta'izz, but these maps are not sold anywhere. I hope that the unification of the two Yemens has reduced the number of enemies to the point that maps can now be declassified.

MEDIA

Newspapers & Magazines

Yemeni newspapers are government controlled: *al-Jumhuriya* (The Republic) and *ath-Thawra* (The Revolution) were run by the former YAR but I wonder what will happen to the former PDRY's *14. Uktubir* (14 October).

Also widely available in central areas of Yemeni cities are a couple of Saudi Arabian English-language dailies – *Arab News* and

Saudi Gazette. Arab News is recommended reading for those interested in religious questions because of its twice-weekly page 'Islam in Perspective'. This features scholarly advice on applying the principles of faith to daily questions such as divorce, breast-feeding, heritage and so on.

Perhaps most interesting is the weekly *Middle East Times*. It has a Yemen edition that you can buy at the newsstands in the bigger cities. Started in late 1989, this paper packs the front page with Yemen-related news stories, with an occasional feature on some aspect of life in Yemen.

Also available in Yemen are *Time* and *Newsweek* magazines. You'll find them at some centrally located newsstands in the bigger cities (San'a, Ta'izz, al-Hudayda, probably Aden by now) and at a couple of luxury hotels in San'a.

Radio & TV

Radio broadcasts in Yemen are exclusively in Arabic.

There is one TV channel for the entire country and all programmes are in Arabic, except for the 7.30 pm news which is broadcast in English.

FILM & PHOTOGRAPHY

Photographers will find that film is readily available in bigger cities, though not in remote villages.

Taking photos of people in Yemen is tricky because Islamic tradition explicitly prohibits the making of portraits of people. Don't snap a photo of anybody without first asking permission. It is not customary to photograph women, even veiled ones. If you do, you must always ask permission from a woman's male companion, not from the subject herself. Generally, photography is more acceptable in the Tihama than in the mountains, and you'll find that people are most reserved about it in the northern mountains.

In the past, tourists taking photos of Yemenis without prior negotiations have lost their equipment – the subject has simply snatched the camera from the foreigner's hands and thrown it violently down against rocks. Show your camera and utter the phrase *mumkin sura*. Many will not grant your request and, if they refuse, you should point your camera in some other direction.

On the other hand, many Yemenis, especially those belonging to the TV generation, not only tolerate posing for pictures but insist on being photographed. The problem with these people is that their idea of a good photo is very different from yours – they will grin in horrible poses, pretending to kill each other with their daggers or playing tricks, to the accompaniment of uncontrolled laughter. It seems that only a true professional or a devout amateur can take good pictures of merry Yemenis.

If someone poses quietly for you and, after the click of your camera, stretches out a hand, they are *not* asking for money. The custom of posing for money is nonexistent in Yemen and you should not establish it – Yemenis are quick to learn new habits, so be careful not to encourage any decadent behaviour. The subject is asking for the picture, which they probably want to keep. Yes, instant photography has arrived in Yemen and that kind of equipment may have been their only exposure to cameras. Be careful not to offend.

It is also easy to run into difficulties when you aim your camera at an inanimate object. Military installations and buildings are strictly prohibited subjects and, in a country ruled by the military, there are plenty of them around. You are bound to come across this situation if you do some photographing outside tourist groups, so you'd better know the Arabic word for 'forbidden': *mamnu'*.

It is easy to understand why airports, checkpoints and communications stations are all mamnu' – they are sensitive subjects in most countries. The old fort on top of the hill, half of it in ruins, is probably still in use, so it is also mamnu'. A soldier passing by may forbid you to take a picture of a mosque not because of the mosque itself but because of the neighbouring police station, which is (of course) mamnu'.

HEALTH

Travel health depends on your pre-departure preparations, your day-to-day health care while travelling and how you handle any medical problem or emergency that does develop. While the list of potential dangers can seem quite frightening, with a little luck, some basic precautions and adequate information few travellers experience more than upset stomachs.

Travel Health Guides

There are a number of books on travel health:

Staying Healthy in Asia, Africa & Latin America, Volunteers in Asia. Probably the best all-round guide to carry, as it's compact but very detailed and well organised.
Travellers' Health, Dr Richard Dawood, Oxford University Press. Comprehensive, easy to read, authoritative and also highly recommended, although it's rather large to lug around.
Where There is No Doctor, David Werner, Hesperian Foundation. A very detailed guide intended for someone, like a Peace Corps worker, going to work in an undeveloped country, rather than for the average traveller.
Travel with Children, Maureen Wheeler, Lonely Planet Publications. Includes basic advice on travel health for younger children.

Pre-Departure Preparations

Health Insurance A travel insurance policy to cover theft, loss and medical problems is a wise idea. There are a wide variety of policies and your travel agent will have recommendations. The international student travel policies handled by STA or other student travel organisations are usually good value. Some policies offer lower and higher medical expenses options but the higher one is chiefly for countries like the USA which have extremely high medical costs. Check the small print:

1. Some policies specifically exclude 'dangerous activities' which can include motorcycling or even trekking. If such activities are on your agenda you don't want that sort of policy.
2. Policies which pay doctors or hospitals direct are probably useless in Yemen, as are policies which ask you to call a centre in your home country for an assessment of your problem. Instead, you should be prepared to pay on the spot; keep all relevant documentation, and claim when you return home.
3. Check if the policy covers ambulances or an emergency flight home. If you have to stretch out you will need two seats and somebody has to pay for them!

Medical Kit A small, straightforward medical kit is a wise thing to carry. A possible kit list includes:

1. Aspirin or Panadol – for pain or fever.
2. Antihistamine (such as Benadryl) – useful as a decongestant for colds, allergies, to ease the itch from insect bites or stings or to help prevent motion sickness.
3. Antibiotics – useful if you're travelling well off the beaten track, but they must be prescribed. Bring the drug with you: thee prescription would probably be useless in Yemen due to differences in brand names.
4. Kaolin preparation (Pepto-Bismol), Imodium or Lomotil – for stomach upsets.
5. Rehydration mixture – for treatment of severe diarrhoea, this is particularly important if travelling with children.
6. Antiseptic, mercurochrome and antibiotic powder or similar 'dry' spray – for cuts and grazes.
7. Calamine lotion – to ease irritation from bites or stings.
8. Bandages and Band-aids – for minor injuries.
9. Scissors, tweezers and a thermometer (note that mercury thermometers are prohibited by airlines).
10. Insect repellent, sunscreen, suntan lotion, chap stick and water purification tablets.

Ideally antibiotics should be administered only under medical supervision and should never be taken indiscriminately. Overuse of antibiotics can weaken your body's ability to deal with infections naturally and can reduce the drug's efficacy on a future occasion. Take only the recommended dose at the prescribed intervals and continue using the antibiotic for the prescribed period, even if the illness seems to be cured earlier. Antibiotics are quite specific to the infections they can treat, stop immediately if there are any serious reactions and don't use it at all if you are unsure if you have the correct one.

Health Preparations Make sure you're healthy before you start travelling. If you are embarking on a long trip make sure your teeth are OK; in the Yemen, a visit to the dentist would be the last thing you'd want to do.

If you wear glasses take a spare pair and your prescription. Losing your glasses can be a real problem, since getting new ones in Yemen could turn out to be next to impossible.

If you require a particular medication take an adequate supply, as it may not be available locally. Take the prescription, with the generic rather than the brand name (which may not be locally available), as it will make getting replacements easier.

Immunisations Vaccinations provide protection against diseases you might meet along the way.

No vaccinations are required to get an entry visa into the Yemen, as long as you don't come from or through a country infected with yellow fever or cholera. Smallpox is still mentioned in the official visa regulations, although the disease apparently no longer exists. Proof of vaccination is not required but, as the Yemeni officials advised us, 'for your own sake, do some vaccinations'. Tropical diseases can be hard to eradicate, especially in the heat of Tihama or the southern coast, and a tourist passing through is just as likely to develop them as the Yemenis.

All vaccinations should be recorded on an International Health Certificate, which is available from your physician or government health department.

Plan ahead for getting your vaccinations: some of them require an initial shot followed by a booster, while some vaccinations should not be given together. Most travellers from Western countries will have been immunised against various diseases during childhood but your doctor may still recommend booster shots against measles or polio, diseases still prevalent in Yemen. The period of protection offered by vaccinations differs widely and some are contraindicated if you are pregnant.

The possible list of vaccinations includes:

Cholera Some countries may require cholera vaccination if you are coming from an infected area, but protection is not very effective, only lasts six months and is contraindicated for pregnancy.

Tetanus & Diptheria Boosters are necessary every 10 years and protection is highly recommended.

Infectious Hepatitis Gamma globulin is not a vaccination but a ready-made antibody which has proven very successful in reducing the chances of hepatitis infection. Because it may interfere with the development of immunity, it should not be given until at least 10 days after administration of the last vaccine needed; it should also be given as close as possible to departure because of its relatively short-lived protection period of six months.

Yellow Fever Protection lasts 10 years and is recommended. You usually have to go to a special yellow fever vaccination centre. Vaccination is contraindicated during pregnancy but if you must travel to a high-risk area it is probably advisable.

Communal Hygiene

To understand the Yemeni concept of public hygiene, we must remember that, as recently as the early 1960s, the Yemeni economy was completely based on recyclable materials. No 'waste' existed; everything was usable and anything that was thrown away was immediately absorbed in a process of natural circulation. This applied not only to rural agricultural communities but also to cities where cattle have always been raised. So, for example, in San'a, even the human excrement was dried, carefully collected and used as fuel in public bathhouses. The ashes were, in turn, sold to gardeners to be used as fertiliser.

The revolution brought the 20th century to this medieval society but has so far been unable to change the habits of 4000 years. Waste is still treated as though it were organic and gets thrown around in all neutral, loosely defined areas such as streets and roadsides; it's a pity that tin cans, plastic bags and used cars are of no use to the ecosystem! Water pipes have been introduced to the towns and villages before sewage systems; the result is that what was previously dried up into neat cakes now flows along the streets. The problem is considerably worse in the northern part of the country than in the once centrally planned PDRY.

All this tends to shock some Westerners, who interpret the ubiquitous 'wrecking yards in the streets' as a sign of an uncivilised society. It is not. Rather, it is the outcome of a violent collision between two cultures. The West has taken several hundred years to solve this problem; eventually, the Yemenis will also come to terms with it. In fact, they have already started. The old part of San'a today is a much cleaner place than it was in the mid-1980s.

Personal Hygiene

The most important thing to realise is that what you see on the roadsides is not threatening to your health. The Yemenis do wash themselves and epidemics no longer scourge the country. This is certainly an aspect of life that has radically changed for the better since the revolution. Tap water is now available throughout the country and the thumping of water pumps in the modern Yemeni countryside is as characteristic a sound as the chirping of crickets.

In the restaurants, soap and tap water are available for customers to wash their hands before the meal. Since Yemenis eat with their fingers instead of with knives and forks, they tend to use the tap for washing after the meal, too. But don't jump to the conclusion that

they are overly hygienic in their everyday routines; it is still best to exercise some caution when choosing your food.

Basic Rules

Care in what you eat and drink is the most important health rule; stomach upsets are the most likely travel health problem but the majority of these upsets will be relatively minor. Don't become paranoid, trying the local food is part of the experience of travel after all.

Water The number one rule is *don't drink anything but bottled water and soft drinks.* Streetside vendors offering tempting cold fruit juices make their ice from tap water, and their products should be avoided – the same applies to any ice-cooled drinks, even if served in the better hotels.

Mineral water, including Shamlan and Azal, and soft drinks, including Canada Dry and Coca-Cola, are available all over the country, even in the smallest villages. At many rural road intersections there are tiny shacks selling biscuits, water and soft drinks. You don't need to bring any means of water purification to Yemen unless you intend to do extensive trekking in very sparsely populated areas.

Mineral water comes in handy plastic bottles of 0.75 or 1.5 litres. You should always carry a couple of them with you. Beware of bottles refilled with tap water, occasionally sold in more remote places; always check that the cap of the bottle has the plastic seal intact.

Tea or coffee should always be OK, since the water should have been boiled. Only boiled milk should be drunk; yoghurt is safe.

Food Salads and fruit should be washed with purified water or peeled where possible. Prepackaged ice cream is OK but rare in the Yemen. Thoroughly cooked food is safest but not if it has been left to cool or if it has been reheated. Take great care with shellfish or fish and avoid undercooked meat. In general, places that are packed with travellers or locals will be fine, while empty restaurants are questionable. Bread is best bought from bakeries or streetside vendors when it's newly baked and hot.

Nutrition If your food is poor or limited in availability, if you're travelling hard and fast and therefore missing meals, or if you simply lose your appetite, you can soon start to lose weight and place your health at risk.

Make sure your diet is well balanced. Eggs, beans and lentils are all safe ways to get protein. Fruit you can peel (bananas, oranges or mandarins for example) is always safe and a good source of vitamins. Try to eat plenty of grains (rice) and bread. Remember that although food is generally safer if it is cooked well, overcooked food loses much of its nutritional value. If your diet isn't well balanced or if your food intake is insufficient, it's a good idea to take vitamin and iron pills.

In the hot climate of the Yemen, make sure you drink enough – don't rely on feeling thirsty to indicate when you should drink. Not needing to urinate or very dark yellow urine is a danger sign. Always carry a water bottle with you, several on long trips. Excessive sweating can lead to loss of salt and therefore muscle cramping. Salt tablets are not a good idea as a preventative, due to the danger of overdosing; it is better to carry table salt with you and add it to your food. If you suddenly feel tired after sweating a lot, try putting some salt on your palm and licking it.

Everyday Health A normal body temperature is 98.6°F or 37°C; more than 2°C higher is a 'high' fever. A normal adult pulse rate is 60 to 80 per minute (children 80 to 100, babies 100 to 140). You should know how to take a temperature and a pulse rate. As a general rule the pulse increases about 20 beats per minute for each °C rise in fever.

Respiration (breathing) rate is also an indicator of illness. Count the number of breaths per minute: between 12 and 20 is normal for adults and older children (up to 30 for younger children, 40 for babies). People with a high fever or serious respiratory illness (like pneumonia) breathe more quickly than normal. More than 40 shallow breaths a minute usually means pneumonia.

Many health problems can be avoided by taking care of yourself. Wash your hands frequently – it's quite easy to contaminate your own food. Clean your teeth with purified water rather than straight from the tap. Avoid climatic extremes: keep out of the sun when it's hot, dress warmly when it's cold. Avoid potential diseases by dressing sensibly. You can get worm infections through walking barefoot. You can avoid insect bites by covering bare skin when insects are around, by screening windows or beds or by using insect repellents. Seek local advice: if you're told the water is unsafe due to sharks, don't go in. In situations where there is no information, discretion is the better part of valour.

Medical Problems & Treatment
Potential medical problems can be broken down into several areas. First there are the climatic and geographical considerations – problems caused by extremes of temperature, altitude or motion. Then there are diseases and illnesses caused by insanitation, insect bites or stings, and animal or human contact. Simple cuts, bites or scratches can also cause problems.

Self-diagnosis and treatment can be risky, so wherever possible seek qualified help. Although we do give treatment dosages in this section, they are for emergency use only. Medical advice should be sought before administering any drugs.

An embassy or consulate can usually recommend a good place to go for such advice. So can five-star hotels, although they often recommend doctors with five-star prices. (This is when that medical insurance really comes in useful!) In most parts of Yemen standards of medical attention are so low that for some ailments the best advice is to return to San'a (or even to get on a plane and leave the country).

Climatic & Geographical Considerations
Sunburn In Yemen you can get sunburnt

surprisingly quickly, even through cloud. Use a sunscreen and take extra care to cover areas which don't normally see sun – eg, your feet. A hat provides added protection, and you should also use zinc cream or some other barrier cream for your nose and lips. Calamine lotion is good for mild sunburn.

Prickly Heat Prickly heat is an itchy rash caused by excessive perspiration trapped under the skin. It usually strikes people who have just arrived in a hot climate and whose pores have not yet opened sufficiently to cope with greater sweating. Keeping cool but bathing often, using a mild talcum powder or even resorting to air-conditioning may help until you acclimatise.

Heat Exhaustion Dehydration or salt deficiency can cause heat exhaustion. Take time to acclimatise to high temperatures and make sure you get sufficient liquids. Salt deficiency is characterised by fatigue, lethargy, headaches, giddiness and muscle cramps and in this case salt tablets may help (see the Nutrition section as well). Vomiting or diarrhoea can deplete your liquid and salt levels. Anhydrotic heat exhaustion, caused by an inability to sweat, is quite rare. Unlike the other forms of heat exhaustion it is likely to strike people who have been in a hot climate for some time, rather than newcomers.

Heat Stroke This serious, sometimes fatal, condition can occur if the body's heat-regulating mechanism breaks down and the body temperature rises to dangerous levels. Long, continuous periods of exposure to high temperatures can leave you vulnerable to heat stroke. You should avoid excessive alcohol or strenuous activity when you first arrive in Yemen's hot climate.

The symptoms are feeling unwell, not sweating very much or at all and a high body temperature (39°C to 41°C). Where sweating has ceased the skin becomes flushed and red. Severe, throbbing headaches and lack of coordination will also occur, and the sufferer may be confused or aggressive. Eventually the victim will become delirious or convulse.

Hospitalisation is essential, but meanwhile get patients out of the sun, remove their clothing, cover them with a wet sheet or towel and then fan continually.

Fungal Infections Hot weather fungal infections are most likely to occur on the scalp, between the toes or fingers (athlete's foot), in the groin (jock itch or crotch rot) and on the body (ringworm). You get ringworm (which is a fungal infection, not a worm) from infected animals or by walking on damp areas, like shower floors.

To prevent fungal infections wear loose, comfortable clothes, avoid artificial fibres, wash frequently and dry carefully. If you do get an infection, wash the infected area daily with a disinfectant or medicated soap and water, and rinse and dry well. Apply an anti-fungal powder like the widely available Tinaderm. Try to expose the infected area to air or sunlight as much as possible and wash all towels and underwear in hot water as well as changing them often.

Diseases of Insanitation
Diarrhoea The disease you are most likely to catch in Yemen is some form of diarrhoea. The usual cause is eating something contaminated. The best precaution is to avoid everything that is not hot when brought to your table. Fresh vegetables and unpeeled fruits are the most common source of problems – don't eat them. Nor should you drink anything but bottled water or soft drinks. Bread is usually safe – either dry bread from stores or the greasy bread that is baked in the outdoor restaurants just before you eat it.

If you get diarrhoea, take things easy and rest. Don't try to complete your sightseeing schedule by climbing the Shihara mountain with diarrhoea; you might not make it.

It is probably not serious at all, though it is a nuisance. Charcoal tablets are recommended for the unpleasant side effects. Drink a lot to keep yourself from dehydrating and keep your salt intake up. Fluid replenishment is the number one treatment. Weak black tea with a little sugar, soda water, or soft drinks allowed to go flat and diluted

50% with water are all good. With severe diarrhoea a rehydrating solution is necessary to replace minerals and salts. You should stick to a bland diet as you recover.

Lomotil or Imodium can be used to bring relief from the symptoms, although they do not actually cure the problem. Only use these drugs if absolutely necessary – eg, if you *must* travel. For children Imodium is preferable, but do not use these drugs if the patient has a high fever or is severely dehydrated.

Antibiotics can be very useful in treating severe diarrhoea especially if it is accompanied by nausea, vomiting, stomach cramps or mild fever. Ampicillin, a broad spectrum penicillin, is usually recommended. Two capsules of 250 mg each taken four times a day is the recommended dose for an adult. Children aged between eight and 12 years should have half the adult dose; younger children should have half a capsule four times a day. Note that if the patient is allergic to penicillin ampicillin should not be administered.

Three days of treatment should be sufficient and an improvement should occur within 24 hours.

If your disease is severe and lasts longer than a week, it is probably serious. There are plenty of possible causes but you should see a doctor. It is recommended that you fly directly to your home country but, for severe cases, an immediate cure may be needed; try the al-Kuwayt Hospital (Mustashfa al-Kuwayt) in San'a.

Giardia This intestinal parasite is present in contaminated water. The symptoms are stomach cramps, nausea, a bloated stomach, watery, foul-smelling diarrhoea and frequent gas. Giardia can appear several weeks after you have been exposed to the parasite. The symptoms may disappear for a few days and then return; this can go on for several weeks. Metronidazole known as Flagyl is the recommended drug, but it should only be taken under medical supervision. Antibiotics are of no use.

Dysentery This serious illness, which some

foreigners have caught in the Yemen, is caused by contaminated food or water and is characterised by severe diarrhoea, often with blood or mucus in the stool. There are two kinds of dysentery. Bacillary dysentery is characterised by a high fever and rapid development; headache, vomiting and stomach pains are also symptoms. It generally does not last longer than a week, but it is highly contagious.

Amoebic dysentery is more gradual in developing, has no fever or vomiting but is a more serious illness. It is not a self-limiting disease: it will persist until treated and can recur and cause long term damage.

A stool test is necessary to diagnose which kind of dysentery you have, so you should seek medical help urgently. In case of an emergency, note that tetracycline is the prescribed treatment for bacillary dysentery, metronidazole for amoebic dysentery.

With tetracycline, the recommended adult dosage is one 250 mg capsule four times a day. Children aged between eight and 12 years should have half the adult dose; the dosage for younger children is ⅓ the adult dose. It's important to remember that tetracycline should be given to young children only if it's absolutely necessary and only for a short period; pregnant women should not take it after the 4th month of pregnancy.

With metronidazole, the recommended adult dosage is one 750 mg to 800 mg capsule three times daily for five days. Children aged between eight and 12 years should have half the adult dose; the dosage for younger children is ⅓ the adult dose.

Cholera One of the most serious diarrhoeal diseases is cholera, which is often fatal. Although it is not very common in Yemen anymore, precautions against the disease are still recommended. The disease is characterised by a sudden onset of acute diarrhoea with 'rice water' stools, vomiting, muscular cramps, and extreme weakness. You need medical help – but treat for dehydration, which can be extreme, and if there is an appreciable delay in getting to hospital then begin taking tetracycline. See the Dysentery section for dosages and warnings.

The violent form of diarrhoea affects your digestive system to such a degree that a mere sip of water has immediate effects. It is not harmful to your stomach or intestines but its violence may cause death by stress.

The standard precaution against cholera is vaccination. If you have never been vaccinated against cholera, you get two injections – an initial one and a booster after one week. The inoculation's period of effectiveness is counted as starting one week after the booster. The cholera vaccination offers only a short period of protection (six months) although, after that, you only need boosters to get another six months. Unfortunately, the vaccine does not give you complete protection – it is only about 50% effective.

Viral Gastroenteritis This is caused not by bacteria but, as the name suggests, by a virus. It is characterised by stomach cramps, diarrhoea, and sometimes by vomiting and/or a slight fever. All you can do is rest and drink lots of fluids.

Hepatitis Hepatitis A (infectious hepatitis) is a severe disease of the liver, again occurring under conditions of poor hygiene. Tourists get it from infected food and the most likely source is shellfish. Symptoms include fever, general weakness, scanty and dark-coloured urine and, in later phases, yellow skin and eyes. Although rarely fatal, hepatitis may last for several weeks and will ruin your holiday.

You should seek medical advice, but in general there is not much you can do apart from resting, drinking lots of fluids, eating lightly and avoiding fatty foods. People who have had hepatitis must forego alcohol for six months after the illness, as hepatitis attacks the liver and it needs that amount of time to recover. Lying in bed, weak, with a fever is hardly a way to enjoy Yemen – but there is no immediate cure.

The usual precaution is a gamma globulin injection a few days before your trip. Protection lasts for about six months but is far from guaranteed – some say the gamma globulin

has no effect at all. The injection is not a vaccination against hepatitis but a stimulator of your body's immune system.

Hepatitis B, which used to be called serum hepatitis, is spread through sexual contact or through skin penetration – it could be transmitted via dirty needles or blood transfusions, for instance. Avoid having injections where you have doubts about the sanitary conditions. The symptoms and treatment of type B are much the same as for type A, but gamma globulin as a prophylactic is effective against type A only.

Salmonellosis This is another disease of the digestive system and it is common in Yemen. You probably get it from unsafe food – something which has not been heated enough. The agents of the disease pass from the body of a patient through excrement, so they might get into your food through polluted water or the unwashed hands of a cook. There are 1000 or so variants of this germ. Some variants are harmless; some have potentially fatal after effects. The only precaution is to avoid unsafe food and drink. No vaccination is available.

Typhoid Typhoid fever is another gut infection that travels the faecal-oral route – ie, contaminated water and food are responsible. Vaccination against typhoid is not totally effective and it is one of the most dangerous infections, so medical help must be sought.

In its early stages typhoid resembles many other illnesses: sufferers may feel like they have a bad cold or flu on the way, as early symptoms are a headache, a sore throat, and a fever which rises a little each day until it is around 40°C or more. The victim's pulse is often slow relative to the degree of fever present and gets slower as the fever rises – unlike a normal fever where the pulse increases. There may also be vomiting, diarrhoea or constipation.

In the second week the high fever and slow pulse continue and a few pink spots may appear on the body; trembling, delirium, weakness, weight loss and dehydration are other symptoms. If there are no further complications, the fever and other symptoms will slowly go during the third week. However you must get medical help before this because pneumonia (acute infection of the lungs) or peritonitis (burst appendix) are common complications, and because typhoid is very infectious.

The fever should be treated by keeping the victim cool and dehydration should also be watched for. Chloramphenicol is the recommended antibiotic but there are fewer side affects with ampicillin. The adult dosage is two 250 mg capsules, four times a day. Children aged between eight and 12 years should have half the adult dose; younger children should have ⅓ the adult dose.

Patients who are allergic to penicillin should not be given ampicillin.

Diseases Spread by People & Animals

Tetanus Tetanus is a severe disease common in all parts of the world and is spread by bacteria from soil and dirt. It causes violent muscle cramps that may be fatal or render you an invalid for the rest of your life. Tetanus occurs when a wound becomes infected by a germ which lives in the faeces of animals or people, so clean all cuts, punctures or animal bites. Tetanus is known as lockjaw, and the first symptom may be discomfort in swallowing, or stiffening of the jaw and neck; this is followed by painful convulsions of the jaw and whole body.

Vaccinations are readily available and will protect you for 10 years. It is worth being covered by a tetanus vaccination at any time but it is especially important when you travel to hot lands where cuts take longer to heal – in Tihama, I developed a purulent discharge in my leg and carried it around Yemen for more than a month before it healed.

Rabies Rabies is found in Yemen as in many countries and is caused by a bite or scratch by an infected animal. Dogs are a noted carrier. Any bite, scratch or even lick from a mammal should be cleaned immediately and thoroughly. Scrub with soap and running water, and then clean with an alcohol solution. If there is any possibility that the animal

is infected medical help should be sought immediately. Even if the animal is not rabid, all bites should be treated seriously as they can become infected or can result in tetanus. A rabies vaccination is now available and should be considered if you are in a high-risk category – eg, if you intend to work with animals or investigate the rare Yemeni widlife closely.

Tuberculosis Tuberculosis is a lung disease commonly spread by coughing or by unpasteurised dairy products from infected cows. Milk that has been boiled is safe to drink; the souring of milk to make yoghurt or cheese also kills the bacilli. It is also passed by sharing unclean eating and drinking utensils and the like, so if you enjoyed chewing qat with Yemenis in a dormitory of a cheap hotel and smoking that huge *mada'a* (water pipe), I'd advise that you check your lungs when you get home. The disease is curable.

Young children are more susceptible than adults and vaccination is a sensible precaution for children under 12 travelling in endemic areas.

Bilharzia Bilharzia is a liver fluke which you can get by swimming in slow-moving waters such as ponds in wadis or using water from cisterns for bathing. It lives in snails and gets into your body through any small cracks in your skin, migrating to your liver.

The first symptom may be a tingling and sometimes a light rash around the area where it entered your body. Weeks later, a high fever may develop. A general feeling of being unwell may be the first symptom; once the disease is established abdominal pain and blood in the urine are other signs.

Curing the disease may take quite some time and liver damage may be permanent. As the disease is common in the Yemen, you should resist the temptation to join Yemenis having a great time swimming in a wadi.

Seek medical attention if you have been exposed to the disease and tell the doctor your suspicions, as bilharzia in the early stages can be confused with malaria or typhoid. If you cannot get medical help immediately, Niridazole is the recommended treatment. The recommended adult dosage is 750 mg (1½ tablets) taken twice daily for a week. Children aged between eight and 12 years should be given 500 mg (one tablet) twice daily for a week.

Diptheria Diptheria can be a skin infection or a more dangerous throat infection. It is spread by contaminated dust contacting the skin or by the inhalation of infected cough or sneeze droplets. Frequent washing and keeping the skin dry will help prevent skin infection. A vaccination is available to prevent the throat infection.

Sexually Transmitted Diseases Sexual contact with an infected sexual partner spreads these diseases. While abstinence is the only 100% preventative, using condoms is also effective.

Gonorrhoea and syphilis are the most common of these diseases; sores, blisters or rashes around the genitals, discharges or pain when urinating are common symptoms. Symptoms may be less marked or not observed at all in women. Syphilis symptoms eventually disappear completely but the disease continues and can cause severe problems in later years. The treatment of gonorrhoea and syphilis is by antibiotics.

There are numerous other sexually transmitted diseases, for most of which effective treatment is available. However, there is no cure for herpes and there is also currently no cure for AIDS. Even though the latter is common in nearby parts of Africa, there are no reported cases from Yemen so far. Using condoms is the most effective preventative.

AIDS can be spread through infected blood transfusions; Yemen, like most developing countries cannot afford to screen blood for transfusions. It can also be spread by dirty needles – vaccinations can potentially be as dangerous as intravenous drug use if the equipment is not clean. If you do need an injection it may be a good idea to buy a new syringe from a pharmacy and ask the doctor to use it.

Sexual contacts between visitors and locals are extremely improbable.

Insect-Borne Diseases

Malaria Malaria occurs mainly in the Tihama, where it is spread by mosquitoes; they transmit a parasite causing the disease. This is a fever disease that rarely kills you at first but may be fatal in the long run. Symptoms include headaches, fever, chills and sweating which may subside and recur. It is worth defending yourself against malaria since it can seldom be completely cured and the attacks can recur after years of apparent health, more probably in a hot climate than in a mild or cold one.

No vaccine exists but, fortunately, the precaution is simple: take regular antimalarial pills. There are several antimalarial drugs available but, since very few Chloroquine-resistant malaria has yet been reported in the Yemen, Chloroquine is the most common variety used. A tablet is taken once a week for two weeks prior to arrival in the infected area and six weeks after you leave it. Unfortunately there is now a strain of malaria which is resistant to Chloroquine and if you are travelling in an area infected with this strain an alternative drug is necessary. Where resistance is reported you should continue to take Chloroquine but supplement it with a weekly dose of Maloprim or a daily dose of Proguanil.

Chloroquine is quite safe for general use, side effects are minimal and it can be taken by pregnant women. Maloprim can have rare but serious side effects if the weekly dose is exceeded and some doctors recommend a check-up after six months continuous use. Fansidar, once used as a Chloroquine alternative, is no longer recommended as a prophylactic, as it can have dangerous side effects, but it may still be recommended as a treatment for malaria. Chloroquine is also used for malaria treatment but in larger doses than for prophylaxis. Doxycycline is another antimalarial for use where Chloroquine resistance is reported; it causes hypersensitivity to sunlight, so sunburn can be a problem.

Mosquitoes appear after dusk. Avoiding bites by covering bare skin and using an insect repellent will further reduce the risk of catching malaria. Insect screens on windows and mosquito nets on beds (rare in Yemen) offer protection, as does burning a mosquito coil. Mosquitoes may be attracted by perfume, aftershave or certain colours. The risk of infection is higher in rural areas and during the wet season.

Cuts, Bites & Stings
Cuts & Scratches Skin punctures can easily become infected in hot climates and may be difficult to heal. Treat any cut with an antiseptic solution and mercurochrome. Where possible avoid bandages and Band-aids, which can keep wounds wet.

Bites & Stings Bee and wasp stings are usually painful rather than dangerous. Calamine lotion will give relief or ice packs will reduce the pain and swelling. There are some spiders with dangerous bites but antivenenes are usually available. Scorpion stings are notoriously painful and can be fatal to children and elderly people. Scorpions often shelter in shoes or clothing.

Snakes There are several poisonous species of snakes in Yemen. To minimise your chances of being bitten always wear boots, socks and long trousers when walking through undergrowth where snakes may be present. Don't put your hands into holes and crevices, and be careful when collecting firewood.

Snake bites do not cause instantaneous death and antivenenes are usually available. Keep the victim calm and still, wrap the bitten limb tightly, as you would for a sprained ankle, and then attach a splint to immobilise it. Then seek medical help, if possible with the dead snake for identification. Don't attempt to catch the snake if there is even a remote possibility of being bitten again. Tourniquets and sucking out the poison are now comprehensively discredited.

Bedbugs & Lice Bedbugs live in various places, but particularly in dirty mattresses and bedding. Spots of blood on bedclothes or on the wall around the bed can be read as a suggestion to find another hotel. Bedbugs leave itchy bites in neat rows. Calamine lotion may help.

All lice cause itching and discomfort. They make themselves at home in your hair (head lice), your clothing (body lice) or in your pubic hair (crabs). You catch lice through direct contact with infected people or by sharing combs, clothing and the like. Powder or shampoo treatment will kill the lice and infected clothing should then be washed in very hot water.

Women's Health
Gynaecological Problems Poor diet, lowered resistance due to the use of antibiotics for stomach upsets and even contraceptive pills can lead to vaginal infections when travelling in hot climates. Keeping the genital area clean, and wearing skirts or loose-fitting trousers and cotton underwear will help to prevent infections.

Yeast infections, characterised by a rash, itch and discharge, can be treated with a vinegar or even lemon-juice douche or with yoghurt. Nystatin suppositories are the usual medical prescription.

Trichomonas is a more serious infection; symptoms are a discharge and a burning sensation when urinating. Male sexual partners must also be treated, and if a vinegar-water douche is not effective medical attention should be sought. Flagyl is the prescribed drug.

Pregnancy Most miscarriages occur during the first three months of pregnancy, so this is the most risky time to travel. The last three months should also be spent within reasonable distance of good medical care, as quite serious problems can develop at this time. Pregnant women should avoid all unnecessary medication, but vaccinations and malarial prophylactics should still be taken where possible. Additional care should be taken to prevent illness and particular attention should be paid to diet and nutrition.

WOMEN TRAVELLERS

Women can visit Yemen without a male companion. However, Western feminist attitudes are simply irrelevant here. Respect the values of your host country. A woman's place in Yemeni society is, by and large, at home with the family and there is nothing you can do about this.

Dress appropriately and behave modestly. Naive Western women have attracted sexual harassment by smiling at men or looking them in the eyes in public. For young teenage boys in the streets of the cities, a lone Western woman is an interesting challenge. Avoid physical contact with them and don't hesitate to show your anger if one actually touches you. Not showing your anger is seen as encouragement.

In the area of transport, buses are preferable to long-haul service taxis. If the bus is full, you will be seated next to another woman. If you have to use a taxi alone, you might want to buy both of the front seats so you can sit alone with the driver. Be prepared to be asked some extra questions at the checkpoints, though.

Some hotels and restaurants do not serve lone women at all. Choose the more expensive hotels of the two-sheet category at least and restaurants frequented by tourists. In shops, you may be served only after the men, including those who enter after you.

DANGERS & ANNOYANCES

Tourism has had its negative effects on Yemen and what was valid a few years ago is not necessarily true any more.

The late 1980s saw an unprecedented tourist boom in the YAR. In 1989, there were 37,000 visitors from Europe and America, more than double the number of five years earlier. Some travellers may not have shown appropriate respect to the Yemeni way of life or, perhaps, the sheer weight of numbers has been too much for the villagers. In any case, children in some regions have taken to throwing rocks at tourists without even

talking with them first. Whether they are just playing *intifada*, with tourists in the role of Israeli soldiers, or whether they are being encouraged by their parents is unclear. The net effect is that some much-visited highland towns and villages – Manakha, Hajja and Shihara, for example, or Sa'da in the north – are no longer as enjoyable. While the rocks hardly ever hurt you physically, they can certainly spoil your humour.

In the northern provinces (Ma'rib and al-Jawf, parts of Sa'da and Hajja), there is even a genuine security problem. During the late 1980s, the present government's popularity waned somewhat among the Bedouins and mountain-dwellers of these areas, and tourists may inadvertently become involved in local incidents. Reports of cars stolen at gunpoint circulate. One American group's driver was seriously wounded by bandits on the road to Ma'rib in 1989. So, if you don't have a tour permit to someplace around these provinces, don't play Lawrence of Arabia and go by yourself!

Attitudes towards Westerners

Most Westerners were evacuated from Yemen before and during the 1990/91 Gulf War, after some Western embassies were attacked. However, people's feelings towards Westerners seems to have gone back to normal now.

Finnish development aid workers have returned to Yemen and so far no problems have been reported.

Beggars

The Muslim religious requirement to give alms means that beggars appear here and there in the Yemen. However, they seem to have been told that non-Muslims do not know about the obligations written in the Koran, so they are not likely to bother you. If someone tries to get some baksheesh from you, they will usually be steered away by an embarrassed Yemeni.

You will definitely come across more beggars in the Tihama than in the highlands. Probably due to African influences, the coastal beggars are more pushy than those in the highlands. But, even here, you should have no difficulties with them.

ACCOMMODATION

In Arabic, there are two words for hotel: *funduq* and *u:ti:l (util)*. These words have equivalent meanings and can be used interchangeably; the latter is a borrowed word while the former is original. The international word is most often seen (also in the Latin alphabet) above the entrances of newer hotels on the assumption that foreign visitors will represent significant market potential in the near future.

Some Westerners believe that funduqs constitute a special family of traditional Arabic inns, while utils are more modern, Western-style hotels. This misconception is actively supported by Arab tour organisers, who recognise here a chance to charge more for something seen as traditional, exotic accommodation. Funduq can only be translated as 'hotel' and is the word you should use when trying to find one.

The traditional form of accommodation is the so-called one-riyal funduq, well known to the few travellers who visited the YAR in the 1970s. You may have heard or read stories about these or about the legendary hospitality of Peninsular Arabs in general. According to these stories, cheap hotels abound even in the remotest and tiniest tent villages and, should there not be one, villagers will compete for the honour of being accepted as host for a traveller, the sheikh (the elected elder in the village) usually winning the contest. The overall atmosphere is warm and kind, the visitor will be served free tea or coffee and there is always excellent food ready.

Despite this image, Yemen has never been a predominantly Bedouin society and the inhabitants of stable agricultural settlements are traditionally more reserved towards strangers. Moreover, motorised vehicles, especially 4WDs, have virtually eliminated the need for an extensive network of cheap hotels. It is sad but true that, nowadays, on the outskirts of Yemeni villages, you will hardly ever find those small groups of beds

under big trees that once offered the cheapest possible accommodation. Still, there is a good choice of reasonably priced hotels in the northern provinces.

The former PDRY, on the other hand, has an acute shortage of accommodation. All hotels and resthouses in the centrally planned country were state owned and most stemmed from the colonial era. The country did not welcome individual travellers at all, allowing in only tourist groups paying some US$2000 per person per week, so the demand for hotels was very low. In the entire country, there were only some 20 hotels and these mainly served foreign delegations involved in special development or research projects. Today, however, the situation has changed and we can expect more private hotel ventures.

In classifying Yemeni hotels, we must replace the conventional no-star to five-star system with the Yemeni no-sheet to two-sheet system (based on what you will find on the beds).

No-Sheet

The lowest level of accommodation is still cheap by Western standards. In any town or bigger village in the northern provinces, you should be able to find a place to stay for YR 20 to YR 50 a night. For this price, you will get a bed with no sheets but plenty of blankets and pillows. The bed may have legs or it may be just a mattress on the floor. It is always absolutely filthy; the bedding is never washed during its lifetime – Yemen is an arid land and precious water is not wasted on this kind of thing. You will not know the true meaning of the word 'filthy' until you have stayed in no- sheet accommodation.

Despite the general filth, these inns can be used if you bring your own sheets (or just don't mind the dirt!). For many people, a sleeping bag does the job of sheets quite comfortably but, as you don't need it for warmth, it may be needlessly heavy to carry around. Even though the nights can be rather chilly in the mountains, there are always more blankets available than you will need and, in the coastal areas, you'll prefer some form of cooling. All that is required is something to separate you from the hotel bedclothes.

As for your own hygiene, *hammam* in these places usually means a toilet, not a bathroom. In bigger towns, running cold water is usually available. Sometimes, there's even a cold shower but, more often, you'll only get a tap and bucket. In smaller towns, running water is seldom available and the innkeepers provide full buckets of water in the hammam. In the one-storey houses of the Tihama, there is seldom any sewage system and the toilet consists of a small hole dug in the ground. You hardly need to be advised about using plenty of water here to wash yourself.

The beds – 10, 20, 30 or even more – are usually in one large hall. This means no women. In some places, there are also smaller rooms with only four or six beds and, if the inn is not full, you may have such a room all to yourself (and your companion). You often have to pay for every bed, however, though that may not be too bad if the cost is YR 20 a bed and you have no choice.

Getting a private room is a good idea even for males; the big dormitory is going to be noisy late at night and early in the morning. You can be sure that a TV set will be watched keenly until midnight and will be played at full volume to keep it audible over the general conversation. The air is not polluted only by noise; the smoke from waterpipes is heavy. After a few weeks in the Yemen, you will appreciate some privacy anyway.

There are inns of this category in all the bigger northern towns, usually concentrated near the bus and taxi stations and the central markets. Though they seldom have signs, even in Arabic, the inns are easy to find – when you arrive in a town, just ask the driver for a *funduq rakhi:s* (cheap hotel). If you don't look too rich, you will be shown a nearby house.

In many of these inns, the main dormitory is on the ground floor and is wide open to the street. Wherever you see a large hall with Yemeni men lying on beds, watching the street life and smoking those ubiquitous waterpipes, you know you have found a chance for a cheap overnight stay.

One-Sheet

The next step upwards is a one-sheet hotel, with beds at about YR 40 to YR 80.

The single sheet is placed on the mattress and is often no wider than the mattress itself – it does not necessarily resemble what you know as a sheet. Sometimes, there are even two sheets. The essential thing about hotels in this category is that the sheets are changed not when the customers change but according to a set schedule – once a week in busy seasons and about once a month when the occupancy level in the hotel is low.

The hammams in this kind of hotel usually offer facilities undreamed of a mere 20 years ago. Tap water is always available, cakes of soap may appear by the sink and, increasingly often, small boilers offer you the luxury of a warm shower. The bathrooms are not clean and you won't want to enter one barefoot. However, with suitable equipment, you can get yourself very clean quite comfortably here. The bathrooms also have doors and locks so that females can use them. After a few days excursion in the countryside, it will look like paradise.

Otherwise, hotels in the no-sheet and one-sheet categories are pretty similar. Both may have large dormitories, though the one-sheet variety is more likely to have rooms as well and may even have just smaller rooms. Neither category offers single rooms and even doubles are rare; rooms with three or four beds are usually the smallest available. The pricing is always per bed; if you want the whole room, you pay for every bed in it.

There are no hotels of this standard in villages or smaller towns. On the other hand, where there is demand for this type of accommodation, there is usually also some competition, so you will have a choice.

Two-Sheet

This kind of hotel is usually found only in cities and big towns. The prices range from YR 60 to YR 200 per person per night. In the south, most hotels run by the Public Corporation for Tourism (the sole hotel owner in the former PDRY) fall into this category, with prices varying between YD 7 and YD 12 a double.

In a two-sheet hotel, the two sheets look like Western-style sheets and are changed at least with changes of guests, perhaps even every other day. There are no big dormitories – only rooms. Double rooms are usually the smallest, though singles are sometimes available. Prices are set by the room.

What you should look for, of course, is hygiene. If you choose a clean hotel in the lower price range intending to pay YR 100 to YR 180 for a double, *don't* choose one with private bathrooms. A common bathroom in the corridor is usually much better because it gets cleaned every day and, if you are not satisfied with it, you can try another bathroom further down the corridor.

A private bathroom will cost you at least YR 50 and delivers its distinctive stench (and, possibly, its cockroaches) directly to your room. If you invest in one, what do you do when the toilet refuses to flush? The staff suddenly won't speak English and, even if you can get somebody to have a look at it, there will be nothing they can do to fix it – why don't you take the bucket and flush it yourself? Moreover, the sewage system is slow to suck away any water so, when you take a shower, the excess water streams under the door and comes to rest in a pool next to your bed. No, private bathrooms belong to the luxury category in the Yemen.

In the Tihama and on the southern coast, you will probably be willing to pay for air-conditioning. In no-sheet and one-sheet categories, air-conditioning is generally unknown but even the most basic two-sheet hotels offer you some kind of fan, with or without cooler (the price is different, of course). In some cheaper hotels, you will find rooms with or without a fan; you will probably automatically be offered one with a fan but, if you don't feel like paying the extra YR 30 to YR 50, you could ask if they have rooms without air-conditioning. You won't find air-conditioning in two-sheet hotels in the highlands – during winter, you'll hope for heaters instead but they, too, are nonexistent.

There are restaurants in some two-sheet hotels but meals are not included in the room prices. The general rule seems to be that, if the restaurant is at the top of the hotel building, it has few customers and the food will be tasteless and pricey (this applies also to all hotels of the former PDRY are in this category).

However, if the restaurant is on the ground floor and opens onto the street, it may be rather good. If plenty of locals eat there, you can bet that the food is cheap and tasty; if there are also plenty of foreign diners, it may even be safe to eat.

Deluxe

Although many Yemeni hotels bear the name *diluks*, there are not too many luxury hotels here. If you're willing to pay YR 500 to YR 2000 and up per night for fabulous Western-style service, you can do that in San'a and, in a less opulent style, in Aden, Ta'izz and al-Hudayda.

General Thoughts

Room Inspection When choosing a hotel in the Yemen, it is quite acceptable to take a look at the rooms offered before making a decision. In the bigger towns, there are plenty of alternatives and it might be worth wandering around and making some price and quality comparisons. When you have asked about the availability and prices of rooms, simply say *mumkin ashuf* to the person at the desk; they will be all too glad to show you the room. Saying *mumkin ashuf al-hammam* will get you a look at the bathroom if it is in the corridor.

Bathrooms In the more basic hotels, the bathrooms are exclusively Yemeni style, with squat-type toilets. In some two-sheet hotels, there may be a choice between this 'Arabic' variation and the 'French-style' bathroom, with sit-down toilet and, perhaps, a bathtub. There may even be a bidet. The Arabic-style bathroom is recommended;

French toilets require you to show quite a bit of flexibility and balance to maintain an acceptable standard of hygiene.

When you are offered facilities, *don't* accept anything without trying it. Check that turning the taps does produce a flow of water and that the drain actually takes it away. It is quite common to see a water heater hanging on the wall but, to get warm water, it must be connected. The thermometer needle on the side of the boiler may point to 60°C but the water may actually be icy. *Don't* believe them if they say it can be fixed; if it is not fixed then and there, it will not be fixed at all. A boiler with no red light on is a dead boiler.

Prices In the older one or two-sheet hotels, prices only seem to have increased by about 20% since our first visit in 1984. This means that, in the biggest towns, you can get a reasonably clean double for about YR 150. In contrast, the lowest and highest price categories seem to have seen spectacular price hikes of about 300% in six years, with new hotels seldom doing business below YR 100 per person per night.

A sad but inevitable consequence of increased tourism is that hotels in some remote but much-visited villages are charging absolutely ridiculous sums for basic accommodation. The hotel in Shihara, for example, falls into the no-sheet category but its prices belong to the upper two-sheet category. The house is a nice, traditional stone tower with plenty of rooms from which to choose, the atmosphere is friendly and you will be served tea and genuine Yemeni food. Nevertheless, charging YR 100 per person is simply ridiculous and a Yemeni would never accept it. This is not the worst example; sometimes, the price is not twice or thrice but 20 times too high.

Some innkeepers seem to think that foreigners come to Yemen because they have run out of ways to spend their money. With this in mind, they try to help by charging the highest possible price when they would give similar services to a Yemeni for free. The illusion that all travellers are wealthy is

maintained by the drivers who bring tour groups from San'a to distant destinations and boast to locals about the high fees.

This is not something to get angry about. However, it is important that you refuse to pay unreasonable prices for anything; otherwise, you just make it difficult for the travellers who arrive there next week. If you have any choice, it is better not to even try bargaining; simply make it clear that the price is insane and leave.

Sleeping Outdoors

Some people have slept out in a sleeping bag under the big Yemeni sky. While their letters describe overwhelmingly positive experiences, these individuals have taken quite a risk. Scorpions and snakes are common in Yemen and your warm body certainly attracts them in the cold of a mountain night.

It is advisable to bring a tent, however small, if you plan to rely on your own lodging. Erecting a tent near a village is, however, likely to attract considerable attention among the local children. In a few places, such as al-Khawkha or Bir 'Ali, tents have been used by tour operators for years and are no longer objects of curiosity.

FOOD

The Yemeni diet is simple. Sorghum and other cereals constitute the bulk of the daily diet, while fenugreek (the celebrated *hilba* soup), vegetables, rice and beans are also common. Meat, milk, eggs and fruit are traditionally the food of the upper social classes but labour emigration and the resulting influx of money to village families have brought these items to the tables of most Yemenis. Fish is a natural part of the diet in the Tihama and along the southern coast.

The most important food in Yemen is bread. The Yemenis prefer warm bread and, where wood for the ovens can be afforded, baking is done once or twice daily. There are several varieties of bread: *khubz tawwa* (ordinary bread fried at home), *ruti* (bought from stores) and *lahuh* (a festive pancake-type bread made of sorghum).

As in all Middle Eastern countries, *kebabs*

are cheap and readily available but Yemen also has its own culinary treats. The national dish is a thick, fiery stew called *salta*. It contains lamb or chicken with lentils, beans, chickpeas, coriander, spices and any other kitchen leftovers and is served on a bed of rice. Yemenis also like their *shurba* – a cross between a soup and a stew. Varieties include *shurba bilsan* (a lentil soup) and *shurba wasabi* (lamb soup). They are served with a thin Arabic bread brushed with clarified butter and a paste made from fenugreek and coriander. In the heat of the afternoon, *shafu:t* (a green yoghurt soup) is refreshing.

A typical Yemeni dessert is *bint al sahn*, an egg-rich, sweet bread which you dip into a mixture of clarified butter and honey. Yemeni suqs, particularly in the Tihama, have many delicious fruits on offer. Peaches and figs have been cultivated here for thousands of years; bananas, papayas, melons and mangoes are more recent introductions.

The main meal in the day of a Yemeni is lunch. You can verify this if you're in a bus or shared taxi at noon; the bus will stop in a village and discharge all the locals into the snack bars, leaving disoriented tourists to wait in their seats, wondering whether to join the Yemenis or play it safe and stay by the bus. Dinner, served after the sunset prayer, is more modest.

Restaurants

In the Yemen, restaurants are places to eat; they are not places of social interaction, as you might expect if you have visited some other Arab countries. Most socialising in Yemen happens at qat parties (see the Facts about the Country chapter).

Bad news for the homesick: there are almost no Western-style restaurants in the Yemen. There are no McDonald's, no bratwurst and no continental breakfasts, though there are a couple of Kentucky Fried Chicken outlets in San'a. Only the restaurants in the most expensive hotels (and most hotels in the south) serve Western-style food and their idea of Western-style is simple: no spices.

Good news, though, for the connoisseur: there are plenty of restaurants everywhere serving tasty Yemeni food. Yemeni men never seem to eat lunch at home and restaurants are also crowded at dinnertime. Restaurants abound in big cities as well as in the smaller towns. In San'a, you will even find a few foreign restaurants that serve Lebanese or Vietnamese food.

Tourists may find that eating in restaurants is a somewhat risky business. Restaurants are no exception to the general standards of hygiene in the Yemen. Choosing the most crowded places at least ensures that the food is not tainted but, even then, you should be careful when choosing your meal. Not only are you forced to refrain from eating fresh vegetables; you should also avoid eating anything that isn't hot when brought to your table, though bread is usually safe. *Never* drink water from the standard plastic jars on the table – always order Shamlan or Azal or whatever brand of bottled water may be available. Canada Dry is safe, too.

This shouldn't stop you from eating out – just don't take unnecessary risks. Yemeni restaurants have many pleasant surprises but even experienced travellers can easily develop diarrhoeal diseases if they are careless with their diet.

Many restaurants hang the menu on the wall; only a few bring a conventional written menu to your table. Generally, the menu is in Arabic only, often hastily written with a ballpoint pen. Sometimes, though, you may encounter minor calligraphic wonders. The selections are usually huge; even tiny restaurants often sport menus of 30 dishes. This doesn't mean they are all available – some may be reserved for holidays only. If you ask the waiter to recommend something, dishes such as liver or meat will probably be suggested.

Table manners are Arabic, that is locals do not use a knife or fork. Sometimes, they eat with a spoon. More often, however, they bring food to the mouth with the right hand and bread. In some big-city restaurants, there may be more Western-style equipment available. The left hand is considered impure and it is customary to refrain from putting it to your mouth.

DRINKS
Nonalcoholic Drinks
Tea & Coffee The everyday drink in Yemen is tea, drunk from small glasses; it's sometimes flavoured with a leaf of mint. *Sha'i talqi:m*, or traditional tea, is delicious and warmly recommended, although *sha'i libtun*, or teabags, are rapidly gaining acceptance. Tea can be enjoyed either without *(sha'i aHmar)* or with milk *(sha'i ma' Hali:b)*. It is always sweet to the extreme; sugar is the first thing Yemenis put in the kettle when boiling water for tea.

Qahwa, or coffee, is not as common as tea, although you can get it too from most retaurants. Coffee is made from either cofee beans themselves *(bunn)* or from coffee-bean shells *(qirsh)*. Coffee, too, is always very sweet, and is often flavoured with ginger and other spices.

Water Safe drinking water is no longer a problem in the Yemen. Bottled mineral water and soft drinks are now readily available even in the tiniest villages; even mere crossroads have tin shacks selling water to passers-by.

Alcohol
The Koran explicitly rules alcohol out of the lives of Muslims and this rule is easy to follow in Yemen – you simply cannot find alcohol in supermarkets or restaurants. The sweet grapes of Rawdha are grown not for wine but for raisins. Nonalcoholic beer is available in some supermarkets but even this is rare. Liquor is totally forbidden in the northern provinces, as it has been for centuries.

The British, however, depended on beer and built a brewery in Aden during their colonial rule. Strangely, the brewery survived not only the revolution of 1967 but the entire period of Communist rule on the pretext that some inhabitants of Aden follow other religions and, of course, foreign project workers and sailors have to be served, too.

Despite the serious attempts of religious leaders, Seera beer was still available in many southern restaurants in the summer of 1990; it will be interesting to see whether it will also survive the unification.

The ban on alcohol does not mean that you can't find liquor, even in the northern part of the Yemen, if you are sufficiently determined. Muslims know that alcohol is not a sin for non-Muslims and Yemenis feel they must provide full service to tourists. Some top-end tourist hotels in San'a, Ta'izz and al-Hudayda sell alcohol. You don't have to be a hotel resident to buy a bottle; you can simply walk up to the restaurant and place your order. You can drink in a civilised manner while dining in the restaurant or buy a bottle to take away. Whisky is almost always available and beer is also common but wines are rare.

The catch is that alcoholic drinks are intolerably expensive; a can of beer may cost YR 100 in San'a, for example. As it has travelled a long way through innumerable checkpoints, this is understandable. The main smuggling port before unification was al-Makha and, if you drive the Tihama road from Ta'izz to al-Hudayda, many a passer-by will try to attract your attention around Mafraq al-Makha. They are trying to sell you alcohol; presumably, in this region, you should get the best alcohol prices in all of the Yemen.

Some Yemenis working overseas have come to know alcohol as a poor substitute for qat. They know that God is forgiving, so they maintain the habit after they return. Some have driven themselves into a situation where they eat qat in the afternoon like any good Yemeni but drink whisky later in the evening so they can sleep well. It is a sad story; most often, these people have returned home to unemployment and the years abroad have alienated them from farmer's work. So, instead of returning to their home villages, they settle in the big cities, live in cheap hotels and use up their savings on qat and alcohol.

THINGS TO BUY

Yemen is not exactly a popular shopping stop and some visitors find it difficult to find any typical Yemeni products that could serve as nice souvenirs. Yemen lacks many of the traditional 'Arab' items that are popular tourist buys.

Even the most 'Yemeni' objects are often not of Yemeni origin; it is quite possible that your souvenir is made in India or Lebanon. Those huge, richly ornamented waterpipes, so requisite in every Yemeni funduq, usually come from India.

Jewellery

Among the places most frequented by tourists in Yemen are the silver markets in the suqs of San'a and Ta'izz, where old and old-looking silverware is sold. Often, some corals, pearls and pieces of amber, glass and ceramic are combined with the silver. You can find necklaces, earrings, noserings, bangles, chains, amulets and small containers on chains used to carry verses of Koran.

To fully appreciate what you can buy, we must take a look at the interesting history of

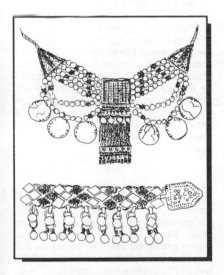

Traditional Silver Jewellery

the Yemeni silverware. The Yemeni class structure has always differentiated people on the basis of occupation. For example, the *jazzars* (butchers) formed one – not particularly highly valued – social group; the *shaqis* (day labourers) made up another low-prestige social group. Although the occupations are not hereditary by definition, it is often impossible for the son of a butcher to get another job and marriages generally are arranged exclusively within the group.

From *himyar* times, or from time immemorial, the Jews of Yemen have served as the country's silversmiths. They were always an extraordinarily important branch of craftspeople in Yemen because silver jewellery has traditionally been a convenient and popular means of paying the bride wealth without which no Yemeni marriage could be arranged. However, the silversmiths were never of high social status, since the Jews were a despised and oppressed people.

When the Jews emigrated from Yemen in 1949 and 1950 to the newly founded state of Israel, the Yemeni imams realised that their country was going to lose an important pool of skilled workers. They therefore declared that no Jewish silversmith could leave the country before teaching their skills to a Yemeni. However, due to the short time available, the Yemeni silversmiths were mere apprentices when the masters left to fulfil Isaiah's prediction: 'They shall mount up with wings, as eagles.' The Yemeni Jews were carried to Israel from Aden in a major airlift operation codenamed 'Magic Carpet'.

The quality of the workmanship was never quite regained, as anyone who visits the suqs of the Yemen's larger cities can verify. The silversmiths' shops abound in old and old-looking silverware but, if you take a closer look at the objects for sale, you may find defects: a missing piece here and a broken joint there, often some missing chains replaced by threads of cloth or other substitutes. The shopkeeper may volunteer to fix these if you point them out, immediately finding spare parts below the counter. The result is a 'perfect' piece that will not fall apart when you wear it but you are left wondering how original it is.

Indeed, it is a fact that most Yemeni silverware isn't very old. When a Bedouin woman dies, all her silverware is melted down to make new jewellery. On the other hand, the townspeople and farmer families keep their precious things for several generations; the women own their jewellery and it functions as their insurance in case of divorce or similar catastrophe. It is passed along in the family in the form of gifts, bride wealth and inheritance, always at the woman's discretion.

The third main group of jewellery consumers is the religious elite. They demonstrate their status with fashionable clothing, elaborately embroidered belts for their silver *dhumas* (daggers), and other ceremonial weapons.

Today, Yemeni tastes have shifted from silverware to gold jewellery. Much of the silverware is offered only to tourists and is made to look old by treating it with chemicals. The 'silver' is never very pure and many

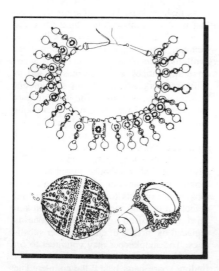

Traditional Silver Jewellery

pieces have hardly any silver content at all. Many wares made of tin plate are not intended to be sold as silver but, since they are sold in silversmiths' shops, tourists often wish to believe more than they are told. But why worry? If you like it, buy it. Do some bargaining – the Yemenis won't lower the price much, if at all, but there are plenty of shops to choose from.

A special form of silverware is the Maria Theresa thaler, originally brought to the Middle East from Austria by Napoleon, who conquered Egypt in 1798. The Ottoman Turks brought the coin to the Yemen, where it served as the currency until the end of the Imamate; it has remained in limited use even since the revolution. This imported coinage was far from ideal as a form of currency; its supply depended on the condition of trade routes from Austria and its value fluctuated with the international value of silver. You can buy this genuinely Yemeni item for a few tens of riyals. Don't be fooled by the date on the coin, though; all Maria Theresa thalers bear the date 1780 even though they were minted in the 1900s.

Nowadays, gold jewellery is very popular among the Yemenis and goldsmiths abound. However, the objects do not look very 'Yemeni'. Some people say that gold can be bought at rather low prices in Yemen when compared to Western countries, so there is a chance for profit. This is because gold is sold by the gram, with no value added for the workmanship, and no import taxes are imposed. If you want to explore this, you'd better know your prices. Gold is probably cheaper in al-Hudayda or Ta'izz than it is in San'a.

Jambiyas

An object that is indisputably typical of countries in southern Arabia is the curved dagger worn by men on a special belt at their waist. The make and look of the dagger differs greatly according to the region and the tribe, as well as the social status of the owner. The tradition was banned in the south during the period of Communist rule but has been continued in the northern provinces without a break.

In the Yemen, the sharply curved tribesman's dagger – called a jambiya – is kept at the front of the body with the tip of the sheath pointing to the right. The elite, such as a qadhi or a sayyid, wear their daggers on the right side of the body. These daggers are called dhumas and their design is more slenderly curved. Dhumas and their belts are usually richly ornamented with silver and gold, while jambiyas often expose the base materials, cloth and leather, beneath sparse cloth ornaments.

Dhumas and jambiyas serve mainly ceremonial purposes and are not meant for actual use (although Yemeni men are all too eager to demonstrate their ability to fight). The design of the blades ensures that you can't do anything with them. They are objects of pride and are often inherited. The prices of these pieces are absolutely insane; while you may obtain a simple jambiya for a couple of hundred riyals, more ornate dhumas with silver and gold decorations can cost thousands of riyals. An old one once owned by a much-respected qadhi may cost hundreds of thousands of riyals.

The most highly valued daggers have handles made from African rhinoceros horn. In fact, Yemen is the chief consumer of this rare material, jeopardising the survival of the entire species.

Guns

The second Ottoman occupation of the northern part of Yemen relied heavily on the use of modern firearms imported from Western Europe. Germany, Italy and France supported Turkey's colonisation of the Arabian Peninsula in order to weaken the British influence in the Middle East. Accordingly, plenty of firearms flowed into Yemen from these countries and, of course, many ended up in the hands of the rebelling Yemenis.

Due to this history, there are lots of old guns in the Yemen, sold today in the silver suq of San'a. You can find French-made Gras Cavalry carbines, Italian Vetterli-Vitali

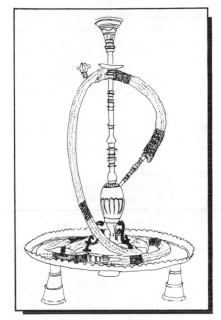

Mada'a - waterpipe made in India

rifles and German Mauser rifles, all from the 1870s or later decades. Prices are reasonable compared to those current in middle Europe. A 100-year-old rifle in working condition may be sold for a couple of hundred riyals. Old pistols and swords may also be offered for sale.

I am not recommending that you buy these rifles, so don't complain to me if you have difficulties with the customs office in your home country or Yemen or other countries you may pass through with this equipment. Also remember that, although the shopkeepers will happily sell you objects they claim to be antique, it is against Yemeni law to export objects over 40 years old without specific permission.

Waterpipes

To continue with impractical souvenirs, how about those huge waterpipes (called mada'a) you see men smoking in every funduq of the country? The equipment includes a brass tripod stand onto which the water bowl is placed and which also serves as a support for the hose (up to two metres long) when it is not being used. On top of the vertical tube is the funnel-shaped tobacco and coal-holder, which is made of pottery.

A typical mada'a is about one metre high with a tripod stand some three-quarters of a metre in diameter. Prices vary according to the materials and workmanship.

Music Cassettes
Local music is one of the best souvenirs you can find. In the Yemen, the locals listen to Arabic and Yemeni styles rather than to Western-style disco or rock music. Musical traditions differ greatly in various parts of the country, with Tihami, San'ani and Hadhrami styles clearly distinguishable from each other.

As in most Arabic countries, records do not exist in Yemen and most music is sold in cassette form. There are three reasons for this. First, electronic sound reproduction arrived late in these countries, during the phase when portable cassette players were 'hot' in the Western world. Second, records adapt poorly to daily use in an arid country, where dust and sand are carried everywhere by the wind – cassettes are much less prone to damage.

The third reason is more subtle: the vast majority of all recordings sold in the Arabic world are bootleg copies, so cassettes are the only practical form of music. This has nothing to do with law or morality – it is just the way things are done. If you listen to a recording in a suq cassette stand and decide to buy it, the owner of the shop will probably record a new copy for you then and there (so don't think you can purchase your audio souvenir on your last hurried morning before leaving the country).

One benefit of this is that recordings are fairly inexpensive in the Yemen; the price of a cassette should not exceed YR 12.

A drawback is that the quality of sound ranges from barely satisfying to incredibly bad. There are examples of Yemeni music in my collection that you simply cannot listen to. My advice is to purchase more cassettes than you actually want, and from several vendors. The cost will be negligible anyway when compared to the expense of getting to the country.

Everyday Items
Of course, commonplace consumer goods produced locally, though not exactly spectacular, often make nice, useful souvenir. In many suqs, you can find beautiful and very colourful fabrics, baskets and clay pots. A variety of spices is readily available, as is *bunn* (coffee) and *qirsh* (coffee bean shells that the Yemenis use just like the beans themselves, making a surprisingly tasty drink).

Another sensory indulgence, frankincense, is still available in the Yemen. In San'a, you can see Black African ladies selling *luba:n* and other varieties of incense for a few tens of riyals per small lump. Smell it or chew it; when burned, it releases its fragrance very efficiently – a cool alternative to the Indian 'dhoops' so loved by the hippies of the 1960s.

Things You Won't Buy
Many things that you would expect to be sold in an Arab country are not to be found in the Yemen. For example, there are no Oriental-looking Yemeni carpets. Almost all rugs with some colour are imported and many can only be described as tasteless. A carpet featuring puppies dressed as humans in a London-style pub looks very strange as a piece of interior decoration in a Yemeni house!

You probably won't buy Yemeni clothes, either – at least if you are male. Typical male attire is a futa, or skirt, ending a little below the knees and worn with a shirt and jacket that look as though they were imported from the Western world (but really aren't). This is a nice combination but not one that is likely to become fashionable elsewhere.

For women, a much better variety is available, from the urban black veils and dresses in the suqs of San'a and Ta'izz to the very colourful garments in local markets. Expect to draw loud and excited attention if you try those pieces on and, once you do so, don't expect to be able to bargain much – by your actions, you have already accepted the price.

Getting There & Away

AIR
To/From Europe
Direct flights from Europe to San'a are offered by Yemenia from Amsterdam, Frankfurt, Larnaca, London, Paris and Rome; there are one to three flights a week. Air France flies weekly from Paris and Lufthansa has twice-weekly flights from Frankfurt. Economy-class return fares to San'a are typically US$1000 to US$1500 plus. Many of the Arab countries' national carriers also offer flights from Europe to San'a via their respective capitals; Saudia is probably the most convenient, while the fares of EgyptAir are among the most economical.

Surprisingly, one of the cheapest ways to fly to Yemen from most West European countries has been with the Soviet carrier Aeroflot. The fare from Moscow to either Yemeni capital was US$800 to US$900 (the fares are fixed in rubles; it is the exchange rates that fluctuate) for a 10 to 35-day excursion ticket. Connecting flights to and from European centres are free, so the trip is cheap even from Paris. Given the continuing upheaval in the USSR, it is hard to tell how long the system will remain the same but the Soviets will continue to badly need the hard currency for some time to come.

Don't go to the Aeroflot office yourself; you will be charged a fare that is the same as your own national carrier would charge in business class (should it fly the route). Instead, find a travel agent specialising in cheap flights to Asia and/or Africa; they will probably offer Aeroflot flights. Be prepared to reserve your ticket several months before your trip because the flights are usually fully booked well in advance.

Aeroflot flies directly from Moscow to most capitals in Europe, Africa and Asia but there are hardly any direct connections; everything goes via Moscow. In the 1980s, Aeroflot had one weekly flight to San'a and three flights a week to Aden.

If you use this kind of service, you will have to stop in Moscow and, since the timetables are not necessarily synchronised with connecting flights between your country and the Yemen, you may have to stay overnight (or even two or three nights) in Moscow. This is not as bad as it sounds. Accommodation is free in the Sheremetyevo airport hotel, which is probably luxury class when compared to the places where you will stay in the Yemen.

If you have plenty of time in Moscow, you might also want to visit the city. I heartily recommend this but, as you'll need to reserve one or two hours for customs and another two hours for the bus/metro ride to the centre of Moscow, the excursion will take at least one whole day. You have to apply for a transit visa before you start off. This usually takes at least a week to be issued; you need a photo and US$10 to US$20. The dates and hours of your visit will be written onto the visa, so you have to decide your date of return beforehand.

To/From Africa
From East Africa, it is easy and relatively cheap to reach Yemen by air. The national carrier of the Yemen, Yemen Airways, flies directly to Khartoum, Addis Ababa, Djibouti and Mogadishu from San'a and Aden. Prices for a one-way economy-class flight should be well under US$200, though local variations are significant.

Ethiopian, Sudanese, Djibouti and Somali airlines also serve the country.

To/From the Middle East
You should have no difficulties reaching Yemen from Middle Eastern countries. If Yemen Airways or the national carrier of the other country does not offer a direct flight, the connection will certainly be made by Saudia.

To/From Asia

Yemen Airways flies directly to Karachi and Bombay. You can look for cheaper fares from various other airlines flying either directly from India or Pakistan or via more circuitous routes. Aeroflot, for example, flies from Singapore or India to Moscow and then connects to San'a. A flight to Amman in Jordan and a connection from there to Yemen is another possibility.

Pakistan International Airlines has a weekly flight from Karachi to San'a, continuing to Nairobi, and back.

To/From Australia

There are no direct connections between Australia and Yemen and, although many flights between Australia and Europe operate via the Gulf states in the Middle East, that route is likely to be expensive. Qantas offers perhaps the best deal: an excursion fare to anywhere in Middle East for A$1850 return (with slight variations depending on your point of origin). This ticket entitles you to a stopover and a change of planes in each direction. The fare includes hotel accommodation if an overnight stop is necessary in, say, Bahrain (but does not cover some A$15 for visa and departure tax in Bahrain).

When planning your flights, take care not to get a stopover in Saudi Arabia as you will not be allowed to change to a Saudia flight in Jedda or Riyadh.

To/From the USA

There are no direct flights from the USA to the Yemen; it is probably best to fly to your destination through Europe. Combination flights are offered by major airlines.

LAND

To/From Europe

An alternative to flying is to drive your own car. This is interesting but impractical and could be very costly. Occasionally, the Yemen's relationship with its neighbours makes the option impossible.

Indeed, with the border between Oman and Yemen virtually closed, the only land connection with Yemen has been through Saudi Arabia and it is here that your difficulties begin. First of all, you will need a transit visa to Saudi Arabia (no tourist visas are available), which you can obtain only if you have an entry visa to the Yemen. Of course, if you already happen to live in Saudi Arabia (because you've worked there, for example), all you will need are exit and re-entry visas.

The transit visa is valid for three days only, so you *must* get through this vast country within that time. This shouldn't be a problem – Saudi Arabian highways are asphalted and in good condition and your car is obviously in excellent shape or you wouldn't even think about driving in the Yemen! In practice, you can get only Toyotas repaired in the Yemen, since other makes of car are rare here. Diesel engines are not recommended because it is difficult to find fuel for them in either Saudi Arabia or Yemen – they were even forbidden a few years ago, as were Fords. For the trip to and from the Yemen, an ordinary car will do but, if you plan to visit smaller villages in the Yemen, you will definitely need a 4WD. No matter what your vehicle, you must get a Carnet de Passages.

One final piece of paperwork is essential: hefty insurance. Should you be involved in an accident in which a Saudi or Yemeni citizen dies, you will be held liable for considerable compensation and may end up paying tens of thousands of dollars to the victim's family. As you might have major problems trying to get your insurance work done in the Yemen, check the procedures with your insurance company beforehand in case you have to leave your vehicle in the Yemen.

In principle, there are two routes from Saudi Arabia to the Yemen: the Tihama route, Jizan to Bajil, and the mountain route, Najran to Sa'da. The latter is closed for the moment, partly because of bad road conditions and partly because of government problems in controlling the area. This leaves you with only one option.

The Tihama road is asphalted and presents no problems. Yemeni customs and immigration formalities are handled in Haradh. The paperwork is extremely time-consuming –

expect to spend anything from a few hours to a full day at the border. In San'a, you'll have to obtain a separate permit to return to Haradh.

SEA

To/From Africa

Yes, there are ship connections between Africa and the Yemen. While Aden is the most widely served port in the country, there are also regular cargo ships from Port Sudan to al-Hudayda and, from Djibouti to al-Makha, a most erratic smuggling trade flourishes. Schedules, prices and ticket conditions are available locally.

TOURS

Several tour agents in middle Europe, especially in Germany, organise tours to the Yemen. A typical package tour takes two weeks, hurries through half or two-thirds of the towns and villages described in this book and costs anything from US$2000 upwards. Some examples are:

Deutsch-Arabisches Reisebüro from Köln, Germany, offers 16 days in Yemen for just under DM 5000 (telex 8-883514).

Minitrek Expeditionen Heidelberg from Heidelberg, Germany, offers 16-day tours to both the northern and southern parts of the country for DM 5,500 to DM 6,500 respectively (fax (6221) 402688).

Ökumenische Studienreise GmBH from Frankfurt, Germany, offers 12-day tours for groups of 10 or more people for DM 4000 (fax (69) 281197).

SSR-Reisen from Zürich, Switzerland, offers 16 days in the northern part of the country for SwF 3990 and 14 days in the south for SwF 4300. A combination four-week tour is available for SwF 5950 (☎ (1) 2423000).

Italian Adventures Association from Rome, Italy, had an ad on the door of a restaurant in Sa'da. I have no information on their services but their address is: Via Cino Da Pistoia, 7-00152 Roma.

LEAVING YEMEN

The departure procedure is straightforward enough: customs, ticket check and passport control. You are required to arrive at the airport two hours before the scheduled flight time.

The airport tax is YR 115 for foreign destinations and is paid at the check-in counter. By the way, this is all the Yemeni money you should have left by now. You can't count on being able to exchange your extra riyals at the San'a airport, and the chance of using them there for any reasonable purpose is limited in the extreme: there is no restaurant, the tea shop sells soft drinks at prices five times the local ones and the tax-free shop is also very expensive. The souvenir shop exhibiting Yemeni handicrafts is occasionally open in the mornings but I wouldn't bet on it. It is therefore best to solve the problem before getting to the airport.

The situation is not much better at the Aden airport. Here, the selection at the tax-free shop appears to have been designed according to some Brezhnevian rules. They will probably improve the shop because this is now the commercial capital of the Yemen.

At passport control, you must fill in the green departure card, which has the same questions as the arrival card.

Getting Around

AIR

For the average independent traveller, flight services inside Yemen are only to be considered if you are in a hurry and plan to combine Hadhramawt with a visit to the highlands. Otherwise, ground transport is cheap, frequent, reasonably fast and offers a chance to see the unforgettably varied Yemeni landscapes on the way.

The two independent Yemens each had a national carrier – Yemenia in the YAR and al-Yemda in the PDRY. After unification, these companies announced that they would unite to form a company called Yemen Airways.

Both companies operated domestically as well as abroad. On internal routes, no big changes are to be expected. There were good links between the capitals and with the countries' other large cities, with several flights a day (usually morning and afternoon, plus occasional midday departures) between San'a and Aden, Ta'izz and al-Hudayda, as well as return flights from Aden to al-Mukalla and Say'un.

Domestic economy-class tickets invariably cost about three times as much as ground transport fares. First-class flights are available only from San'a to Ta'izz and Aden, obviously for connecting international flights. Add to this the exorbitant taxi fares to and from the airports and you will easily end up spending another 50%, so you must have a good reason to fly in Yemen.

During the flights, nonalcoholic beverages are served. The service is standard; there is nothing to complain about except perhaps that there is nothing exotic about it.

In fact, one of the wonders of the postcolonial era is the fact that setting up modern national airlines is one of the very first activities of even the world's most underdeveloped countries after they gain independence or throw out a despot. Clearly, this cannot happen without outside technical and monetary aid and, since there aren't too

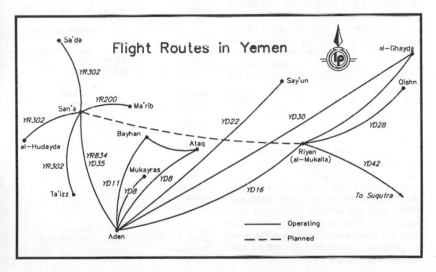

Flight Routes in Yemen

many sources of such help, the result is highly standardised carriers; you'll usually find that only the appearance of the flight attendants varies.

In the case of Yemenia, the San'a International Airport was built by West Germany in 1973. The planes came from Saudi Arabia which, in 1977, helped to found Yemenia and owns 49% of the company. The Aden International Airport was expanded in the late 1980s with Soviet aid and sports a huge, modern terminal building. However, in 1990, the company still operated a fleet of ancient de Havilland DHC-7 propeller-powered aircraft, alongside some more up-to-date Boeing 707s and 737s.

You should have no difficulty getting tickets. There are plenty of travel bureaus and airline offices in San'a, Ta'izz and al-Hudayda, fewer in Aden, and most of them sell Yemen Airways tickets. English is widely spoken in these places.

In such an office, you will probably first be given a Yemen Airways schedule to check the departure and arrival times. Don't be astonished to see some strange destinations mentioned there: Sa'da, Ma'rib, al-Buq, al-Jawf. This doesn't necessarily mean that you can actually fly to these places. The Ma'rib airport is, for the time being, used for military and industrial purposes only and no passenger flights were in operation when we asked ('There is a problem with the airport in Ma'rib – why don't you use a taxi?'). Al-Buq (near al-Baydha) and al-Jawf (north of Ma'rib) are also not for civilian use – at least, not for the use of foreign civilians ('These places are not for tourists').

BUS

There are two main forms of land transport in Yemen: bus and service taxi. Of these, taxis are the more original and you should at least try them – they have a real Arabic feel. Buses were introduced to Yemen in the mid-1980s and are rapidly expanding their services. The General Transport Corporation fares are cheap and constant, and the buses are punctual and reliable; you should have no difficulties in using them.

On the other hand, the bus windows are made of grey or brown glass to reduce the heat of the sun and, often, they cannot be opened. This means that, whatever wonders you see en route, you can't take a photo – when you're sitting in the 20th row of a full bus, you can't just yell at the driver to stop for a minute so that you can step out for a picture. Furthermore, the buses are filled with unbearably heavy tobacco smoke.

The buses go wherever there are asphalted roads. This means that new bus routes have been opened yearly during the 1980s. The list given here simply cannot be complete by the time you arrive in the country – use it as a reference but check the routes you intend to use. While it is unlikely that any connections will have been withdrawn, new bus lines will have been added and schedules amended.

Route 1:	San'a to Ta'izz
Stops:	Ma'bar, Dhamar, Kitab, ad-Dalil, Ibb
Departures:	6.30, 7, 9 am; 1.30, 2 pm (from Ta'izz also 8 am, 3 pm)
Prices:	YR 90
Duration:	4½ to 5 hours

Route 2:	San'a to al-Hudayda
Stops:	Mafhaq, Manakha, al-Qadm, Bajil or Ma'bar, Madinat ash-Sharq, Bajil
Departures:	6.30, 7, 8 am; 1.30, 3 pm
Prices:	YR 90 to 100
Duration:	4½ to 5 hours

Route 3:	San'a to al-Baydha
Stops:	Ma'bar, Dhamar, Rada', as- Sawadiyya
Departures:	7 am, 2 pm
Prices:	YR 90
Duration:	4½ to 5 hours

Route 4:	San'a to Sa'da
Stops:	'Amran, Khamir, al-Harf
Departures:	7 am, 2 pm
Prices:	YR 90
Duration:	5 hours

Route 5:	San'a to Hajja
Stops:	'Amran, Mafraq Kuhlan
Departures:	8 am, 2 pm
Prices:	YR 65

Top: Shining white old port town of al-Mukalla
Left: Orchids in Wadi Dhahr
Right: Goats leaving Thilla through its southern gate

Top: Fetching water from a cistern in Shihara
Left: Street scene in Old San'a
Right: Selling tobacco under the eyes of the president

Duration:	2½ to 3 hours

Route 6: San'a to Ma'rib
Stops: none
Departures: 8, 9 am; 2 pm (from Ma'rib 8 am; 2, 3 pm)
Prices: YR 75
Duration: 3 hours

Route 7: San'a to Rada'
Stops: Ma'bar, Dhamar
Departures: 1.30 pm (7.30 am from Rada')
Prices: YR 60
Duration: 3 hours

Route 8: San'a to Qa'taba
Stops: Ma'bar, Yarim, Damt
Departures: 7 am; 2 pm (from Qa'taba 7 am, 1.30 pm)
Prices: YR 80
Duration: 5 hours

Route 9: al-Hudayda to Ta'izz
Stops: Bayt al-Faqih, Zabid, Hays, al-Juma'a, Mafraq al-Makha
Departures: 7, 8 am; 2 pm
Prices: YR 90
Duration: 4 hours

Route 10: al-Hudayda to Harad
Stops: al-Qanawis, Suq al-Khamis, Suq 'Abs
Departures: unspecified
Prices: YR 60
Duration: 3 hours

Route 11: Ta'izz to ar-Rahida
Departures: 7, 10 am; 2 pm
Duration: 1 hour

Route 12: Aden to Ta'izz
Stops: Lahej, ar-Rahida
Departures: 7 am
Prices: YD 4
Duration: 3 hours

Route 13: Aden to 'Azan
Stops: Lawdar, Habban
Departures: 6.30 AM
Prices: YD 3
Duration: 6 hours

Route 14: Aden to Ataq
Stops: Lawdar
Departures: 6.30 am
Prices: YD 3
Duration: 6 hours

Route 15: Aden to al-Mukalla
Stops: Lawdar, Habban, 'Azan, Bir 'Ali
Departures: 6 am
Prices: YD 5
Duration: 12 hours

Route 16: al-Mukalla to Say'un
Departures: 6 am
Prices: YD 3
Duration: 5 hours

The buses follow the same timetable for travel in the opposite direction. In cases where the departure times differ, they are indicated in parentheses. Note that during our visit no bus lines were opened between Aden and Ta'izz or Aden and San'a; only service taxis operated those lines.

Buses are best suited to long-haul travel – from San'a to Ta'izz or from Aden to al-Mukalla for instance. You can easily use them to get from a terminal city to a smaller town en route (from Ta'izz to Ibb, for example) but you may find that a trip from, say, Yarim to Dhamar is best done by taxi.

Usually, you cannot buy tickets on the buses – you have to buy them from ticket offices beforehand. There are ticket offices at every bus terminal and, occasionally, at stops along the way. Timetables exist only for departures from terminals, not for those from intermediary stops. Ticket offices are usually open about 30 minutes to an hour before bus departure times and close immediately after the bus leaves. At an intermediate stop, the ticket office may only be open for the time the bus stops there. If there is room in the bus, you may succeed in halting it almost anywhere by the roadside, though you can't count on this.

You will find it hard to locate a ticket office much in advance of your planned departure. You are not expected to do such advance planning in Yemen; you should act in a more Yemeni, spontaneous manner. We had the following conversation with a local informant and it illustrates a profound difference between Yemeni and European ways of thinking:

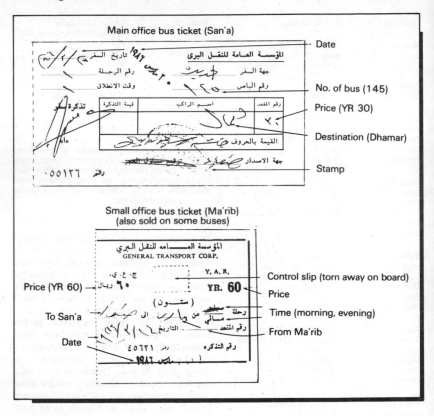

Main office bus ticket (San'a)

Date
No. of bus (145)
Price (YR 30)
Destination (Dhamar)
Stamp

Small office bus ticket (Ma'rib)
(also sold on some buses)

المؤسمة العـــامه للنقل البري
GENERAL TRANSPORT CORP.

Price (YR 60)
To San'a
Date

Control slip (torn away on board)
Price
Time (morning, evening)
From Ma'rib

– Where can we find the bus ticket office here?
– There is none here.
– But can we get a bus here?
– No, the bus has gone already.
– But can we get a bus tomorrow morning?
– Yes, of course.
– So can we buy the ticket in the bus?
– No, you must buy them in the ticket office.
– You said there is no ticket office here?
– Tomorrow there will be.
– Where, then?
– Just here.

Some words of advice: in the terminal cities, you should arrive well before the bus is due to leave. On crowded lines like those in San'a, Aden, al-Hudayda and Ta'izz, this may mean getting there a full hour before the scheduled departure time, especially on weekends. There may be one or more buses going to your destination but all tickets may already be sold 30 minutes before the bus leaves. If you arrive late, you may not get a good seat – on certain routes, the side of the bus you sit on matters, since the scenery is much better on one side of the road than on the other.

The main San'a bus station, Bab al-Yaman, may be confusing and you might have some problems finding the right bus. The destinations are marked on most buses but, if your knowledge of Arabic is limited to what you've read in this book, you probably won't be able to recognise the one you want. Moreover, there may be more than one bus going to a particular city and, if you take the wrong one, you will be politely asked to move over just before the bus leaves and you could end up sitting in a much worse seat than you had intended. Although the seats are not reserved, the tickets are sold for specific buses anyway – as many tickets per bus as it has seats. The bus number is marked on the front bumper, again in Arabic only. You should be able to compare this with the number on your ticket (see illustration).

City Bus

In cities and major towns, you can find minibuses (called *dhabar*) and larger buses to serve very local transport needs. The fares are a few riyals per person. The cheapest buses link San'a's major gates and squares; these city buses wait until they are full, with the driver shouting the name of the destination to everyone who passes by. Once full, they drive fast and charge everybody YR 1.

The cities of the north also have plenty of black-striped minibuses that drive along predefined routes and pick up passengers from the streets. The drivers are very alert; if you simply stand by the roadside waiting for the chance to cross the street, they will swarm around you offering their services. Prices are generally YR 2 to YR 4 per person. This is an ideal form of public city transport – cheap, reliable and fast. You'll find that the only problem is not knowing the routes, which makes it difficult to find the right bus. Generally, any minibus will become a private taxi if you mention a destination that is not on the route, so remember to check the price before getting into the car.

In the cities of the south, large and small blue buses operate on more regular schedules and charge two or three shillings per trip.

TAXI

There are two types of taxi in Yemen: *sarwis*, or service (shared) taxis, and *inqiz*, or private taxis.

Service Taxi

Service taxis are well known in many Arabic countries. In Yemen, they run on predetermined routes, say, from San'a to Shibam or from Shibam to at-Tawila. All bus routes are also served by service taxis and the taxis travel on nonasphalted roads as well. Service taxis have no timetables – they wait until full and then leave. This may take anything from a few minutes to a few hours. Usually, service taxis have seats for four or six people but they are not considered full until they have six or 10 passengers, respectively. More people are sometimes crammed in if the passengers know each other. Once, I saw a man, his two wives and three children in the front seat in addition to the driver – nobody complained.

Taxis are invariably so old that you can't help wondering what keeps them going. Strangely, they do. Although their maintenance may seem to have been totally neglected, the driver makes the interior of the taxi very cosy: dashboards are decorated with fancy Arab-style textiles and the mascots that hang from the rearview mirror include classic calligraphy, such as 'Allah' or 'Muhammad', etched in brass.

The atmosphere in a service taxi is very warm and positive. Passengers often form a spontaneous community, enjoying lunch and prayers together during stops (which are inevitable if the trip takes more than a couple of hours). It pays to make an effort to communicate with the other passengers. If you do, you will be more easily accepted and will be granted privileges otherwise not available, such as views of remarkable mosques and villages by the road or extra photo stops. Yemenis like talkative people, especially in the afternoon.

Service taxis use different stations to the buses. Often, a service-taxi station is a little way from the centre of town along the road the taxis take so, depending on traffic routes, there are usually a few stations in each town.

Taxis are easy to recognise in Yemen: they are painted white with broad horizontal stripes and a big circle on the front door. Often, the taxi's route is painted in Arabic inside the circle. Ordinary city taxis and short-haul service taxis have black stripes, while the stripes on long-haul service taxis are coloured according to the route served. For example:

Route	Stripe Colour
San'a to al-Hudayda	blue
San'a to Sa'da	brown
San'a to Ma'rib	yellow
San'a to Ta'izz to Aden	green
Ta'izz to al-Hudayda	red
al-Hudayda to al-Harad	red

Fares There are a couple of important things to remember about taxi fares. First, you always pay for a seat in the taxi – that is, the fares are per person. Second, the price must always be negotiated before you sit down. If you are part of a couple or group and you ask for the fare to a particular destination, the driver will give you a price and then multiply it by the number of persons in your group to get the total fare.

Generally, service taxi fares are fixed and non-negotiable. Nevertheless, a Westerner is likely to be charged something extra by way of a 'foreigners' tax', so be wary. If there are local passengers around, you will almost certainly get the right price the first time. If you are alone, you will probably be quoted a price that's too high. It might be a good idea to loiter around for a while, ask the fare from different individuals (such as drivers to other destinations) and listen keenly when locals ask the same question.

If you agree on an amount and get into the car, no more bargaining can be done; you have to pay the agreed fare. An agreement must always be honoured in Yemen. If you accept a price and sit in the car alone, and the taxi then starts off immediately without waiting for other passengers, you are paying for all the empty seats as well (about five to 10 times the cost of a single seat). The driver is not cheating you; rather, you are being given especially good service because you seem able to afford it.

If you want to complain, you should have some idea about the prices beforehand. Distances don't tell the whole truth because road conditions vary widely in Yemen. To estimate the cost yourself, ask the driver how long it will take to reach your destination. They will probably not want to give you an overestimate, since you might then abandon the trip altogether, but too short a time would show that the price is too high. You are therefore likely to get a reasonable answer.

A rule of thumb is that a car should cost something in excess of YR 100 per hour. A journey from San'a to al-Hudayda (240 km on a winding but good asphalted road) takes about five hours, so a fare of YR 100 per person is typical for an eight to 10 passenger taxi. Here, the price is somewhat high because it is a bus route; Yemen is consider a service taxi more comfortable than a bus, so you can expect the taxi fare to be 10% to 15% higher than the corresponding bus fare. On some less-traversed routes, a regular taxi service may not exist but locals may offer a 4WD Toyota and a driver at a price that works out at around YR 150 to YR 200 per hour.

Sometimes, after waiting at the station for a couple of hours, it is agreed that there just won't be enough passengers for the taxi to be considered full. In such cases, an extra charge is calculated and added to each passenger's fare.

Even when you are not going to ride the whole distance, you will often be asked to pay the full fare; this depends on how confident the driver is of picking up new passengers at the place where you'll be getting out.

Use your judgement in deciding whether to accept these kinds of conditions; often, you'll be able to find alternatives. If you get into a taxi at a halfway point, you should always be entitled to a rebate.

Private Taxi

The distinction between public buses and private taxis is very vague in Yemen. Some small taxis drive, mostly along certain cheap routes, seeking extra passengers on every street corner ('public'), while others will drive you anywhere, treating you as the owner of the car ('private'). Each charges appropriately. Even a huge bus will some-times turn into a private taxi when a tourist is obviously at a loss and keeps asking how to get to a certain place. You should be able to get almost anywhere within the city boundaries for well below YR 30 in San'a, less than YR 20 in Ta'izz or al-Hudayda and YD 1 in Aden, though some patience may be required to find the right taxi.

Sometimes, private taxis can be a nuisance because drivers love to offer you better service than you actually need. Suppose you want to get to a service-taxi station to leave a city for some distant destination but you don't know where the station is. From any point in any city, the appropriate fare should be no more than YR 5. However, the driver may insist on driving you right to your final destination for around YR 1200. Don't try to argue; just take another taxi – there are always plenty of them around.

CAR RENTAL
Car with Driver
Car rental in the Western sense of the term is now and rare in Yemen. Cars are usually hired complete with driver and are available either on the streets or from local travel agencies. A 4WD vehicle with a driver will cost you at least YR 1200 a day and, if you travel long distances (for example, to Ma'rib and back within a single day), expect the cost to be well over YR 1500.

If you are alone or with a small group, these prices are vastly above those you would be charged for using service taxis or buses. However, if you are with five or more people, it might be a good idea to check some of the travel agencies. An additional benefit is that the driver will act as a guide; some travel agencies have English, German or French-speaking drivers. This can also be a nuisance, though, since the driver may insist on taking an active part in your decision-making on where to go next, how long to stay in each place, where and what to eat, where to stay overnight and so on. You will proba-bly pay the driver's expenses, too, since it is courteous to express your gratitude for good

service, so include that in your estimate of the costs.

Yemen Tourism Company (☎ 770628/9), PO Box 1526, San'a, and Yemen Arab Tourism Agency (☎ 224236), PO Box 1153, San'a, are two of the many travel and tourist agencies in San'a. There are plenty of others around Ali Abdul Mogni and az-Zubayri streets. Phone them first to get current street addresses. (This will also give you a sample of the staff's knowledge of English.)

Car without Driver
Renting cars without drivers is a concept that didn't reach Yemen until the mid-1980s but there are already some offices on az-Zubayri and Hadda streets in San'a. This is a cheaper way to rent and you can get a car for YR 500 to YR 700 a day. The smallest 4WD vehicles cost about YR 600. To this, you must add the cost of fuel (about YR 60 per 20 litres).

Gasoline is *bitru:l* in Arabic. Petrol station procedures are universal and you should experience no difficulties. The gauges come from Saudi Arabia, so don't be surprised to see riyals and halalas on the display. These are Saudi riyals; one Saudi riyal is 1000 halalas, while one Yemeni riyal is 100 fils. In any case, the gauges are calibrated to show the cost in Yemeni riyals.

Warning Don't think about renting a 4WD vehicle unless you know what you're doing. If you are driving yourself, you should be very experienced in handling such a vehicle because the mountain tracks could not be described as roads. A Yemeni driver seems to be able to get a car across anything a goat can climb but they have been doing so for years. Driving for hours and hours along such routes is exhausting. There are no reli-able maps because tracks in the lowlands often change seasonally. Never rely on meeting friendly souls at every crossroad to show you the right track – Yemen is a most unevenly populated country and, in some areas, you can drive for hours without seeing a human being.

Another warning: when driving along Yemeni roads, you are subject to Islamic and tribal law. This means, among other things, heavy financial penalties if you happen to harm somebody through careless handling of the car. In the case of a lethal accident, the foreigner is always assumed to be guilty of carelessness. You may have to pay hundreds of thousands of riyals to the family if you caused the death of a man, half the amount if you killed a woman and less again for children. During Ramadan and the pilgrimage season, the penalties are doubled.

And remember: you can't expect local shepherds to fix the car if something goes wrong with it.

BICYCLE

Of all the improbable means of transport, some people have chosen cycling. No bicycle rental services exist in Yemen but what follows is an excerpt from a letter by Ms Gill Farjounel of France about her six-week holiday in 1989:

A lot of people don't realize it is very easy to take a bicycle on the plane as part of the 20 kg baggage allowance. Obviously this limits what else you can take, which is probably a good thing, and we took all our heavy luggage in our cabin baggage. It is advisable to protect the bikes for the flight and deflate the tyres, some airlines provide special cardboard boxes.

In Yemen the hotels were helpful, we were always able to find somewhere safe to leave our bicycles. There didn't seem to be a problem and we often left our bikes fully loaded whilst we wandered off sightseeing, usually asking someone, a shopkeeper for example, to keep an eye on them.

We mainly used the tarmac roads. Although the mountain passes seemed formidable the gradient was rarely more than 5%, they were just very long (we drank litres of water). The rough road riding would require mountain bikes, also on the rough tracks there are no signposts and it is easy to take the wrong turning. A compass is essential as existing maps are not accurate.

Food and water were not a problem, but did require a bit of day to day planning (shopping is easier in the morning and you can't rely on finding anything open in some very small villages on a Friday). Sun protection cream and hat are musts during the hot days.

Cycling was a very special experience. We were encouraged on our way with laughter, shouts and much hooting of horns. Sometimes we were followed for miles by motorbikes or cars, I suppose that a girl on a bike is a rare sight. On one occasion the crowd that gathered to see our bikes blocked the road and a policeman had to sort it out.

My most memorable moments are those of our early morning rides when the roads were deserted, the sun was low in the sky, the air cool and we could really appreciate the splendour of the mountains and it was easy to forget the occasional hardship.

HITCHING

Many people come to Yemen with the principal aim of wandering through the mountains from village to village. The country offers some of the best opportunities in the world for this, especially in the mountains north-west of San'a, or around Ibb and Ta'izz. There, the distances between villages are short, a few hours on foot at most, and there are plenty of open-minded and helpful people to assist you with any problems you might encounter on your trek.

For longer hauls, it is easy to get a ride in Yemen, except on the asphalted roads served by buses and taxis. Many poorer Yemenis rely entirely on cheap (occasionally free) rides on passing vehicles. You'll see plenty of open-platform trucks travelling along the highways, roads and tracks of Yemen carrying anything from one to 20 people in addition to their cargoes. Often, you will find it easy to join these passengers – just wave the vehicle down and greet the driver and passengers cordially before asking where they are going and whether it is OK to climb onto the platform. Usually, it will be. Sometimes, you will even be invited to have a seat, and somebody will move over to the platform to make room for you.

It is perfectly possible to get a ride in any vehicle. Soldiers and police often pick up tourist hitchhikers, while well-educated Yemenis may want to practice their English. You are less likely to get a ride on a busy route frequented by buses and service taxis than on quieter roads or tracks. On the other hand, in remote areas where tourists are rare, people may worry about their own safety and avoid contacting strangers, which may make it difficult to get a ride. After a few very positive experiences, don't jump to the conclusion that Yemen is a paradise for the budget traveller – it isn't.

One thing is important: you should not behave as though you are taking the driver's hospitality for granted. They expect you to talk with them and to answer their questions. If they don't ask any, volunteer information about yourself. If they speak only Arabic and you don't, talk with them in your own language; at least you have body language in common. If, for some reason, they don't want to talk with you, they will let you know but it is better if they decide this, not you.

After the ride, always offer some money; not too much, definitely less than you would pay for a seat in a service taxi, but not too little either – be careful not to make your offer an offence. They may not take it or they may take it without a word of thanks – either way it's alright.

Some Yemenis have heard wild rumours about foreigners paying astronomical amounts for rides of a few km; they may ask crazy prices when you ask for a ride, such as hundreds of riyals for a 30-minute drive. Fortunately, these people are still rare, at least for the time being, and you should not add to their number. Turn them down. This kind of situation is not good for you, it is not good for Yemen and it is not good for those who will come after you. The phenomenon of Western tourists paying far too much for basic services is a modern form of colonialism, transforming once proud nations into pitiful crowds of beggars. This has not yet happened in Yemen and there is no reason why it should happen here at all.

San'a

Yemen's capital, San'a (san'a; Sana, Sanaa), is in the northern provinces. San'a is a unique city. As the bustling capital of a not-so-small country, it has the usual traffic jams and environmental problems, yet it is simultaneously one of the biggest open-air museums in the world. Rather than displaying lifeless relics, San'a preserves the age-old way of living itself. For 1500 years it was a legendary town; few Europeans had ever visited San'a and it earned fame as a city never exposed to foreign influence. Then, all of a sudden, in the latter half of the 20th century, it became an integral part of the modern world.

The Pearl of Arabia Felix still exists, perhaps in more fascinating form than ever. San'a may no longer be a quiet, small city in the midst of fields under blue sunny skies but the old San'a is still there, hiding in the midst of modern suburbs and beneath the dust clouds raised by motor vehicles.

History

According to Yemeni folklore, San'a was founded by Noah's son Shem and is one of the first sites of human settlement. Legend says that Shem came to Yemen from the north seeking somewhere to settle and chose the place shown to him by a bird. The legend still flourishes in San'a and the town bears the nickname 'Sam City'.

After Shem, other religious notables (Jewish, Christian and Muslim) lived here. At one point the city was called Azal, after the sixth son of Biblical Joktan (Qahtan in Arabic) to whom all Arab tribes trace their origins. Today, Azal is the brand name of a bottled mineral water.

Spoken tradition also tells us that, at some point during the Sabaean and Himyarite times, around the beginning of Christian times, there was a huge palace somewhere in or near present-day San'a. The palace, Ghumdan, was said to be 20 storeys high. Bronze lions guarded each corner and the alabaster roof was apparently so thin and translucent that the unnamed king could see the birds flying above the palace.

In the 10th century AD the famous Yemeni historian al-Hamdani reported on developments some 800 years before his time. According to his account, it was the Sabaean king Sha'r Awtar who, in the late 2nd century AD, built a wall around the palace of Ghumdan, thus starting the tradition of making the city a walled one. The name San'a literally means a fortified city.

The oldest reliable records of San'a date from the 1st century AD; however, these give us little information about the city's changes in status. A few centuries later, San'a suddenly appeared as the capital of the Himyarite kingdom. Exactly when Dhafar lost its place to San'a is not known, but in 525 AD, when the Aksumites from Ethiopia conquered the Himyarites, San'a had served as the capital during the reigns of more than one king.

Scriptures from that period describe the Qalis in San'a as a splendid cathedral built of teak with gold and silver nails, housing an ebony pulpit with gold and silver plating. It was a place of pilgrimage for the Christians of Arabia; even today, some inhabitants of old San'a may stop a tourist and point out the place where the Qalis is supposed to have stood. (The word 'Qalis' is derived from the Greek word 'ecclesia', which means church.)

Nothing is left of these monuments. Some 50 years after the Ethiopians came the Persians, and again only scriptures testify to their presence in San'a. In the course of only a few years following the arrival of Islam in Yemen in 628 AD, the palaces of non-Muslims were destroyed, as were many of the city's other buildings. The Great Mosque of San'a was built using the stones.

During subsequent centuries San'a often served as a capital, either of the whole of Yemen or of a small region in the midst of the highland plains. The city prospered greatly at these times. Often, however, it was humiliated and destroyed by new sultans seizing power from old rulers and moving the throne elsewhere.

The first troubles occurred soon after the Islamic expansion. Early in the 9th century, Yemen is fought to free themselves from the rule of the Abbasid caliphs of Baghdad; San'a was destroyed by the troops of the legendary Caliph Harun ar-Rashid in 803 AD. About 100 years later, destruction came at the hands of a closer rival: in 901 AD the emerging Zaydi state conquered San'a for the first time. The year 1187 AD was another black year for San'a – a series of dynastic battles for power severely damaged the city.

At the beginning of the 16th century, Mamelukes from Egypt briefly occupied Yemen and succeeded in taking San'a. In 1548 came the Turks. They held the city for some decades and left in 1636, only to return to Yemen 200 years later, in 1849, conquering San'a in 1872. Again, their power was highly disputed and they had to give up San'a several times while fighting against the troops of the Zaydi imams. San'a again suffered greatly from recurring battles.

It was only after the 1912 treaty of Da''an (in which the Turks agreed to retreat from the Yemeni highlands, leaving the region under the rule of Imam Yahya) that San'a started to enjoy the benefits of peaceful development. In 1918 the city became the capital of the independent Kingdom of Yemen.

San'a's next crisis came in February 1948, when the so-called 'Free Yemenis', a group of Shafa'i merchants and other opponents of the imamic rule, killed Imam Yahya outside San'a. They proclaimed Abdullah al-Wazzir the new imam. However, with support from the Saudis, Yahya's son Ahmad recaptured power, killed al-Wazzir and let Zaydi tribespeople loot the city. Al-Wazzir's head was staked on top of a flat rock near the Bab al-Yaman gate, where it stayed for weeks as a warning to others. A main street in San'a was later named after Muhammad Mahmud az-Zubayri, a leader of the revolutionary group.

After the coup attempt, Ahmad moved the capital to Ta'izz. However, San'a remained an important highland centre and, shortly after the 1962 revolution, it again became the capital of Yemen . In fact, the 1962 revolution began in San'a when Imam Ahmad's son Muhammad al-Badr was proclaimed the new imam following his father's death. On 26 September, a week after the transfer of power, the newly appointed head of the imam's bodyguard, Abdullah as-Sallal, ordered army tanks to shell al-Badr in his palace in San'a. Next day, Yemen was proclaimed the Yemen Arab Republic.

Al-Badr survived, fled to the mountains and, from there, organised armed resistance against the new leaders. The resulting civil war lasted through the rest of the 1960s, success fluctuating between the Royalists and the Republicans. On 1 December 1967 the Royalists laid siege to San'a. The siege lasted for 70 days but ultimately failed and the civil war was finally brought to an end in 1970.

Since the civil war San'a has experienced unprecedented growth, doubling in size every four years. In 1962 the city wall was completely intact, embracing the whole city and separating it from the green fields immediately outside. A 1964 map shows that large sections of the city wall had been destroyed and new suburbs built; by the mid-1980s the city had spread in all directions, swallowing the nearby villages and covering hundreds of hectares of fertile fields. During the same period the population of the city grew from 55,000 to almost 500,000.

In 1990, when the two Yemens united, San'a became the capital of the new Republic of Yemen.

Architecture

Despite the furious pace of recent urban development, the old San'a, especially the eastern part, has remained relatively intact. The city wall has been broken in several places to let cars and motorcycles enter the narrow streets, and steel waterpipes crisscross both the lanes and the outer walls of the houses. Even with these modern additions,

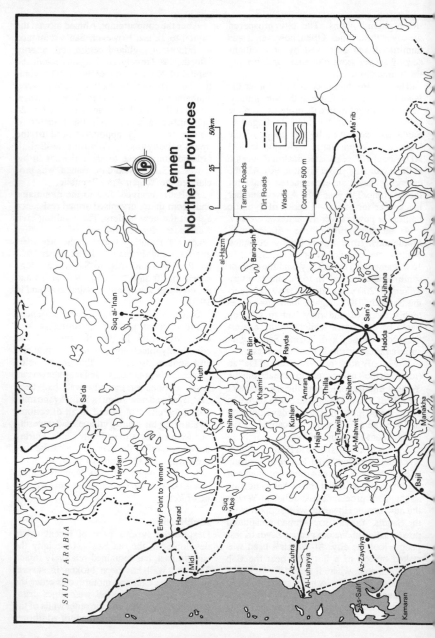

**Yemen
Northern Provinces**

Tarmac Roads
Dirt Roads
Wadis
Contours 500 m

0   25   50km

SAUDI ARABIA

Suq al-'Inan

Sa'da

Haydan

Entry Point to Yemen

Harad

Midi

Suq Abs

al-Hazm

Baraqish

Huth

Shihara

Dhi Bin

Khamir

Rayda

Amran

Kuhlan

Hajja

At-Tawila

Al-Mahwit

Thilla

Shibam

San'a

Hadda

Ma'rib

Al-Jihana

Manakha

Bajil

Az-Zuhra

Al-Luhayya

As-Salif

Kamaran

Az-Zaydiya

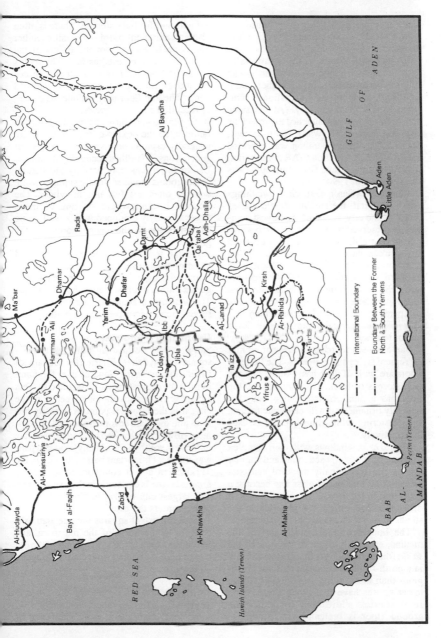

San'a is a remarkable town; many houses are more than 400 years old and all are built in the same 1000-year-old style.

In fact, old San'a is internationally regarded as such a unique part of the human cultural heritage that, in December 1984, UNESCO launched an international campaign to safeguard the city. (At the same time, a campaign was launched to protect the city of Shibam in Wadi Hadhramawt, PDRY.) The San'a operation was expected to cost US$223.5 million (YAR contribution US$500,000) and take five years but it was still going on in 1990.

What makes San'a so special? Two things stand out. First, the *medina*, or old walled centre of the city, is one of the largest completely preserved medinas in the Arab world – from Suq al-Baqr in the centre of the old city, you can walk more than half a km in any direction without encountering 'Western' or 'modern' architecture. Second, the architecture of San'a is distinctly different from that found anywhere else in the world; there are comparable gems elsewhere in Yemen but they are smaller and more difficult for a visitor to reach.

San'a houses represent a fascinating mix of Yemeni styles and materials. The first few floors are built of dark basalt stone and the next storeys of brick. Occasionally the top floor has a mud coating. Outer walls are typically ornamented with elaborate friezes, and plastering with white gypsum is used imaginatively.

The *takhrim* windows, with their complex fretwork of superimposed round and angular shapes, are traditionally made of alabaster panes, though coloured glass has become a substitute in the 1990s. The small panes of different colours make a night walk in the streets of San'a an unforgettable experience.

The houses of the eastern part of the medina, especially those to the east of the *sa'ila* (the seasonal river that crosses the city in a north-south direction), are more prestigious than those in the western part. These tower houses have five or six floors, each floor serving a different function. The ground floor is typically used to house animals and for bulk storage. There is often also an excrement room – a small chamber that collects waste from the toilets of the upper floors, to be used as fuel. The rooms on the 1st floor often serve as storage spaces for agricultural products and household items. The 2nd floor may include the diwan, or reception room for guests.

Yemeni tower houses belong to extended families, so the next two or three floors are generally used as bedrooms for the several generations of families occupying the house. Use of the rooms may vary by the season: colder rooms are used during summer while warmer ones get full use in winter. The kitchen is somewhere on one of these storeys, usually equipped with a well going straight through the lower storeys to the ground.

On the top floor is the most privileged room of the house: the large *mafraj*, or the 'room with a good view', where the owner's guests gather to chew qat in the afternoons. The *manzar*, a separate attic on the roof, serves the same purpose as the mafraj.

Orientation & Information

San'a is best defined in terms of its main squares. Maydan at-Tahrir (the Square of Liberation or Tahrir Square) is at the point joining the separate parts of the old city. This square is the postrevolutionary centre of the city; it is the terminal point of intracity bus lines and there are several important government offices nearby. Bab al-Yaman, the Gate of Yemen, south of the old city's eastern part, was the most important part of the city in the Turkish era and it continues to gather the greatest crowds of people in their spare time. The largest city market in Yemen , Suq al-Milh, borders the gate.

Less important squares include Bab ash-Sha'ub, to the north of the old town, and Maydan al-Qa', in the western part of the old city. These, too, are connected to Maydan at-Tahrir by bus.

Tourist Office The office of the General Tourist Corporation (spelt Cooperation on some local maps) is at the western end of

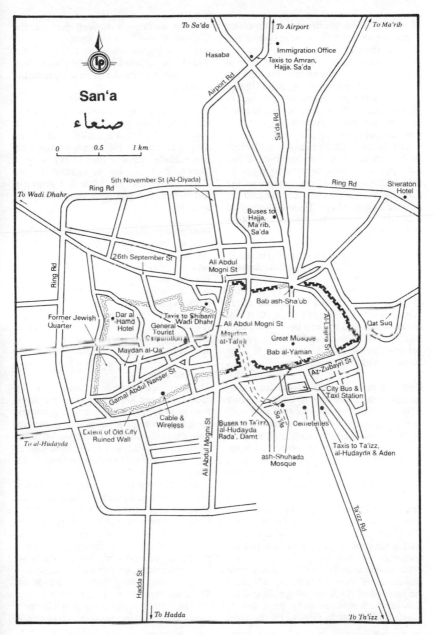

San'a

صنعاء

0   0.5   1 km

Maydan at-Tahrir. You have to visit the office to get your tour permits to other parts of the country. The office is open from 9 am to 1 pm and tends to be pretty crowded. You should reserve at least an hour for the visit because each passport is individually checked, although groups get a common permit. Tour guides with thick piles of passports are frequent customers, so your wait may turn out to be long indeed.

The Handicraft Exhibition (souvenir shop) there is worth checking; even if you don't purchase their silvery jambiyas or colourful Tihami clothes, you can get all the maps the Yemeni officials have decided are suitable for general sale. There is also a good selection of postcards, posters and other works of art.

Money Exchange There are plenty of banks in the vicinity of Maydan at-Tahrir, dealing with both cash and travellers' cheques. In Suq al-Milh (the central suq by the Bab al-Yaman gate) you can find private enterprisers exchanging cash only. US$100 banknotes tend to get you better rates than smaller notes, even though the moneychanger probably has only thick piles of 5, 10 or 20 riyal notes to offer in return.

Post The main post office is at the southeastern corner of Maydan at-Tahrir. You buy stamps from the counter and drop your mail in the mailbox yourself; there are separate mailboxes for domestic mail, mail to Arab countries and mail to all other countries. Postcards can be purchased from sellers at the main entrance (or cheaper from the General Tourist Corporation).

Telephone For calls inside Yemen, use the coin-operated phones in the main post office. No phone directories are available but the staff at the counter will gladly find you the numbers.

For overseas calls, there's a handy card phone service some 10 minutes walk from the junction of Ali Abdul Mogni St and az-Zubayri St. It was set up by the Cable & Wireless Company in the late 1980s. Walk west on az-Zubayri St until you see the Chinese Embassy to the right, on a small street crossing az-Zubayri St. It is open from 8 am to 10 pm and for YR 150 you can buy credit card type plastic cards to operate the phones.

Maps The Survey Authority in San'a has published a very good map of San'a, with scales of 1:10,000 and 1:2500. It describes the city as it was in 1982 and is probably the best publicly available map of any place in Yemen. It is sold by the General Tourist Corporation for YR 12 and I strongly recommend that you get a copy, if any are available.

Immigration Should you need a visa extension, the Immigration Office is in Hasaba, in the northern part of town. It is halfway between Maydan at-Tahrir and the San'a International Airport, near the station for taxis to Sa'da and other northern destinations. A taxi takes you there from Maydan at-Tahrir for YR 6 per person – ask for *Hasaba, maktab al-jawa:za:t* (passport office). This is simple to pronounce and the drivers will probably understand you.

The Old City

The most imposing sight in San'a is the city itself. You can walk around it for days, finding more and more fascinating houses, mosques and suqs. Many places in the city have distinctly different characters at different times of the day and on different days of the week – it is the people who bring San'a alive.

The eastern part of the old city is a good place to explore. Make sure you carry twice as much film as you think you will need. Plenty of mosques raise their minarets high above the roofs of the beautiful tower houses; unfortunately, though, entering a mosque is practically impossible for a Westerner. Hammams, or bathhouses, abound in the city, many dating from the Turkish era. There are separate hammams for men and women, and it is perfectly possible for a visitor to have an inexpensive bath in one. A local guide may make you feel more comfortable in these places.

Don't ignore the gardens of San'a – there are hectares of them within the walls of the old city, although they might easily escape your eyes because they are private and mostly walled, visible only from the backyards of the houses or mosques. They are improbable oases in this vast urban environment. In previous times the city was self-sufficient in vegetables and fruit, and the gardens are actively cultivated to this day.

Although the old city covers a large area, you hardly need a map. For one thing, the streets are so winding that following a map is no easy task. However, the overall structure of the city steers you along the main routes. If you enter the smaller alleys, you may soon find they are dead ends. Before you reach that point, though, some friendly souls approach to ask where you want to go; boundaries between public streets and private courts are vague here and you are being gently reminded that the privacy of homes is inviolable in an Arabic city.

The paving of the main streets of old San'a is of recent origin, having started in the late 1980s with Italian aid. Before the introduction of motorised vehicles, paving was unnecessary; people, goats, camels and donkeys trampled the soil down, so dust was no problem until 1962. With only 30 or so rainy days per year, mud was no problem, either; the torrential rains were hardly enough to wash away loose debris from alleys.

Unfortunately, after the revolution, modern technology began to pulverise the streets of San'a. An encounter with a single Toyota jeep on an unpaved street leaves you spitting dust and the traffic raises giant dust clouds that constantly blanket the city. This phenomenon is greatly amplified by the cement factories just outside the city.

The other part of the old city, to the west of Ali Abdul Mogni St, has newer buildings and is less likely to elicit gasps of admiration. Its many grocery stores, supermarkets and electronic shops abound in imported goods, from Japanese Nikon cameras to Dutch Philips vacuum cleaners, from Finnish Kantolan biscuits to Australian nonalcoholic Swan beer, demonstrating a prosperity that makes it hard to believe that Yemen still ranks among the least developed countries in the world.

Nevertheless, a walk in this part of the city is rewarding; most of the old embassies have their offices in Bir al-'Azab (at the westernmost end) and many beautiful old houses remain. The former Jewish quarters, Qa' al-Yahud (also called Solbi), can be found south-west of Maydan al-Qa'. Many houses have been destroyed, but with luck, you can still find an original one, identifiable by the Star of David above the door or windows. Otherwise, these clay houses are modest in the extreme. Under imamic rule, Jews were not allowed to build houses higher than nine metres, so these houses often had basements, a rarity in Yemen.

City Wall

San'a's city wall is largely history today. The best remaining examples of it are by the western side of the Sa'ila and by az-Zubayri St, between Sa'ila and Bab al-Yaman. The wall was originally built of mud only; the stony part was built in 1990 as an act of restoration, preserving the structure but destroying its spirit.

Parts of the wall also exist on the northern side of the medina, near Bab ash-Sha'ub. On the south-eastern tip of the walled city, the old citadel stands on an elevation, surrounded by massive walls. It is used by the military forces and cannot be visited.

Suq al-Milh

The central market area begins at Bab al-Yaman and extends all the way past the Great Mosque, half a km to the north from the Bab. Bab al-Yaman itself was built in the 1870s by the Turkish occupiers and looks almost as alien as the fountain in front of it, built by South Koreans in 1986.

The suq is open daily but is best visited in the morning, when activity peaks, or between 6 and 7 pm. After entering Bab al-Yaman, you encounter an ever-expanding variety of commodities for sale. Although the area is called Suq al-Milh, or the Salt Market, salt is a minor sales item in this market. The market zone actually consists of some 40 smaller suqs, each specialising in a clearly defined sector of business.

Traditionally, each suq was under the control of the *shaykh as-suq*. Within each suq there was (and still is) a *samsara* (plural *sama:sir*), a building that served as both storehouse for the wares and inn for those bringing the wares for sale. Today these buildings have largely fallen into disuse, and there are restoration projects for the most important sama:sir. Fifteen important sama:sir can still be found next to the corresponding suqs, recognisable by their decoratively tiled brick facades and their location within the suq area.

Many of the goods are left out in the open overnight; men called *shaykh al-layla* guard them from small watchtowers.

There used to be a central samsara (Samsara Muhammad Ibn al-Hassan) for storing money and other precious things but this tradition ended in 1948; after a murder attempt, Imam Ahmad ordered his tribespeople to loot San'a, including the samsara.

Near Bab al-Yaman, jambiyas, music cassettes and other items from the past and present are sold. Deeper in the suq better defined sub-suqs emerge, many of them selling mainly traditional products, although imported wares are not uncommon. In the actual Jambiya Suq you have a good opportunity to watch the complicated manufacture of the ceremonial weapons. The silver market largely bases its prosperity on tourists paying high prices but many of the silver goods on sale have been made in the suq or imported from India. You may be lucky enough to see a genuinely old piece brought from the Yemeni countryside, distinguished by its astronomical price.

The spice market is by far the most pleasantly scented place in Yemen. Vegetables, qat, corn, raisins, pottery, clothes, carpentry and copper, to mention just a few – each product has a suq of its own.

Qat Suq

To the east of the old city is a more modern market, the walled Qat Suq. This vast wholesale market primarily sells qat but has a range of other products, from chickens to cows and from grain to firewood. Warehouses and restaurants replenish their stocks here.

Open every day, the Qat Suq is recommended if you enjoy crowds and a busy atmosphere.

The Great Mosque

For Muslim visitors, the place to visit in San'a is, of course, al-Jami' al-Kabir, or the Great Mosque, on the westernmost side of Suq al-Milh.

The mosque was built around 630 AD, in the very first years of Islam's presence in Yemen, when the Prophet Muhammad was still alive. Since then it has been severely damaged and restored many times; by 705 the original building was greatly enlarged, in 875 it suffered severe flood damage, and in 911 it was badly damaged during wars against the Qarmatians. In the 12th century the mosque and both its minarets were restored. It is from this period that most of the present structures date, although even the Turkish occupiers later contributed to the mosque's inner decorations.

The Great Mosque is built in strictly Islamic style. Within the great square of walls are all the requisites of a Muslim place of worship: it has a fountain and an ablution pool for the ritual washing before prayer; the most richly decorated *mihrab* wall indicates the direction of Mecca; the imam conducts the Friday worship from the *minbar*, or pulpit, by the mihrab wall; and the muwadhdhin responds to the imam during the sermon from the *dikka*, or platform, in the centre.

Entrance is usually not granted to non-Muslims. The straight walls effectively hide the mosque's beauty from outsiders and even the minarets are difficult to see because the densely built city makes it impossible for you to observe them from a distance. You could take a hasty peek through the main door, into the solid hall of columns, but the believers will soon inform you that you'd do better somewhere else.

Other Mosques

Of greater interest to non-Muslims are those mosques that reveal their beauty to the outside. You can choose from quite a variety in this 'city of 64 minarets'.

Salah ad-Din Mosque, in the eastern part of the city, is built in pure Yemeni style, while the Qubbat Talha, in the western part of the medina, shows Turkish influence in its cupolas.

The small al-'Aqil Mosque raises its beautiful minaret, brightly lit at night, over Suq al-Milh. The relatively recent al-Mutwakil Mosque on 5th November St, near the northernmost corner of Maydan at-Tahrir next to the National Museum, was built in Turkish style by Imam Yahya in the early 20th century.

The Qubbat al-Bakiliya, in the easternmost part of the old city, is perhaps the most imposing of all, partly because of its location by broad al-Laqiya St, where the mosque is easy to inspect from a distance. It was built in the early 1600s, during the first Turkish occupation, and was restored when the Turks returned to Yemen in the latter part of the 19th century. Its many cupolas are built in Turkish style, while the brick minaret is Yemeni.

In the late 1980s several new mosques were built in the modern parts of San'a. The sheer size of these massive concrete constructions makes them striking but not exactly pleasing to the eye. A very good example is the ash-Shuhada Mosque, next to the taxi stations south of Bab al-Yaman.

National Museum

The National Museum is by Ali Abdul Mogni St, some 100 metres north of Maydan at-Tahrir, next to al-Mutwakil Mosque. It is housed in Dar as-Sa'd (House of Good Luck), a former royal palace built in the 1930s. The museum moved there in 1987 from Dar ash-Shukr (House of Thanks), an older and smaller imamic palace in the Mutwakil estate, when its collection grew too big.

The museum is open daily from 9 am to noon and from 3 to 5 pm, except on Friday when it's open in the morning only. The entrance fee is YR 10 per person. The museum occupies five floors, each with several rooms and a different theme. The small ground floor is for foreign exhibitions; when we visited, we saw ancient European items, including old Roman statues lent by Germans, with labels in German and Arabic only.

The 1st floor houses a permanent exhibition of the pre-Islamic history of Yemen, with rooms dedicated to ancient kingdoms such as Saba, Ma'rib, Ma'in and Himyar. Plenty of finds from archaeological excavations are on show here, along with interesting maps.

The 2nd floor presents Yemen's Islamic past. Rooms on this floor feature Koranic calligraphy, mosques, copperware and coins, as well as towns of significant Islamic achievement, such as Dhafar, Dhi Bin and Zabid. A slide show runs hourly.

The 3rd floor showcases 20th-century Yemeni folk culture. In this ethnographical section there are plenty of traditional scenes that can still be seen in the Yemeni countryside (though they are vanishing fast). Agriculture, fishing, jambiya-making, carpentry, pottery, carpet-weaving, costumes, jewellery, even San'a weddings each have a small room here.

While the 1st, 2nd and 3rd-floor exhibits are labelled in English and Arabic, the 4th floor is obviously meant exclusively for Arabs, since all labels are in Arabic only. Among other things, there is a collection of photographs of Yemen and of (currently) friendly Arab countries; at the time of our visit, Egypt and Iraq had permanent rooms.

Military Museum

The Military Museum, by the south-western corner of Maydan at-Tahrir, is easy to spot: the building is exuberantly decorated with military hardware. The museum tells the story of Yemen, as seen by the government of the YAR – I wonder if the peaceful unification of the country will eventually bring some changes to the story! Plenty of equipment is on show in the two storeys and in the small courtyard of the building, and major historical events are described in both text and photographs.

The museum is open daily from 9 am to noon and from 4 to 8 pm; it is closed on Fridays and on the last Thursday of each month. The entrance fee is YR 10, and you can get your camera in by paying another YR 10.

Arts

Traditionally, visual arts in Yemen are Islamic only – calligraphy, jewellery and architecture. Depicting living things, especially human beings, was prohibited by the Islamic faith for centuries and this ban has only recently been selectively lifted. TV and the ubiquitous portraits of political leaders have made it possible for art in the Western sense to enter Yemen.

The pioneer of San'a's art scene, German-educated artist Fuad al-Futaih, owns Yemen's first art gallery, opened in 1986. Gallery Number One displays the work of both Yemeni and visiting artists. You will find it some 15 minutes walk from the junction of az-Zubayri St and Ali Abdul Mogni St: walk south on Ali Abdul Mogni St until you reach Khartum St (formerly al-Mujahid St). Turn right and, after a couple of blocks, you will come across the tiny gallery.

Other art galleries in the city have proved short-lived. The newest (and hopefully successful) venture, San'a Art Gallery, opened in May 1990 near Gallery Number One. Occasional exhibitions of various Yemeni and non-Yemeni artists are also held in the deluxe hotels. The centrally located Taj Sheba hotel is easily checked. Mr al-Futaih himself had plans to open an arts and crafts centre in an old San'a samsara.

Places to Stay

San'a offers the widest variety of hotels in Yemen. Prices range from YR 40 to YR 2000 per night, though it is probably not a good idea to choose the cheapest alternatives here since, elsewhere in the country, you may not have a choice.

There are many reasonably priced hotels in the immediate environs of Maydan at-Tahrir and Bab al-Yaman.

Places to Stay – bottom end

If you want to spend the night in a dormitory, don't need to wash anything but your hands and face and don't mind cold water, there are several bargains to be found. For rock-bottom prices try the no-sheet *Funduq Wadi Bana*, opposite Bab al-Yaman, in the corner where the city buses arrive from Maydan at-Tahrir.

A little better is the one-sheet *Hotel as-Salam*, on the other side of az-Zubayri St. Triples are YR 80 and hot water was available 'tomorrow'.

Slightly better again is the *Funduq an-Nazir*, in a side street off Ali Abdul Mogni St, opposite the post office by Maydan at-Tahrir. In this one-sheet hotel, four of you can share one room for YR 20 each. Amazingly, hot water was available for a shower in the public bathroom.

Places to Stay – middle

Most hotels in central San'a are in the YR 40 to YR 90 per person range. At this price you get one or two-sheet beds in double or triple rooms; singles are occasionally available. Hot water should go without saying but it doesn't; check the bathroom before moving

1	Funduq Wadi Bana
2	Hotel as-Salam
3	Funduq an-Nazir
4	Funduq Reidan
5	Himyar Land
6	Middle East Tourist Hotel
7	Funduq ash-Sharq (Orient Hotel)
8	Funduq az-Zahra
9	Hotel al-Makha
10	Hotel Shuhara
11	Funduq al-Iskandariya
12	Hotel Arwa
13	Hotel al-Khayam
14	Taj Sheba
15	Hotel al-Ikhwa

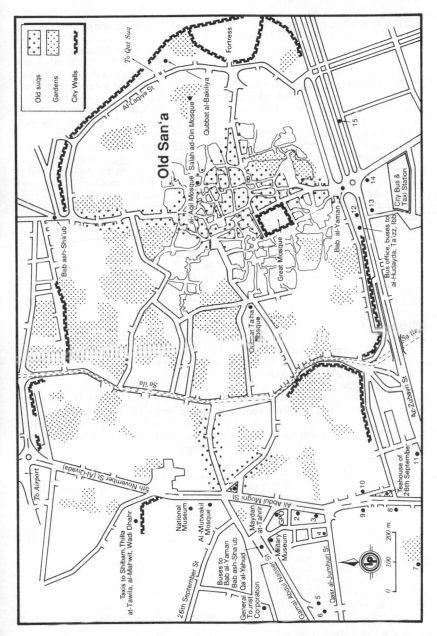

in. Here is a selection, moving from Bab al-Yaman to Maydan at-Tahrir and beyond.

Funduq Reidan is a little way off Bab al-Yaman; walk east on either of the streets extending az-Zubayri St. Triples (YR 120) are the minimum room size in this hotel. Its public bathrooms feature warm showers and a cleanliness that is exceptional in the one-sheet category.

The *Himyar Land*, opposite Bab al-Yaman, stands in an excellently central but exceptionally noisy place. In this one-sheet hotel, you get doubles for YR 100 and a level of hygiene that is very Yemeni.

The *Middle East Tourist Hotel*, or *Funduq ash-Sharq al-Awsat as-Siyahi*, is on az-Zubayri St, between the Sa'ila and Ali Abdul Mogni St. Doubles with private bathroom cost YR 160. This is quite a clean two-sheet hotel.

Ali Abdul Mogni St has several two-sheet hotels with fully equipped shared bathrooms. These places offer doubles for about YR 120 to YR 150. They were built in the early 1970s in contemporary Egyptian style and have not been renovated since. *Funduq ash-Sharq (Orient Hotel)* (☎ 74226) and *Funduq az-Zahra* (☎ 72550) are on opposite sides of the street, while *Hotel al-Makha* (☎ 72242), with hot water in the mornings only, and *Hotel Shuhara* (☎ 78502) are near the main post office. *Funduq al-Iskandariya (Hotel Alexander)* (☎ 72330) is a couple of blocks off the main street, on Qasr al-Jumhuri St, and offers singles and triples also.

Continuing along Qasr al-Jumhuri St a few blocks and turning right, you come to *Hotel Arwa* (☎ 73838) and *Hotel al-Khayam* (☎ 75272). Both are two-sheet hotels with doubles for YR 160 to YR 180 and both are relatively clean. I prefer the Arwa because of its shared bathrooms.

There is also a selection of less centrally located but newer and clean hotels along Ta'izz Rd, to the south of Bab al-Yaman. The big two-sheet *Hotel Two Paradise Land* offers triples with private bathroom for YR 150 and doubles with shared bathroom for YR 100.

Places to Stay – top end

If money is not a concern and your travel agent has made advance reservations, you'll stay at *Taj Sheba* (☎ 272372), by Ali Abdul Mogni St. This gorgeous hotel belongs to an Indian hotel chain and has everything you'll ever need in a hotel. In addition to the room charge (in the over YR 1500 realm), you can spend a few thousand riyals to join their health club so you can use the sauna.

At the lower top end there is the *Hotel al-Ikhwa* (☎ 74026), a couple of blocks behind Taj Sheba. At YR 280 for a modest double with private bath and TV, this hotel is hardly worth the money.

If you don't want to stay in the city centre, you could choose the modern *San'a Sheraton* (☎ 237500, telex 2222 SHSAN YE), on Ring Rd in the eastern suburbs; doubles were YR 1860 here in 1990. *Ramada Hadda Hotel* (☎ 215214, telex 2227 RAMADA YE) is on Hadda St. These are international hotels – the names should tell you everything.

High-quality hotels in traditional-style houses include the *Rawdha Palace Hotel* (☎ 34022, telex 2498 YEMTOR YE) in the nearby village of ar-Rawdha, eight km north of San'a's centre. Singles/doubles with bath cost YR 300/400 and you must have advance reservation.

Another such hotel is *Dar al-Hamd* (☎ 74864, telex 2270 ALHAMD YE) in the western centre of San'a, only a km from Maydan at-Tahrir – many visitors have liked this hotel, which charges only YR 600 for a double.

Places to Eat

Yemeni men like to eat out so San'a is full of restaurants. There are not too many of them in the old city but, immediately outside it along the main streets, you will find innumerable small eateries that would be called snack bars in the Western world. Further off in the suburbs, restaurants also prosper. All have basic Yemeni menus and are not exactly exotic.

Middle Eastern Food The best selection of

restaurants can be found near Bab al-Yaman and Maydan at-Tahrir.

The *Shazarwan Restaurant* is by the Funduq ash-Sharq, opposite the cinema on Ali Abdul Mogni St and very near the Teahouse of 26th September. It is clean and busy; anything you can buy here is probably safe and the cooks certainly know their job. The grilled chicken is some of the best you will find in Yemen.

Opposite the Shazarwan, next to the cinema, you can find the *Palestine Restaurant* with a vast chicken-grill by the door. Their shawarma (the huge vertical spit of lamb meat) is tasty and so popular that portions seem to be carved out often enough to ensure the freshness of the meat. However, most of the traveller feedback about people getting sick after eating in a restaurant has been generated by this one.

On az-Zubayri St between Ali Abdul Mogni St and the Sa'ila, there is another shawarma restaurant. Menus written on pieces of paper are brought to the tables. This is a very rare occurrence in Yemen; usually there is just one menu (in Arabic) hanging on the wall.

In the small street parallel to Ali Abdul Mogni St, between the post office and Qasr al-Jumhuri St, there are a couple of inexpensive fish restaurants.

On Hadda St, a few blocks from the az-Zubayri St junction, the *Peacock Restaurant* offers Ethiopian food and excellent cappuccino. One block from the junction, towards Maydan al-Qa', *al-Bustan* is a recommendable garden restaurant serving Lebanese food.

Western Food You won't find hamburgers or pizzas in Yemen as yet, nor bacon and fried eggs. The only Western-style fast-food chain is *Kentucky Fried Chicken*, which has two branches in San'a, one on az-Zubayri St, near Hadda St, and the other by 5th November St, near the now-closed Sam City Hotel.

In Ali Abdul Mogni St, next to the Palestinian Restaurant, *Snack-88* serves modest food in a Western-style interior. Here and there in the streets of the newer parts of

San'a, you can find small stalls serving takeaway french fries.

First-class hotels have restaurants serving Western-style food with prices to match. *Taj Sheba* hotel, for example, has a Western (as well as Yemeni) buffet every night for YR 150.

Sweets Near the junction of Hadda St and az-Zubayri St are several shops selling Arabic sweets. The *Lebanese Pastry Shop* has a variety of Middle Eastern desserts as well as ice cream.

Tea If all you want is a glass of tea, you might enjoy the balcony on the 1st floor of the hotel by Bab al-Yaman; it has excellent views of the bustling square. Other recommended places abound in the city, most of them on ground level and halfway into the street. Many serve excellent greasy loaves of bread (khubz) for YR 1 in the evenings; we became fond of the place behind the main post office.

The real place to be is the *Teahouse of 26th September*, where the local low-income intelligentsia gather with their newspapers and course books to see and be seen. It's on Ali Abdul Mogni St, opposite the Taj Sheba Hotel, halfway between Bab al-Yaman and Maydan at-Tahrir. The place is a park restaurant (relatively rare in Yemen); it's enjoyable to sit in the shade of the trees, sipping *libtun* and watching the crazy traffic of San'a's main street. Too bad the comfortable old chairs were replaced with concrete nonremovable ones in the late 1980s.

On the opposite corner of the junction of Ali Abdul Mogni and az-Zubayri streets, there is the *Officers' Club*, also visitable by nonmilitary personnel.

Getting There & Away
There are a few bus and taxi stations in San'a, each serving a different direction.

South & West Buses to Ta'izz and al-Hudayda leave from Bab al-Yaman (actually, from a couple of hundred metres west of the Bab, on az-Zubayri St). You can't miss the station as there are plenty of buses there. Taxis leave from the huge taxi station on Ta'izz Rd, just south of az-Zubayri St behind the houseblocks.

North-West If you are going in the direction of Wadi Dhahr, Thilla, Shibam, at-Tawila and al-Mahwit, you'll find the taxi station a couple of hundred metres north of Maydan at-Tahrir. The short-haul taxis bear black stripes, just like city taxis. No buses run in this direction.

North Brown-striped taxis going to 'Amran, Hajja and Sa'da leave from Hasaba, at the junction of the Sa'da and airport roads. (Black-striped minibuses will take you there from Maydan at-Tahrir for YR 3 per person.) Buses in the same direction leave from the station in al-Jomhuriyya St, half a km north of Bab ash-Sha'ub, where the city bus leaves you. Buses actually start from Bab al-Yaman and stop at this station on the way.

East If you get a tour permit to Ma'rib, you can find buses leaving from the same station as the northbound buses. Yellow-striped taxis operate from the square next to the bus station.

Getting Around

To/From the Airport Until recently only private taxis served the airport, with all drivers charging the 'standard' (official) fare of YR 150! This was clearly absurd but the system managed to flourish for decades. Recent traveller reports, however, suggest that it is now possible to use shared taxis for YR 20 per seat.

If you can't find a shared taxi from the city to the airport, you can always take a black-striped minibus from the Maydan at-Tahrir to Hasaba for YR 3 per person, walk across the Sa'da Rd junction and catch another minibus to the airport for the same price. Obviously you aren't in a hurry if you choose this option and it's certainly not practical if you have plenty of luggage or your plane leaves at an odd hour.

Bus San'a is an easy place to move around

because the public transport system is extremely comprehensive. The most important subcentres, around Bab al-Yaman, Bab ash-Sha'ub and Maydan al-Qa', are linked with Maydan at-Tahrir by city buses. These buses wait at the stations for passengers and the drivers stand beside their buses, yelling their destinations. Buses leave when all seats are full and cost YR 1 per person. The route between Maydan at-Tahrir and Bab al-Yaman is served most frequently.

Black-striped minibuses shuttle along main streets such as az-Zubayri St, Ali Abdul Mogni St (the airport road), Hadda St and parts of Ring Rd. The usual fare is *riyalayn*, or YR 2 per person, but it may be up to YR 6 for longer hauls. Beware of empty minibuses whose drivers agree to take you wherever you want to go; they quickly turn into private taxis charging YR 50 or more. Check the price before entering the vehicle.

Taxi Black-striped shared taxis often operate on the same principle as minibuses, driving back and forth along a certain street. The charge may vary from YR 5 to YR 15 per person, according to the length of the ride. Again, bargain before entering the car but don't argue if the price is not right, just choose another shared taxi – at least five others will be there waiting for you.

Almost any black-striped car may choose to operate as a private taxi, charging you a few tens of riyals for the ride. Within the urban area there is no reason to use private taxis, unless you are uncertain about how to get to your destination. Even then, be prepared to encounter a driver no wiser than you.

Around San'a

There are several places of interest on the outskirts of San'a, near the borders of the San'a basin. They are suitable for half or full-day excursions from the capital.

AR-RAWDHA الروضة

(ar-rawza; ar-Rawdah, Raudah)
This village is eight km north of San'a's centre, just to the east of the airport road. It is surrounded by large vineyards and, in earlier times, served as a summer resort for the imam. Today it is a suburb of San'a and highly recommended by Yemeni tourist officials.

Things to See

Apart from the lively market on Sunday mornings, there are a couple of architectural sights in ar-Rawdha.

The Rawdha Palace Hotel, in the middle of the village, was originally built to serve as a residence of the imam. It is a perfect example of San'a's architecture and offers the visitor a chance to see the interior of a multistoreyed house built of stone and clay bricks. You can also admire the beautiful landscapes from its roof.

The Mosque of Ahmad ibn al-Qasim stands very near the palace and is noteworthy for its outer walls and for the minaret, decorated with Koranic verses. Imam Ahmad, a grandson of Qasim al-Kabir, ruled between 1676 and 1681. (The mosque in Dhawran, in the 'Anis Mountains, was built at the same time – see Dhamar.)

Further into the village is an underground building with only cupolas standing. This is the Hammam of ar-Rawdha, a bathhouse built by the Turks in typical Turkish style.

Getting There & Away

The best way to get to ar-Rawdha is to take one of the minibuses that abound in Ali Abdul Mogni St by Maydan at-Tahrir to Hasaba (YR 3 per person). From there take a black-striped taxi to ar-Rawdha. A seat in a shared taxi costs only YR 5 but you will gladly be offered a whole taxi for YR 50, so be careful.

The best day to visit ar-Rawdha is Sunday, the village market day, when buses shuttle from Bab al-Yaman to ar-Rawdha and back between early morning and noon. A ticket costs a mere YR 5.

BAYT AL-HUQQA الحقة

(bayt al-Huqqa)
Some 23 km north of San'a, in the direction of 'Amran, lies a small village named Bayt al-Huqqa. The site of an ancient settlement, it is rich in Himyarite relics. In the 1920s German archaeologists carried out a research project here; the most precious finds are now in San'a's National Museum. However, many stones from ancient temples have been reused in present buildings, and ornaments as well as animal figures can be observed on the walls of the houses in Bayt al-Huqqa.

According to researchers, the temple of al-Huqqa and the water cistern belonging to it were built in the 3rd century BC. The temple was destroyed in an eruption of the nearby volcano in the 3rd century AD.

Getting There & Away

Bayt al-Huqqa is not served by regular taxis. You can reach it by private taxi or you can take a service taxi to 'Amran. Get out where a dirt road starts to the right just before the village of al-Ma'mar, some 20 km from San'a, and walk the last five km. The road leads you past the village of Bayt al-Hawiri and continues to al-Jahiliya – turn left before reaching that village.

WADI DHAHR وادي ضهر

(wa:di: zahr)
Only 15 km or so north-west of San'a lies Wadi Dhahr, a fertile and very pleasant valley of small villages and clay-walled orchards, green all year round and growing all kinds of fruits of the Mediterranean variety. A building that has developed into some kind of symbol of Yemen serves as a landmark in the valley.

You'll find it rewarding to spend a few hours walking in the valley and surrounding mountains, where the green gardens are a striking contrast to the reddish and brownish sandstone of the wadi's rocky edges. Walking upstream (to the west, out of the area covered by the Wadi Dhahr map), you come to the village of Bayt Na'am. Contin-

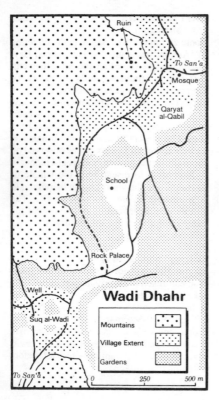

Wadi Dhahr

Mountains	
Village Extent	
Gardens	

uing from there, you can reach the very beginning of the wadi.

Dar al-Hajar

If you have defined your destination only vaguely as Wadi Dhahr, the driver will probably throw you out of the car in front of Dar al-Hajar, the Rock House (or Rock Palace). This remarkable building atop a protruding rock formation is pictured in every other book about Yemen .

The five-storeyed palace was built in the 1930s by Imam Yahya to serve as a summer residence. Building a palace in such an extraordinary place was not his idea; there were already ruins of a prehistoric building

on top of the hill. The well penetrating the rocks by the house is said to be original.

The palace is government property and stayed empty from the revolution to 1990, when a 'renovation and furnishing project' was started. I'm not sure what the outcome will be but rumour has it that the palace will be developed into a 1st-class hotel with a casino (!) on the top floor. A visit (if possible) is worthwhile for the chance to inspect the elaborate takhrim windows and take in the scenery from the roof.

al-Qabil قرية القبل

To the north of Dar al-Hajar Qaryat al-Qabil is a beautiful little village with a small Friday market. It is shadowed by an impressive stone wall formed over millions of years by fast-flowing waters. (You may find it difficult to imagine the fast-flowing waters if you visit during the dry season, but in 1975, the villages in the wadi were severely damaged by floodwaters eight metres high.) Here you can enjoy the Yemeni sense of harmony by observing the way a constructed environment is incorporated into the giant frame of nature; the houses seem to have grown out of the bedrock.

The region was already inhabited in Himyarite times; if you look carefully toward the precipice, you should spot several caves. The ruins of fortifications on nearby hilltops probably date from the days of Turkish occupation but some may have even more remote origins. Continuing north along a path past the village cemetery and through the fields in the bottom of the wadi, you will find some ancient rock paintings of animals and hunters by the wadi bank near a small house. Ask the children for directions.

Heading east from the village, you come to an asphalted road that leads to the San'a-Sa'da highway, offering you an alternative route back to the capital.

Getting There & Away

It is easy to reach Wadi Dhahr from San'a: black-striped taxis leave from the car park a couple of blocks north of Maydan at-Tahrir and will take you to Wadi Dhahr for YR 15 per person. The road down to the wadi branches from the asphalted San'a-Shibam road about nine km from San'a, then descends into the valley at a place called Suq al-Wadi.

THILLA   ثلا

(thilla:; Thulla, Thula)

About 54 km north-west of San'a is a remarkable ancient town, Thilla. It is built at the eastern foot of a mountain, near a large gently sloping basin of terraced fields, with a fortress on the mountaintop to shelter the inhabitants during crises. It is an excellent example of the system of defence that has so efficiently protected Yemenis against foreign invaders.

Thilla is a rare example of an almost perfectly preserved highland town of stone tower houses. The walled town with its paved streets is entirely built with stones from the mountain, so that from a distance you would hardly suspect the presence of a town here. Walking in its alleys, lanes and the old suq is a pleasing experience; friezes and wall textures give the houses variation despite the fact that all are built from the same material.

Thilla has always been a free town. During the Turkish occupation in the 16th century, it remained unconquered, with Imam Muttahir Sharaf ad-Din leading the successful battle against aggressors equipped with firearms.

Near the northern and southern gates you'll find well-preserved aqueducts and beautifully carved water cisterns. More cisterns can be found by the fortress on top of the mountain, which provided the population with drinking water in times of crises. Old domes mark the graves of imams.

Unfortunately the fortification on top of the hill is not easily visited. A walk along the steep path would take only 20 minutes but the guards by the locked gate at the beginning of the path usually won't let you through. If you want to try, walk straight through the town from the eastern gate (where taxis leave you) to find the beginning of the path. We were once permitted to enter for a fee of YR 5.

A visit to Thilla can be combined with a visit to Shibam and Kawkaban (see al-Mahwit) since the towns are so close to each other, but visiting both may turn out to be too much for a single day. There are modest hotels in each of these three towns, so a couple of days for a leisurely trip makes good sense, with a possible extension to at-Tawila and al-Mahwit.

Places to Stay

Thilla has a no-sheet hotel in an old-style tower house. You can find it behind the post office (maktab al-bari:d, sign in Arabic only), which is by the central square, where Thilla's small Tuesday market takes place. The Thilla hotel charges YR 50 for a bed in rooms of various sizes.

Getting There & Away

You can reach Thilla from San'a by taking a taxi from Harat al-Musbana, a couple of blocks north of Maydan at-Tahrir. There are few direct connections to Thilla but the black striped taxis and minibuses leave frequently for nearby Shibam; a seat costs only YR 25. You have to exit at mafraq Thilla, a crossroads a couple of km before Shibam; from there it is nine km to Thilla but you are likely to get a ride to your destination from any car passing by. The road is asphalted all the way to Thilla.

HADDA   حدّة

(Hadda; Haddah)

The village of Hadda, in the foothills of Jabal Hadda, is just 10 km south-west of San'a along a good asphalted road. It is recommended for those on a tight schedule who wish to visit a typical mountainside village by the San'a basin.

Hadda has beautiful terraced almond and walnut orchards as well as peach, apricot and other fruit trees. The orchards are watered by a controlled stream that flows through the village. The path through the orchards to the upper part of the village has several pleasantly shaded resting places suitable for picnicking and it is amusing to witness a Yemeni family with a portable TV set enjoying a holiday in the open .

From the slopes of the mountain, above the village, a grand view towards San'a opens between two mountains. From here you can continue to other mountain villages and even to Bayt Baws (see below), less than 10 km to the east.

Getting There & Away

The cheapest way to travel to Hadda from San'a is to take a YR 2 minibus along az-Zubayri St to its junction with Hadda St, then a black-striped taxi to Hadda (YR 10 at most). The road goes past the Hadda hotel, the oldest of the 1st-class hotels in the northern part of Yemen. On the mountainside east of Hadda you'll see several tiny villages which depend on the small streams that flow down the mountain for their livelihood.

BAYT BAWS

(bayt baws; Beit Baws)
The easternmost of the villages, Bayt Baws, is seven km from Hadda and is the mountaintop village closest to San'a. On top of a small (by Yemeni standards) rocky outcrop, the village is of ancient origin, as the Sabaean inscriptions on a stone near the village gate testify. A small cistern beneath the far side of the village once served as the sole water reservoir, but today, water is carried up by the motorised pumps that are now so common in Yemeni villages.

On the San'a side of the village, near the fields in which the villagers work, there is a newer subvillage with a new school building. Schools and water pumps are ubiquitous in the Yemeni countryside, demonstrating the government's firm intention to preserve the vitality of rural regions and to prevent the movement of the rural population from villages to towns and cities.

However, the people of Bayt Baws have not appreciated the government-donated water pipes and have all but deserted their mountaintop settlement, moving down to the new village in the late 1980s. What was, in 1986, a busy village with glorious traditions had just one house inhabited in 1990; the rest of the buildings were already starting to decay. It remains to be seen if the influx of emigrants returning to Yemen as a result of the Gulf crisis of 1990-91 will reverse this trend.

San'a Province

The province of San'a is the largest in the northern part of the country, stretching from as far south as Kusma, between Dhamar and Bayt al-Faqih, to as far north as Suq al-'Inan, east of Sa'da. A highland province, it has large cultivated plateaus at an altitude of more than 2000 metres and desolate mountains of more than 3000 metres. By the main roads to the west and north, there are a few towns and villages of interest; visits to these can be easily combined with tours to more distant destinations.

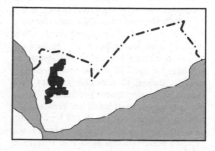

JABAL AN-NABI SHU'AYB

(jabal an-nabi: shu'ayb; Dzebel Nabi Shoeib) جبل النبي شعيب

The highest mountain in the Yemen (actually, in the entire Arabian Peninsula), the 3660-metre Jabal an-Nabi Shu'ayb stands a mere 30 km from San'a as the crow flies. To visit the mountain, take a bus or a taxi heading west from San'a along the old al-Hudayda Rd to the small village of Matna, 25 km away. From there a dirt road leads up to the mountain, branching several times to reach the small villages scattered around the south-eastern slopes.

Further along the al-Hudayda Rd, a bit before the small Thursday market of Suq Baw'an, 34 km from San'a, another scenic road branches off to the right. The road winds 18 km along the western slopes of Jabal an-Nabi Shu'ayb to reach al-'Urr, a village with a Tuesday market.

MANAKHA مناخة

(mana:kha; Manakhah)

In the Haraz Mountains 90 km to the west of San'a stands the proud mountain village of Manakha (altitude 2200 metres). The centre of the intensely cultivated terraced countryside and benefiting from ample monsoon rains gathered by the western mountains, Manakha is an important market town for villages on the surrounding mountain slopes.

The village had a strategic location during the Ottoman occupation of the Yemen; from here it was possible to protect the supply lines between San'a and al-Hudayda, in the Tihama. The Turks installed their cannons in the mountains and effectively blocked the lower roads.

For today's occupiers, Western backpackers, Manakha is an excellent base for trekking. Small villages and hamlets lie scattered everywhere between the terraces that extend across the steepest slopes. Many visitors have suggested that the majestic spirit of the mountains can be felt more intensely in Manakha than anywhere else in the Yemen.

Trekking

Short Treks The nearby Ismaili villages with their decorated houses are usually recommended; al-Khutayb, the place of pilgrimage for members of the small sect, lies only about five km downhill, south-southeast from Manakha. To reach it, walk through Manakha and take the southbound road on the eastern side of the town; keep asking the locals for the right route. The roads, tracks and footpaths uphill to the west lead to other picturesque villages, overlooking both al-Khutayb and Manakha itself. From al-Kahil a steep footpath leads back to Manakha. The highest peak of the Haraz region at almost 3000 metres, Jabal Shibam stands to the south of Manakha, a couple of km south-west from al-Khutayb.

The Haraz region is full of old fortified villages built on hilltops. One of the finest examples, the tightly built al-Hajjara, is five km south-west of Manakha. Take the road that branches from the western side of town, in front of the Manakha Hotel. The four and five-storey stone houses of al-Hajjara can already be spotted in the distance. The village, dating to the 12th century AD, served as an important fortification during the Turkish occupations of the Yemen. Continuing another five km to the west brings you to Jabal Masar (jabal masa:r) and exposes you to several more fine villages in the area.

Long Treks If you came to the Yemen with trekking in mind and with plenty of time and appropriate survival facilities (such as tent, compass, water purifier, suitable shoes and clothes), you might consider leaving Manakha on foot for a trek of several days. This is not like trekking in the Alps: no maps exist, paths are not marked and the locals can't understand why you are walking, showing you the way to the nearest taxi route instead of the village you are seeking. Be prepared to get lost and make sure you are carrying enough food and drinking water (you will drink at least seven litres a day, depending on the time of year).

One possibility is to go south from Jabal Shibam or from al-Hajjara, reaching the village of al-'Urr in a few hours, then turning westwards and following the road by a small wadi. Walking for a couple of days through the green landscape, with its many small villages, will eventually bring you to a suq village called 'Ubal ('uba:l), by Wadi Siham and the Ma'bar to Bajil highway. Here you have a choice of directions: either back to the highlands or onward to the Tihama. By now you have descended almost 2000 metres from Manakha.

On the other hand, you might want to leave Manakha for the north, with al-Mahwit as your destination. This can best be done from Khamis bani Sa'd, 45 km west from al-Maghraba (see al-Mahwit). A much less frequented and much harder route directly north from al-Maghraba to ar-Rujum by the at-Tawila to al-Mahwit road will take several days (or more) and will give you plenty of chances to get lost in this fascinating land.

Recommended for only the most experienced trekkers, the route takes you along Wadi Day'an down to Wadi Surdud (wa:di: surdu:d), a descent of 1000 metres from al-Maghraba. Continuing south-west along the wadi takes you to Khamis bani Sa'd; to the north-east, along Wadi Ahjar, is Shibam. Heading in a generally northerly direction along one of the wadi's side valleys, you will eventually end up somewhere by the at-Tawila to al-Mahwit road, exhausted. Sorry, no reliable maps are available.

Places to Stay

There is an old-style no-sheet hotel in a traditional Manakhan house. This place is frequented by Western tour groups and its prices may be among the highest in the Yemen, varying according to the season (and the customer?) from YR 80 to YR 250 per person. You might want to try bargaining if it is a quiet day but I don't guarantee the results. It's certainly wise to check the price beforehand and avoid unpleasant surprises when you get your bill in the morning.

Just by the entrance of the village, on the right-hand side, next to the gas station, is another hotel, opened in 1988. It is owned by the same family and the prices are similar.

For rock-bottom prices you would not choose Manakha but instead stay in the small no-sign funduq in al-Maghraba, on the San'a to al-Hudayda road. A night in one of their dormitories costs just YR 10.

Getting There & Away

Manakha is only a few km from the old San'a to al-Hudayda road, so it is well served by the buses and taxis operating on that route. An excursion from San'a to Manakha takes at least two days, so you might want to make a detour to the town when travelling from one end of the highway to the other.

Buses and taxis to al-Hudayda leave from

Bab al-Yaman in San'a; buy a ticket to the village of al-Maghraba (82 km from San'a), a small roadside market where buses and taxis usually stop for lunch. The fare to al-Maghraba is YR 45 by bus; a taxi may want to charge you all the way to al-Hudayda, expecting to get no new customers from al-Maghraba.

From al-Maghraba, a six-km road takes you up to Manakha. Local taxis charge YR 15 for the ride, but if you don't plan to do extensive trekking in the region, walking the distance will give you some of the finest photos of your Yemen visit. The not-too-distant village to the west, al-Hajra, is a former market site on the old San'a to al-Hudayda road.

Getting away may involve a long wait for a taxi in al-Maghraba. A better alternative is to take the San'a or al-Hudayda bus. For schedules, remember that al-Maghraba is about halfway between these two cities.

'AMRAN عمران
('amra:n; Amran)

'Amran is a walled town in the middle of fields, 50 km north-west of San'a. It is on the San'a-Sa'da highway, where the modern Hajja road heads west. The fields by the junction were completely built over in recent times, so you see only the modern suburbs of 'Amran unless you get out of the car.

A visit to the old part of the town is well worth it, especially on Friday, 'Amran's market day. The town has mixed stone and clay architecture; ground floors are often built only of stone, higher floors are made of clay bricks and mud, and roof parapets have raised corners. The appearance of the houses has something in common with that of the San'a tower houses, although they are more modest and have features borrowed from the eastern Bani Husaysh style. Some houses have stones with pre-Islamic inscriptions.

'Amran's town wall is made of stone, exceptional in this area of mud architecture. The old suq of 'Amran is also noteworthy because of its round stone columns supporting a roof above the shops. The construction is similar to that found in the market of Kuhlan. The original market is today dwarfed by the streetside market beside the Hajja road.

Places to Stay
You are unlikely to stay overnight in 'Amran, however, there is some very modest accommodation by the highway.

Getting There & Away
'Amran is best visited while travelling to see Hajja to the west or Sa'da to the north. Buses to 'Amran leave San'a from Bab ash-Sha'ub. Brown-striped taxis have their base in Hasaba, by the airport road, and charge YR 25 per seat.

RAYDA ريدة
(rayda; Raidah)

The old Tuesday market of Rayda is 22 km north of 'Amran. Buses and taxis to Sa'da may stop here for cigarettes, qat or water. Rayda is interesting mainly because it is excellent proof that traditional tribal rule is alive and well in Yemeni society. In 1979 Bayt Harash, a new market village with modern facilities, was built just two km off the road to the east. Bayt Harash also functions as a Tuesday market, and contrary to expectation, both markets continue to prosper. The explanation is that the market in Rayda is controlled by the Bakils, while Bayt Harash was founded by Hashid tribes. Despite the apparently bold leap the Yemenis have taken into the 20th century, the old set of values continues to govern their thinking.

DHI BIN ذي بين
(dhi: bi:n)

Thirty km along the dirt road to the north-east from Rayda, you will arrive in the village of Dhi Bin, famed for its 13th century mosque. A few hundred metres before the village, a steep path ascends to the beautiful mountain village of Dhafar and to the ruins of an ancient fortification. The extent of the ruins is huge, second only to that of Baraqish

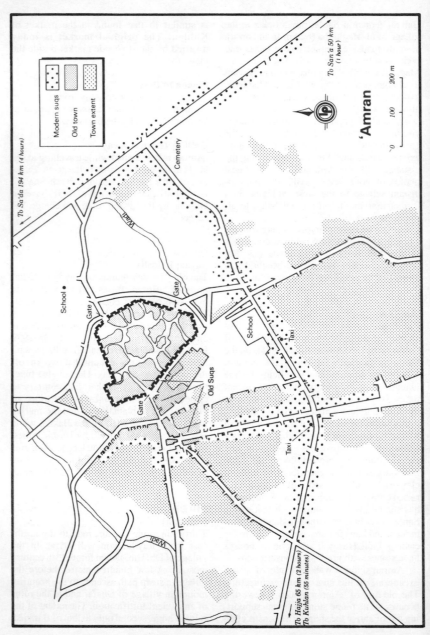

'Amran

To San'a 50 km
(1 hour)

To Sa'da 194 km (4 hours)

To Hajja 65 km (2 hours)
To Kuhlan (55 minutes)

Modern suqs
Old town
Town extent

School

Cemetery

Gate

Gate

Gate

School

Taxi

Old Suqs

Taxi

Wadi

Wadi

0   100   200 m

in al-Jawf, but very little is known about the history of Dhafar. Excavations started in the late 1980s and should shed some light on the site's past.

Although the mosque has been depicted on a postcard published by the General Tourism Corporation of San'a and the Dhafar fort ruins are among the most impressive to see, the place is not officially recommended to visitors due to security problems. Even a tour permit might be difficult to get; in 1990 the only way to visit the place was to hire a car with a driver from a tour company for YR 1200 per day.

KHAMIR خمر

(khami:r)

Khamir is another small market town in the heartlands of the tribal region. It's on the San'a-Sa'da highway, 22 km north of Rayda. Market day is Sunday.

HUTH حوث

(Hu:th)

Huth, the biggest town between 'Amran and Sa'da, has a Friday market and some very modest hotels waiting for misscheduled travellers arriving from Shihara (see the Hajja section) in the dead of night. Huth is 118 km from San'a and 120 km from Sa'da.

SUQ AL-'INAN سوق العنان

(su:q al-'ina:n)

Suq al-'Inan is a village in the Barat Mountains, remarkable for its distinctive architectural style. Houses are built of mud, using the zabur technique common in Sa'da, even though stone is plentiful in the region. The main ornamental effect comes from the striking use of colour, with broad stripes of red and yellow ochre alternating in the facades and round the windows, where white plastering is also used (you may have already glimpsed a few such houses north of Huth from the main road to Sa'da). Suq al-'Inan has a Monday market.

Getting There & Away

The bad news about Suq al-'Inan is that you won't see it: you cannot get a touring permit and visiting on your own would be very difficult. No shared taxis are available in this most sparsely populated region and the local inhabitants tend to be surly towards strangers. In 1990, not even tour operators were willing to risk driving you there.

Should things change, getting to Suq al-'Inan would involve a 36 km drive from Huth in the direction of Sa'da, arriving in the village of al-Harf. From there, a very stony path leads north-east to Suq al-'Inan (65 km).

Al-Mahwit

Although the province of al-Mahwit, north-west of San'a and south of Hajja, has the smallest area of all the North Yemeni provinces, it has several places that are worth a visit. The age-old twin towns of Shibam and Kawkaban are on the agenda of any ready-made tour of Yemen. So are the towns of at-Tawila and al-Mahwit, important market-places of the highlands, although they can't boast a glorious history.

The stone architecture of the province is related to that of Thilla, east of Shibam. Stone decorations include friezes, inlays and carefully worked-out openings: large, beautiful windows are set very low, almost at floor level. The windows are often surrounded by two narrow takhrims, very typical of this area.

Al-Mahwit is also one of Yemen's most beautiful mountain provinces and its many villages and paths make the area excellent for hiking. The inhabitants of the region are among the most friendly in Yemen and are used to backpackers. The many paths and small roads link the towns to each other and to the neighbouring provinces; an intrepid traveller could walk from at-Tawila to Hajja, for example, in a few days.

This is a fast-developing area and the stony path leading from Shibam to al-Mahwit has recently been widened to a major road. I expect it to be asphalted in the very near future, followed by the opening of a new bus line.

SHIBAM   شبام
(shiba:m)

Yes, there is another Shibam in Yemen: the Shibam in the Hadhramawt valley, a town famous for its extraordinary skyscraper architecture. The Shibam of the north is a smaller town with a less shocking appearance but with quite a past. It stands on the edge of the San'a basin, and a mountain with a large flat summit starts its steep ascent just

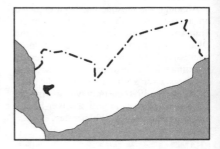

behind the town, rising steeply from 2500 metres to 2850 metres.

The town is worth a visit mainly because of its dramatic location, its sister city, Kawkaban, on top of the mountain and its lively Friday market.

History

Shibam was an inhabited area well before Islam came to Yemen. During the 1st century AD it served as a capital, not of Yemen but of a small and short-lived independent 'state'; these states were common in the highlands during those times when the kingdom of Saba was weakening and the Himyarite state, with its capital, Dhafar, was rising. Both Sabaean and Himyarite inscriptions can be found on stones reused in the city gate of Shibam, in the mosque and in other older constructions; you may be able to spot a few. Some stone pillars in the old market area are of Sabaean origin.

From 845 AD to 1004 AD Shibam was again the capital, this time of much of the highlands, when the Bani Ya'fur dynasty ruled here. They built the Shibam mosque on the site of a Himyarite temple.

The Historic Fart
Shibam has the honour of being the only locality in all of Yemen to host a tale from the *Thousand and One Nights*.

128

In the tale a man fouls up his wedding ceremony by letting out a tumultuous fart at the peak of the festivity. In utmost shame, the man flees the scene, riding his horse all the way to India and finally settling there. Years later he decides to put an end to his exile and returns home to Yemen. On the outskirts of his adored village, he dismounts by a house and happens to overhear a conversation through a window. A young girl asks her mother about her age and is told that she was born 'on the day of Husayn's historic fart'. Facing the horror of the fact that his fart will never be forgotten or forgiven, the man mounts his horse and rides away, this time for ever.

Places to Stay

Many travellers have enjoyed the basic no-sheet *Funduq Hanida*, where you can overnight in traditional Yemeni style at varying prices – YR 30 per mattress should be enough but YR 50 and even more is not uncommon. To find the place, walk down the at-Tawila Rd from the central market square until you see a small arch, some 30 metres on your right. Go through the arch and you will find the modern-looking house directly in front of you.

Getting There & Away

Shibam is served by taxis. Black-striped taxis shuttle to Shibam from San'a. The taxi station is in Harat al-Musbana, next to the National Museum, a couple of blocks north of Maydan at-Tahrir. The fare is YR 25 per person for the one- hour ride and the 45-km road is asphalted.

KAWKABAN كوكبان

(kawkaba:n; Koukaban)

If you don't feel like trekking and climbing mountains, preferring cosy hotel rooms and guided half-day tours instead, Kawkaban is *the* place in Yemen to visit for a taste of the Yemeni passion for building villages on the most inaccessible mountainsides. Here you can enjoy the country from an eagle's point of view.

Kawkaban, on top of the mountain shadowing Shibam, was built to serve as the town's fortification. During crises, the inhabitants were evacuated to the fortress. Several water cisterns carved out of the rock collected water during the rainy seasons,

grain silos were filled during the years of peace and the population was able to survive a crisis of almost any length. The door of the town's only gate is still closed and locked each night.

The only way up – the steep path winding its way from Shibam – was easily defended; many an attacker found their sophisticated guns useless against Yemenis throwing rocks down from the cliffs. It was only during the civil war of the 1990s that Kawkaban was defeated, like many of Yemen's other famous mountain fortresses. Most of its buildings were then bombed from aeroplanes, so today the town is partly in ruins.

From the edge of the cliff there is, besides the sheer 350-metre drop, a very good view over the vast plain of fields below. Far to the left (north), a mountain is visible; the low-lying town of Thilla and its mountain fortress are nine km from Shibam and are heartily recommended for a visit (see the San'a section). On the southern horizon, you may be able to see the peak of Jabal an-Nabi Shu'ayb, the highest mountain in Yemen.

Places to Stay

The *Kawkaban Hotel*, in an old-style Yemeni house, offers charming but very basic (no-sheet class) accommodation for tourists. Some tour organisers use this hotel, so watch the rates – YR 200 has been asked for over-nighting, a price which includes quite an outrageous tax on scenery.

Like many other mountaintop villages, Kawkaban is gradually being deserted as its inhabitants move down to more conveniently accessible quarters. Accordingly, some travellers report the hotel's temporary closure every now and then.

Getting There & Away

The walk from Shibam to Kawkaban takes one hour – probably more because you'll stop every now and then to admire the majestic scenery. Take a good stock of film for your camera. The footpath is paved and easy to walk, though somewhat steep; it starts from behind the big mosque.

There is hardly a village in Yemen that is

not served by 4WD Toyotas, and Kawkaban is no exception. The road starts from Shibam and goes round the mountain but you probably would not enjoy the ride. There is a second footpath up, leaving the road halfway to Kawkaban and offering an alternative walking route.

AT-TAWILA الطويلة
(at-tawi:la; at-Taweelah)

At-Tawila is a smallish town built beside a short ridge of mountains facing south, the houses framed by majestic boulders. Stretched along the slope, the old town is squeezed between the road and the mountain wall, having perhaps earned its name from this feature (*tawila* means long). Newer suburbs have also spread down to the other side of the road.

A walk on the steep mountain paths above the town offers a good view over at-Tawila and a glimpse or two to the other valley behind those huge rocks. The four peaks from west to east are al-Mahdhur, al-Munqur, ash-Shamsan and al-Husn; al-Qarani is further to the north-east. There are old fortifications on most of these peaks but they are made inaccessible by military restrictions.

Places to Stay
There are a couple of modest hotels near the at-Tawila taxi station. The one-sheet *as-Sala:m Hotel* (spelt Alsslam on the sign) has doubles for YR 100, while a no-name no-sheet place across the square charges just YR 30.

Getting There & Away
At-Tawila is easily reached from Shibam in a shared taxi (YR 25, 1¼ hours). There are few, if any, direct connections from San'a, so it is best to first ride to Shibam. Walking the 29 km from Shibam to at-Tawila is highly recommended; between the towns, the road rises to mountains well over 3000 metres high. Around at-Tawila are plenty of small villages and cultivated terraces with shade trees, rare elsewhere in Yemen.

AL-MAHWIT المحويت
(al-maHwi:t; al-Mahweet)

Al-Mahwit is the larger of the province's two towns. It is a beautiful mountain town, with the oldest houses atop the central hills and the new settlement spreading down the slopes. Splendid views over the valleys are often obscured by clouds in the rainy seasons. The mountains around al-Mahwit are just as beautiful as those of the Haraz region around Manakha.

Places to Stay
Al-Mahwit has a few old-style no-sheet hotels with no signs outside. Ask the locals, they will be all too eager to find you a place to stay. Prices range from YR 25 to YR 50 a bed per night, with doubles the smallest rentable rooms. The central *Funduq an-Nil* offers beds in a dormitory for YR 30.

Getting There & Away
The road from Shibam to at-Tawila continues along an agricultural valley, passes by the small Monday market of ar-Rujum and climbs the slopes of the al-Mahwit mountain, eventually reaching the town. The taxi fare for the 26-km ride should not exceed YR 25 per person.

The province also has a narrow projection to the south of al-Mahwit, extending all the way to the San'a to al-Hudayda road, where a small Thursday market village, Khamis bani Sa'd, marks the beginning of the dirt road to al-Mahwit. No taxis serve this route but it is possible to get a ride on the platform of a Toyota. Allocate at least five or six hours (two days if you are on foot) for the 60-km ride; vehicles use the Wadi Sari' as the road, then pass by the Friday market of Juma'a Sari' and start the long ascent to al-Mahwit. The slopes are a perfect example of rural Yemeni landscape: all are terraced and under intense cultivation, with small hamlets scattered everywhere.

TREKKING IN AL-MAHWIT
The province of al-Mahwit is, in my opinion, the area of Yemen best suited to trekking. The distances are not overwhelming, the

mountain scenes are breathtaking and the people are among the friendliest in the country. Many trekking routes will take you to or from a neighbouring province in a few days. The usual precautions apply here: don't expect these routes to be easily followed, equip yourself with a tent, and carry enough foodstuffs and (especially) drinking water. Also, plan your trek carefully beforehand; you should not rush into it unprepared, seduced by beautiful sceenery. Equip yourself with all the necessary tour permits.

From al-Mahwit or at-Tawila, it is possible to head northwards towards Hajja and Kuhlan (see Hajja), crossing the westwards-flowing Wadi La'a on the way. The adventurous will find countless unmapped footpaths and dirt roads here. A good halfway destination is the 3240-metre Jabal Maswar, some 35 km south-east of al-Mahwit. Extraordinarily beautiful terraces abound on the slopes of the mountain. To the east of the mountain, almost directly north of at-Tawila (some 20 km), is a village called Bayt 'Adhaqa.

From here you can continue north-west to Hajja or north to Kuhlan, still using small footpaths. Or, if you prefer the luxury of a Toyota, you may opt for the eastbound dirt road to 'Amran, joining with the 'Amran to Kuhlan tarmac road after 17 km, halfway between the towns.

Still another possibility is the very scenic southern road east from Bayt 'Adhaqa, leading all the way to Thilla, 31 km away (see San'a Province chapter).

Alternative routes to al-Mahwit from the San'a to al-Hudayda road have already been mentioned (see also Manakha). Twenty-six km from al-Mahwit, on the road to Khamis bani Sa'd, the road forks; the right-hand branch winds its way along the northern slopes of the Jabal Hufash and Jabal Milhan mountains, eventually connecting with the at-Tur to Dayr Dukhna road in the at-Tur basin. This is a very long alternative route to Northern Tihama (130 km from al-Mahwit to Dayr Dukhna).

Hajja

The province of Hajja, north-west of San'a and al-Mahwit, is an oddity on the Yemeni map. It is quite a large province, stretching from Yemen's highest mountains to the northern Tihama. The country's road network traverses Hajja in several directions; however, the different parts of the province have little in common, and to get from one town to another, you often have to leave the province and re-enter it by another road.

For a traveller, the most interesting places to visit are Hajja, the provincial capital and Shihara, an extraordinary mountain village in the northern part of the province. The northern Tihama rarely sees tourists other than the few who enter the country by land from Saudi Arabia.

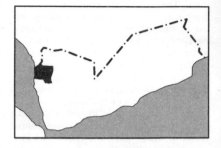

HAJJA

حجة

(Hajja; Hajjah, Haddzhah, Haggah)
Hajja is a modern town, boasting one of the very first traffic lights in Yemen. The town is on top of a mountain; indeed, several peaks are completely built over. It has relatively few attractions; a small market area and some mosques are not enough to draw masses of tourists to the town. Instead, people come to see the environs of the town: countless villages on the tops and slopes of the terraced mountains in the heart of the Yemeni highlands. The Hajja road alone makes a trip to Hajja worthwhile, even if you take the next taxi or bus back.

Despite its modern outlook, Hajja is an old town and once served briefly as the capital of the Zaydi state. Hajja owes its importance to its strategic location, from which it has been possible to control vast areas of the heavily cultivated and populous mountainous Tihama area in the at-Tur basin by Wadi Mawr. The inhabitants of Hajja have paid dearly for this privilege in the course of history; during the Turkish occupation of Yemen, this Zaydi stronghold was often

defeated, and the town was also heavily bombarded during the civil war of the 1960s.

The citadel on top of Hajja's highest peak was built by the Turks and served the Zaydi imams while the country was not occupied. The imamic rule depended heavily on the custom of taking hostages from among rebelling tribes, so the citadel has large underground prisons. Some older houses feature decorations in the Turkish style. New houses sport some very bold colour combinations on their facades, unique in Yemen.

Hajja offers a reasonable variety of accommodation, so it is a feasible base for trekking in the vicinity.

Places to Stay – bottom end

There are some very modest hotels on San'a St, near the central taxi station. *Funduq ash-Sharq*, a one-sheet hotel, offers doubles for YR 80. There are shared bathrooms in the corridor but no shower or hot water.

Places to Stay – middle

Hajja Tourist Hotel (Funduq Hajja Siyaha) (☎ 220196) is a newish two-sheet hotel built in modern Yemeni style to European standards. It belongs in the upper middle class (or, in Yemen, the lower deluxe class), offering very clean doubles for YR 220. The private bathrooms have hot water and showers that work, and there is a restaurant in the hotel.

The Hajja Tourist Hotel is away from the centre of the town, 20 minutes walk from the central taxi station. From the central cross-roads, take the road uphill, to the right from San'a St. The winding road climbs and then drops, going round the mosque, an old cistern and a school. There are a few cross-roads; ask the locals for directions.

Places to Stay – top end

Funduq Ghamdan Hajja (Ghamdan Hotel Hajah) (☎ 220420) stands on top of the hill to the west of central Hajja; you can walk there in 10 minutes from the central cross-roads (take the road left from San'a St). The Ghamdan, opened in the late 1980s, offers doubles for YR 350.

Getting There & Away

Hajja is easily reached from San'a using the tarmac road, finished in 1982. Hajja itself is served by the General Transport Corporation. Buses from San'a to Hajja cost YR 75 and leave at 8 am and 2 pm from Bab ash-Sha'ub. Taxis leave from Hasaba, at the junction of the airport and Sa'da roads, and cost YR 90. The 115-km ride takes 2½ to three hours.

The road offers spectacular views, especially the 65-km stretch between 'Amran and Hajja. The road first climbs to an altitude of 2800 metres, slowly ascending through ter-raced slopes. By the time you reach the outskirts of the 'Amran basin, some of the worst effects of the oil boom in the Middle East are evident – the labour force was sucked from the Yemeni countryside to con-struction projects in Saudi Arabia and the Gulf states, and terraces went untended. After just a couple of years of neglect, heavy rains had washed the fertile soil from the terraces, baring the stones and leaving the form of the terraces visible.

After crossing the highest pass, the road descends in steep serpentines all the way down to Wadi Sharas, a mere 1000 metres above sea level. This descent of almost two km provides quite a variety of climates,

scenery, vegetation and plantations. The Chinese-built road itself warrants a second look; this remarkable feat of engineering is marked by a small observation platform near the village of Kuhlan. Here one can stop to admire the organic alignment and gentle construction of the road.

In Suq Sharas, a small Sunday market built where the road crosses the river at the bottom of the valley, you can enjoy the strik-ing contrast between Yemeni and Chinese aesthetics – a Chinese pavilion stands in the midst of the shopkeepers' modern tin shacks.

After crossing the wadi, the road again ascends to Hajja, 1700 metres above sea level.

Until the 'Amran-Hajja road was built, the only route traversable by car was the dirt road from Dayr Dukhna on the Tihama highway, and this road still offers an interest-ing alternative (see al-Hudayda). The taxi fare between al-Hudayda and Hajja is YR 80.

KUHLAN   كحلان

(kuHla:n; Kohlan)

Halfway between 'Amran and Hajja, just after the observation platform, there are a couple of crossings to the right (northern) side of the road. The signs read 'Kohlan City' (sic). This small mountaintop village is well worth visiting and is highly recommended for those on a tight schedule as it is easily accessible – the roads are good and the village is just behind the mountain.

Kuhlan is a very good example of a Yemeni mountain village. It is built on a slope so steep that the ground floor of one house is above the roof of the next. Monday, market day, is the best day to visit; the road nearer Hajja leads directly to the suq. The shops are framed by porticoes with stone columns, similar in style to those you can find in the suq of 'Amran.

A climb to the top of the mountain involves following serpentine paths through or around the village. The citadel on top of the mountain is for government use and cannot be entered. The path to the left of it leads over the mountain and back to the Hajja road.

SHIHARA شهارة
(shiha:ra; Shaharah)

Shihara is one of the most famous mountain fortress villages in Yemen. Situated on top of the 2600-metre Shihara mountain in an area otherwise averaging an altitude of 1500 metres, the almost inaccessible village of Shihara has long been a base for armed conflict. During bygone centuries it served more than once as an asylum for the Zaydi imams when foreign occupiers threatened their power. The inhabitants of the village have always been suspicious of strangers and eager to defend themselves to the very end if needed. Even today visitors find the Shiharans among the most reserved of Yemenis.

During the 16th and 17th centuries Shihara played an important role as a base for resistance to the Ottoman Turks, who occupied most of the Yemeni highlands at various times. The defence, led by Imam Qasim al-Mansur Bi-llah and completed by his son Imam Mu'ayyid in 1635, was largely conducted from Shihara. The fierce battles of this conflict caused so many casualties among the occupying forces that Yemen came to be known as 'the grave of the Turks'. During the second Turkish occupation, in the 1800s and early 1900s, Shihara remained the western landmark of the area of 'independent tribes' on Turkish maps of Yemen.

During the civil war of the 1960s, Shihara again served as a headquarters, this time for the Royalists in their struggle against the Republicans. This time, however, new technologies of warfare brought defeat to Shihara for the first time – the Republicans used their air strength to heavily bombard the village, inflicting severe damage. Houses that collapsed in the air raids can still be seen today, although many have been rebuilt in traditional style.

The architecture of Shihara does not favour abundant decoration. The stone houses have up to five storeys but feature little more than dented friezes and a few small round or cruciform openings above the upper facade windows. White plastering is often used around the windows, splashed from inside with little care. Here you can find perfect examples of original, almost archaic, Yemeni mountain architecture.

Shihara has plenty of water cisterns, dug in amphitheatre form deep into the rock. By one count, there are 23 water cisterns; one of the biggest is in the centre of the village, near the mosque. These cisterns were built during the first Ottoman occupation so that the inhabitants would be able to survive the dry season while besieged by the enemy.

The village actually consists of two parts, located on neighbouring mountain peaks. They are connected over a 300-metre deep gorge by a stone bridge, a remarkable feat of early 17th century engineering. The bridge construction plans, prepared by famous architect Salah al-Yamani, called for three separate arches, one on top of another, but only the topmost arch remains today.

Places to Stay

The price of an overnight stay in one of the no-sheet dormitories at *Funduq Shihara* varies greatly. Some people tell stories about staying there for YR 25, while others have been charged YR 100 per person. This old-style Shiharan stone house is principally used by tour groups yearning for the 'exotic', so the prices have been inflated. With no tap water in the bathroom, YR 25 would seem about right but foreigners tend to get overcharged for any service around Shihara. Why complain? Tea and simple food are available.

The only other accommodation around Shihara is that offered by people who serve tourists privately. Take care: you could be badly overcharged. Although some travellers tell of the hospitality they received from Shiharan families, this is not the general rule. In al-Qabai, for example, there is a house claiming (rather fancifully) to be a funduq. It charges YR 100 per person for a roof, four walls and earthen floor – nothing else. The nearest modest hotels are in Huth.

Getting There & Away

Shihara is one of the few places in Yemen to have been spoiled by excessive tourism. As recently as the mid-1980s, Shihara was something of a challenge for independent travellers, being one of the hardest places to reach on your own. Today the thrill is all but gone, replaced by compulsory spending. During the tourist 'boom' of the late 1980s the Shiharans converted their hostility and suspicion towards strangers into greed for the travellers' seemingly plentiful money. As a result, the General Tourist Corporation decided in 1989 to impose new travel restrictions which state that you can only get a tour permit to Shihara through a tour operator, who will provide you with a car and driver for YR 1500 a day.

Although Shihara is only 163 km from San'a, you still need a full day to reach it and another day to get back, plus the time you spend there. After 118 km you reach Huth, a smallish town by the San'a-Sa'da highway and 120 km from Sa'da. It is only 45 km from Huth to Shihara but, as road conditions are rather bad here, the journey to the foothills of the Shihara mountain can easily take some hours.

Eighteen km west of Huth along a stony, bumpy mountain road is al-Ashsha, a small village with a few grocery shops. Continuing along the fertile, subtropical Wadi al-Wa'ar, past the date, banana and papaya plantations, you come to the tin shacks of Suq al-Ahad, 12 km south-west of al-Ashsha. This Sunday market serves the surrounding rural area.

The village of al-Qabai, at the foot of Mt Shihara, is 15 km west of Suq al-Ahad. From al-Qabai the 1400-metre ascent to Mt Shihara (2600 metres) begins: it's a very steep road and a very unpleasant drive.

The locals will force a car change at al-Qabai. The San'a tour operators are not allowed to drive you to the top of the mountain, so you have to hire a local car for the staggering sum of about YR 750. This fee is charged for every car load arriving from San'a – if you have hired a car for a small group and happen to meet up with another group here, you can't team up to fill one Shiharan 4WD. Two cars arriving from San'a means two Shiharan Toyotas climbing the mountain, even if each vehicle is carrying just one tourist!

The better option is to walk up, enjoying the extraordinary views from the terraced and qat-growing slopes of the mountain. However, you need to be in excellent physical shape to do this because the trip will take at least five to seven hours. Walking all the way to the top will vividly demonstrate to you why the Turks were not able to conquer the village on top of the mountain!

There are four small villages by the road. Immediately after the third of them, Hababa, the road branches. The road to the right is a very steep path and leads straight to the smaller part of Shihara. The famous bridge that joins this part of Shihara to the main village can already be sighted from near the junction. The left-hand fork is easier but longer; it winds around the mountain and passes the Thursday market of Suq al-Khamis, yet another village of tin shacks. Here the road branches, with the right-hand path starting the final ascent to Shihara through the Bab an-Nakhla gate.

Sa'da

Sa'da, Yemen's northernmost province, deserves respect. Its capital, the town of Sa'da, is the birthplace of Zaydism, the most powerful spiritual school of Islamic thought in Yemen. The province provides a home for numerous mountain tribes still clinging to their independent status – in the 1960s, during the civil war in the YAR, the proud tribes of Sa'da were the last to drop their weapons and accept Republican rule in the new state. It was also here that the 1990 unification of the Yemens faced its most stubborn resistance.

The province's northern border with Saudi Arabia is largely undemarcated, while to the east, the province merges into the sands of ar-Ruba' al-Khali, the vast Arabian desert. Saudi influence, both good and bad, has been visible here throughout the history of independent Yemen. In quiet times, Saudis have actively smuggled consumer goods across the border; in restless times they have provided weapons and ideological support to Yemeni internal resistance.

Most visitors to Yemen come to Sa'da, though some, after visiting other parts of Yemen, are not particularly impressed with Sa'da. For them, it is just another old town with Toyotas and Peugeots cramming its streets. The province is relatively sparsely populated and most of its villages are in the mountains west of Sa'da, where tourists don't go; the highway steers you through the desolate plateaus of Yemen to the town of Sa'da and back again.

Nevertheless, Sa'da is a place worth visiting. Here you can appreciate the solemn traditions of an ancient town that has been abruptly thrown into the late 20th century. Sa'da also has a distinctively original architectural style, which is striving to survive the introduction of concrete and tin.

Small things mean a lot: the lone young soldier walking towards us on top of the city wall, stopping and gesturing for a photo with his Kalashnikov, didn't utter a word – he just

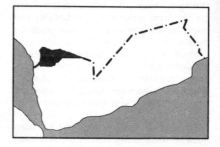

nodded his thanks and hurried past after the click of the shutter. He left us more than a memory on film; his actions carried a culture spanning 1000 years.

SA'DA صعدة

(sa'da; Sadah, Saadah)
The city of Sa'da was originally walled and stood in the midst of fields. It is still a walled city, now in the midst of fields and new suburbs. Although it was badly damaged during the civil war of the 1960s and the city wall was broken in the 1970s to make way for motor vehicles, much of the original town is still intact. The few startlingly modern government houses built next to the city wall really seem out of place here.

History

In Sa'da, as elsewhere in the country, Yemenis are eager to point out that their town was inhabited before the arrival of Islam. Located halfway between the cities of Ma'in (to the south-east) and Najran (to the north), near the beginning of Wadi Najran and in the midst of a basin 35 km long, Sa'da must have been an excellent stopping place for camel caravans on the incense road. But those days have left little behind.

The first written account of Sa'da town

dates back to the 10th century AD, when the famous Yemeni historian and geographer al-Hamdani included it in his description of South Arabia. By that time, Sa'da was already important because of the introduction of Zaydism at the end of the previous century.

In 901 AD, Yahya bin Husayn bin Qasim ar-Rassi (an outsider from Basra, Iraq) proclaimed himself the imam and made Sa'da his capital. He was a highly religious man, representing the Shi'a sect of Islam, and had spent years in Madina learning the teachings of Zayd ibn 'Ali (697-740 AD) – hence the name Zaydism. Yahya had been called to Sa'da from Madina in 892 to mediate between warring Hashid and Bakil tribes; at first he refused but, in 897, he returned and settled the quarrel most successfully, eventually founding a unified state and becoming its head. He was to be known as 'al-Hadi ila-l-Haqq' (the leader to the truth).

Zaydism is a Shi'a subsect and is found only in northern Yemen (see the Population & People section in Facts about the Country). Zaydi teachings are excellent support for the idea of a state, as they emphasise the difference between a person's private and public duties and rights.

The Zaydi state is led by the imam. According to Zaydi principles, anyone who meets certain conditions can be elected to the post of imam. There are 14 conditions on the list, such as being male, being born free and healthy, paying one's taxes and knowing the Koran. The 11th and 12th conditions are the most restrictive of all. They state, in essence, that the imam must be chosen from those descended directly from 'Ali and Fatima, the son-in-law and daughter of the Prophet.

This system effectively created a religious nobility, the sada (see Social Classes in Facts about the Country chapter), a collection of families who had all the power. During the 1000 years of Zaydi rule, the number of members of the sada class rose to 50,000. These people held most of the government positions, while the land remained mostly in the possession of ordinary tribespeople. Tribal justice and imamic rule were often on

a collision course through the centuries, but generally the sada have been highly respected.

Imam Yahya ruled until the year 911. The three imams following him continued to rule from Sa'da but, from then on, the capital was moved to other towns, such as Hajja or San'a. It was not until 1597, when Imam al-Mansur al-Qasim ibn Muhammad made Sa'da his base for the war against the Ottoman Turk occupiers, that the town again became the capital of the Zaydi state. In 1636, when the Turks were finally thrown out of the country, the capital was again moved to San'a. Sa'da, however, remained the spiritual capital of the country, the holy city of the Imamate.

In 1962 the last imam, al-Badr al-Mansur, was dethroned by the revolution that laid the foundation of the YAR. Imam al-Badr fled to the mountain area north-west of Sa'da to lead a fruitless campaign against the new leaders. The civil war lasted for seven years; even today it is in the northernmost part of the country that the power of the Republican government is at its weakest.

At the beginning of the 1990s the Sa'da region was the centre of opposition to the unification of the two Yemens. Indeed, the town and its religious aristocracy were among the biggest losers in the process. The loosening of Yemeni economic ties with Saudi Arabia left Sa'da out in the cold, with the commercial centre of the country moving to the distant port of Aden. Moreover, the unification left the 'liberal' laws of the south intact for the moment, to the dismay of the *ulama* (religious scholars and leaders) of Sa'da, who were horrified by such ideas as educated, unveiled women working for a salary.

Architecture
Sa'da is a perfect example of the *zabur* architecture that is common on the plateaus of the eastern and northern highlands, where stone is scarce but clay is abundant. Zabur means laying clay courses on top of each other,

letting one layer dry as the next one is built. Walls of the houses are typically at least half a metre thick, thinning towards the higher floors.

In Sa'da, the technique has yielded a town unique in style and appearance. The corners of the houses are strongly raised from the very basement. continuing the difference in the levelling of the clay to the roof, contrasting with the horizontal lines of the clay courses. The walls are carefully finished with a mud coating, leaving the courses clearly visible, even emphasised. Small horns mark the roof corners. On the edge of the roof are parapets decorated with a number of small arches, plastered white with lime, like the horns in the corners. Alabaster-paned windows feature elaborate carvings and lime plastering. All this creates a very pleasing effect visually.

Orientation & Information

The carriers leave you in front of Bab al-Yaman, Sa'da's southern gate. The hotels, restaurants, bus office, taxi station, police and hospital are on San'a St, within a few km of the city wall.

There used to be an office of the General Tourist Corporation here, but it has gone with the closure of the mountain road from Saudi Arabia.

Things to See

The holiest place of the Zaydis is the Great Mosque of Sa'da, built in the 12th century. Imam Yahya, the founder of Zaydism, is buried here with 11 later imams, under 12 cupolas. You'll have to be satisfied with looking from the outside; don't even think about entering the mosque. The same applies

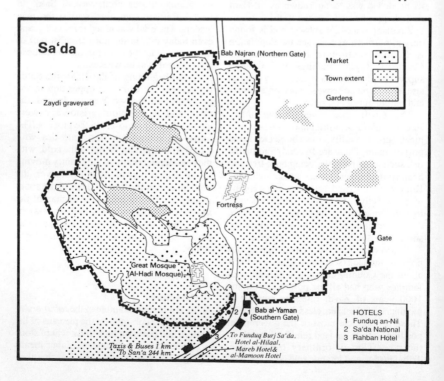

Sa'da

Bab Najran (Northern Gate)

Market
Town extent
Gardens

Zaydi graveyard

Fortress

Gate

Great Mosque
(Al-Hadi Mosque)

Bab al-Yaman
(Southern Gate)

To Funduq Burj Sa'da,
Hotel al-Hilaal,
Mareb Hotel &
al-Mamoon Hotel

Taxis & Buses 1 km
To San'a 244 km

HOTELS
1 Funduq an-Nil
2 Sa'da National
3 Rahban Hotel

to another remarkable mosque, the an-Nisari, further into town. The fortification on the central hill today serves as a government office (read: military base), so it can't be entered, either.

Don't be discouraged – the town itself deserves your attention. Despite some modern buildings just outside the old town, Sa'da is excellently preserved in zabur style and the town wall remains largely intact. Built of clay during the days of Imam Yahya, the wall was originally wide enough for a donkey to draw a cart along.

Although parts of the wall have collapsed into rubble, it is still possible to walk around the town on top of it, and a restoration project is proceeding. You may have to step down here and there but this is the best way to appreciate the beauty of Sa'da. The place to start is by the Bab al-Yaman gate; immediately on entering the old town, take the narrow alley to your right, next to a silver vendor's shack.

Of special interest is Bab Najran, the northern gate, surrounded by imaginatively twisted walls. Enemies fighting their way through the winding alleys by this gate certainly had a problem. Remember to exercise some discretion when aiming your camera at the private clay-walled gardens which are exposed to people walking on the town wall.

The next best way to see Sa'da is to walk the streets of the town, though you see less. In the town, the market is worth seeing. Though permanent, it also functions as a Sunday market, when it is greatly enlarged. From the moneychangers, who lay their wares on cloths spread on bare earth, you can buy a Maria Theresa thaler, the silver coin used as the sole monetary object before the revolution and still in limited use.

Just outside the town, to the west of the town wall, is a huge 'empty' field surrounded by a modest wall. This is the Zaydi grave-yard, by far the biggest and oldest in Yemen. You are allowed to enter, and can observe innumerable elaborately carved stone plates and tombstones. A few small domes here and there mark the graves of the imam's distin-guished relatives and other learned Zaydis.

Places to Stay

There are quite a few hotels on San'a St close to Bab al-Yaman.

Places to Stay – bottom end

The one-sheet *Funduq an-Nil (Nile Hotel)* offers singles, doubles and dormitories but is not among Yemen's cleanest. Shared bath-rooms feature showers, even warm ones if you switch on the boilers and wait a couple of hours. A bed in a double room costs YR 30 to YR 50.

If you are on a really tight budget, you can get a bed in a double for YR 20 by forgoing the luxury of warm water and choosing the *Sa'da National Hotel*, opposite.

Funduq Burj Sa'da has a sign in Arabic only. This no-sheet hotel is on San'a St, 1½ km towards San'a. Triples cost YR 100.

Places to Stay – middle

The *Rahban Hotel* is a two-sheet hotel in a modern house, curved like a dhuma and very conveniently positioned – taxis bring you right to the front door. This was our earlier recommendation in Sa'da but not anymore: in 1990 the staff were most unfriendly and would not accept Yemeni riyals in payment of the insane price they were asking in US dollars – the equivalent of YR 450 a double!

Better alternatives are to be found one or two km along San'a St. *Hotel al-Hiluul*, a traditional one-sheet inn, is remarkably clean for its class. Quadruples are the smallest available rooms; a bed costs YR 30. The *Mareb Hotel* is a bit classier. It offers two-sheet doubles with shared bathrooms for YR 150.

Furthest from the town, the two-sheet *al-Mamoon Hotel* (☎ 2203) is the newest and cleanest of those built at the end of the 1980s. It has very friendly staff, doubles for YR 230 and a bathroom to every three rooms.

Places to Eat

Several eateries along San'a St offer modest but tasty food. Inside the city walls, there are a few places around the market area where you can find something good to eat.

Getting There & Away

From San'a, Sa'da is best reached by bus or taxi. Buses leave from Bab ash-Sha'ub at 7 am and 2 pm; the fare is YR 90. Brown-striped taxis will take you to Sa'da any time for YR 100 a seat; the taxi station is at Hasaba. The 244-km trip takes about four hours.

AROUND SA'DA

You can visit a few places around Sa'da without a separate tour permit. In the immediate environs of the town, there are plenty of very beautiful small villages built in zabur style. It's worth taking a walk along the Wadi Sa'da for a few hours.

Walking a few km south-southeast from Bab al-Yaman along the wadi, you will reach the beautiful village of Raqban (raqba:n). A km or two further on is the mouth of the very narrow Wadi 'Abdin (wa:di: 'abdi:n). On the left bank of the wadi you will see an old fort, as-Sinnara. It is well worth a visit and travellers are occasionally granted entry.

Immediately to the east of Sa'da, some 15 minutes walk from Bab al-Yaman, near some old water cisterns you can find huge pre-Islamic rock engravings with an ibis motif. Six km south-southwest of Bab al-Yaman is the village of Ghuraz. There are rumoured to be pre-Islamic cave drawings seven km north of town; you'll need a local guide.

Suq at-Talh   سوق الطلح
(suq at-talH)

Suq at-Talh, a Friday/Saturday/Sunday market, is some 12 km from Sa'da, in the direction of Najran. This is the biggest market in the province. Here you can buy anything you would expect to find in a Yemeni market, from cattle to qat, from fruit to pottery.

Suq at-Talh used to be one of the most extraordinary places in the entire Yemen. It was the largest market for commodities imported from Saudi Arabia. Hundreds of trucks and jeeps brought the wares across the border and the goods were sold directly from the vehicles. You could buy anything: building materials, automatic rifles, consumer electronics, hand grenades – you name it.

Legal? Well, is smuggling legal in a place where sheikhs of the Bakil tribes have more power than the government? In the late 1980s the governments of the YAR and Saudi Arabia reached an agreement to stop smuggling. The deterioration of Saudi-Yemeni relations during the Gulf crisis of 1990 was another blow for Suq at-Talh, and today, it is a mere shadow of its former self. The border region is still difficult to control, however, and a significant proportion of the cars in use in the northern part of Yemen are driven around unregistered, with no taxes paid on them.

Umm Layla   أم ليلى
The Umm Layla (Mother Night) mountain, some 50 km north-west of Sa'da along the tarmac road that leads to the Saudi Arabian border, is as far north as you can go in Yemen. The sandstone mountain is bizarrely eroded and the drawings sculpted into its rocks date back to the days of the incense trade.

Tihama

For many visitors to Yemen, the coastlands of the Red Sea – the Tihama – constitute an obligatory but minor part of the itinerary. Organised tours often rush through the 'big triangle' of San'a, al-Hudayda, Ta'izz; a typical schedule for the Tihama would consist of an overnight stay in al-Hudayda, Friday morning in Bayt al-Faqih, an afternoon in Zabid, possibly overnight camping in al-Khawkha and a morning visit to al-Makha, then hurriedly back up to Ta'izz. Some do it in reverse order.

It is no coincidence that every major tour organiser seems to follow the same formula. If you haven't seen Tihama, you have seen only half of Yemen. This hot flatlands with its racially diverse population is a striking contrast to the mild climate and more homogeneous people of the highlands; Tihama is an indispensable part of the country.

Economically it is the most important part of Yemen and, in the past, has played major roles in most phases of the country's development. Indeed, with a third of Yemen's population and almost half the country's agricultural output, it is a place that cannot be ignored.

On the other hand, the Tihama is probably not what most tourists are after. Devastated many times in recent history, it has no spectacular ancient architecture, and the landscapes are hardly breathtaking. The hot, humid climate is extreme and uncomfortable sandy winds blow daily.

All hotels outside al-Hudayda are of the lowest standard, and if you are going to catch malaria anywhere in Yemen, it will probably be here. So it would seem a sound strategy to limit your time in the Tihama to the shortest possible period – to minimise complaints from customers, this is exactly what the tour organisers do. But whether or not you like your visit to Tihama, you'll never forget it.

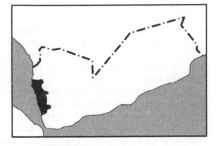

AL-HUDAYDA
الحديدة

(al-Hudayda; Hudaydah, Hodeida)

Al-Hudayda is the capital city of the central Tihama, the province of al-Hudayda, which stretches from al-Luhayya in the north to al-Khawkha in the south. The width of the province averages 50 km, from the coast to the foothills of Yemen's western mountains. The province is widest where major wadis (Wadi Mawr in the north, Wadi Siham just south of al-Hudayda and Wadi Zabid in the south) have eaten their way deep into the mountains, extending the coastal plain.

It is more than likely that you will stay overnight in al-Hudayda, since you can hardly tour Tihama at all otherwise. Al-Hudayda is Tihama's Rome: all roads lead to the city. Since every bus and long-haul taxi line starts or terminates here, it is impossible to pass the city by.

You will probably arrive in al-Hudayda by bus or taxi from the direction of San'a or Ta'izz. The third (less probable) alternative is to approach from the north, from either Hajja or Saudi Arabia.

On the trip from Ta'izz the scenery is quite monotonous: the Soviet-built Tihama highway offers few surprises.

There are two asphalted roads between San'a and al-Hudayda. The northern road, which passes near Manakha, was built in the late 1950s and early 1960s. It is a spectacular feat of Chinese engineering and serves as a model of how to build a mountain road gently, preserving the beauty of the landscape. This is the route taxis usually take; buses use both roads.

The less scenic southern road branches off the San'a-Ta'izz road at Ma'bar, penetrates the mountains abruptly and descends to Madinat ash-Sharq, then follows the vast Wadi Siham to join the northern road before Bajil. The path of this road, built in the early 1980s, treats the landscape much more ruthlessly: rocks have been blasted away wherever necessary, with little attention to aesthetic considerations. Moreover, the agricultural valley of Wadi Siham seems to be a developing area whose small settlements are rarely as eye-catching as those on the northern route.

Wherever you decide to stop en route, don't get your first impressions of Tihama from Bajil. This industrial city demonstrates the worst aspects of poor planning: the neighbouring cement factory has been sited so that the prevailing winds carry cement dust (plenty of it!) all over the town. Instead, if you arrive on a Monday morning, you might want to stop in al-Marawi'a (al-mara:wi'a), just 20 km from al-Hudayda. This lively little village has a Monday market. It serves as a pale substitute for Bayt al-Faqih if visiting that village on a Friday doesn't fit into your schedule.

History

Al-Hudayda is a young city. Although it was a verifiable port in the early 1500s, Carsten Niebuhr, the chronicler of the famous Danish expedition in the 1760s, makes almost no mention of the town, describing al-Luhayya and al-Makha as the ports of Yemen. Al-Hudayda, along with most of the northern Tihama, was destroyed in 1809 when the Wahhabi forces marched south from the Jizan area. It was not until 1830, after the British had started developing Aden, that the Ottoman Turks began to make al-Hudayda an efficient port and thus diminished the importance of al-Makha.

But the Turks were not strong enough to keep enemies from destroying their efforts. Recurrent wars devastated the Tihama for 100 years, peaking around WW I, when the al-Hudayda population dropped from 40,000 in 1911 to a mere 2000 in 1918, after Italians and Britons in turn had bombarded the city from the sea. Peace came to the Tihama only after the Saudi-Yemeni war and since 1934 al-Hudayda has been allowed to develop without disturbance.

The start was slow, however. Imam Yahya ibn Muhammad's isolationist foreign policy was of little use to a port. After his death in 1948 the pace quickened as Imam Ahmad cautiously tried to open some doors to the outside world. Ahmad's achievements include cooperation projects with China (the San'a to al-Hudayda road) and the Soviet Union (the al-Hudayda port).

The real boom for the city began after the revolution and especially after the civil war, in the explosive years of the foreign (import) trade. Since 1970 the port has been among the most congested in the world, with waiting times for unloading of up to six months. The city itself has been evolving rapidly, pushing the reed huts of local fishers out of the path of modern concrete buildings and asphalted streets.

The unification of the two Yemens left al-Hudayda in the position of the second most important port in the new country. Its growth rate is expected to slow down remarkably now that Aden has stolen its place as the trade capital of the country.

Today al-Hudayda is Yemen's fourth largest city, with a population of more than 170,000. Most of the province is rural; the rest of the population of almost 1.3 million lives in towns and villages of less than 20,000 inhabitants. If, while in the Tihama, you need any service outside the area of basic human needs (a shower, film for your camera or money exchange, for example), your best bet is to search for it in al-Hudayda.

On the other hand, al-Hudayda is by far the dullest city in the entire Yemen. It has almost no visible history, most of the city's buildings were built during the last few decades, it is on the coastal plain, with no topographical attractions, and it has absolutely no 'sights' whatsoever. In fact you won't miss much if you manage to avoid visiting al-Hudayda altogether.

Some readers of the first edition report having found al-Hudayda pleasant, though these people did not love the highlands so much. Obviously these are matters of taste.

Orientation & Information

It is fairly easy to find your way around al-Hudayda. Since you'll probably arrive from the east or south, or from the direction of San'a or Ta'izz, you will be left at the main street, San'a St, which enters the city from the east. The most interesting area is between San'a St and the coastline.

Continuing along San'a St to the very end, you will come across what must be the most modern park in all of Yemen: Hadiqat ash-Sha'b (the People's Garden). You can even see people spending their time around the huge fountain, which is gorgeously illuminated at night. Southwards, in the direction of the seashore, there are a couple of similar open spaces, leading eventually to Maydan at- Tahrir (Tahrir Square), just one block from the sea and next to the old suq area.

Everything you need in al-Hudayda lies within one or two km of the People's Garden – bus stations, taxis, accommodation, the 'old' city, shops, markets, pharmacies, banks and the fishing port. Al-Hudayda is a fairly large city and you might easily exhaust yourself walking around the modern suburbs to the north of San'a St.

Tourist Office There is a branch office of the General Tourist Corporation on the southern edge of Tahrir Square (see map). You might want to visit this office if you have run out of copies of your tour permits or if you enter the country from the sea. You can also purchase a 1983 map of al-Hudayda there or at any other branch. Of the three city maps available in Yemen, this one contains the least information. Most travellers spend only a day or so in al-Hudayda, so you will hardly benefit from a detailed map.

Money Exchange There are banks around the People's Garden but many of these seem to concentrate on activities other than exchange. Should you have trouble finding a moneychanging service, the Bank of International Credit and Commerce, to the west of the People's Garden, is a guaranteed one. Another choice is the Central Bank of Yemen office on San'a St, near the Yemen Airways office – this bank also changes travellers' cheques.

Post There is a GPO to the north of the bus station on San'a St, a block off the main street. But remember: any postcards you send out of Yemen go through San'a, so all you get from posting them here is a prolonged transport period.

Telephone For phone and telex services, there is an office of Cable & Wireless a few hundred metres west of the hotel cluster by the People's Garden. It operates like the office in San'a. You can also make overseas calls from the GPO.

Things to See & Do

There aren't many. The architecture mainly consists of concrete and cement blocks dating no further back than the 1960s. Historic mosques? None worthy of a mention. In the heat of the afternoon, there is nothing to see except the Red Sea, which is like any sea but has a warm wind – you might find the wind pleasant if it weren't blowing so violently most of the time.

In the morning you'll probably enjoy walking southwards by the shore, along al-Kurnish St. The fishing port further to the south abounds with fishers coming back from the sea carrying numerous different species of fish and shellfish to the shores. Many fishers still use wooden vessels built in the traditional way. These are very photogenic but be careful not to aim your camera at objects that might be regarded as military – and there is plenty of military interest in a port.

Some visitors have reported swimming a few km further south and also to the north of

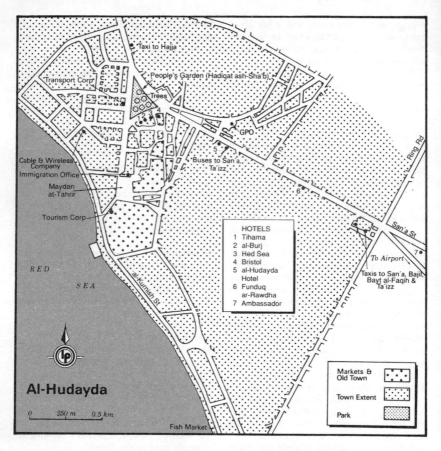

Al-Hudayda

HOTELS
1 Tihama
2 al-Burj
3 Red Sea
4 Bristol
5 al-Hudayda Hotel
6 Funduq ar-Rawdha
7 Ambassador

Markets & Old Town

Town Extent

Park

the city, for a change from the highlands. Females, however, may have some trouble with locals passing by.

The oldest part of al-Hudayda is formed by the Turkish quarters near the old market area and features some beautiful but rotting buildings. The typical old Red Sea house is three or four storeys high with wooden balconies or window covers as signs of Turkish influence and beautifully plaster-decorated walls. One of the best examples faces the Red Sea by al-Kurnish St. This fine building with a rare dome on its roof has not been in use for years and was badly damaged by

moist onshore winds, though it was being restored at the time of our visit in 1990.

Indian influence is also evident in the doorway decorations of some of the older houses. This is hardly surprising, since craftspeople used to follow sailors and traders to the port cities of the Red Coast; the 20th century has seen an end to this kind of cultural exchange.

The market itself is lively as any Yemeni market, with the extra flavour of beggars (there are more of them here than anywhere else in Yemen) and sailors from diverse countries. The oldest market quarters are behind the eye-catching Turkish gate. Some people say that gold jewellery is cheaper here than in San'a or Ta'izz – a chance for a bargain. But remember: if there is a place in Yemen where you may be cheated or robbed, it is al-Hudayda.

Places to Stay

There is quite a variety of hotels in al-Hudayda – you can spend anything from a few tens of riyals to a few hundred riyals for an overnight stay. While there are probably plenty of alternatives elsewhere in the city, there is hardly any reason to look outside the two-km stretch of San'a St from the taxi station to the People's Garden, which contains a representative sample of Yemeni hotels.

Places to Stay – bottom end

If you arrive by taxi from San'a or Ta'izz and walk a couple of blocks along San'a St, you will find a couple of hotels on the left-hand side of the street. A no-sheet, no-sign *dormitory*, wide open to the street and with doors the size of the wall, offers the chance of modest lodging for males who arrive late in the evening, start again early in the morning and have no need of any luxury.

Another choice is the legendary one-riyal *hotel* by the market area, a noticeable white building. The huge dormitory on the 1st floor has no walls, so the warm Red Sea winds caress you to sleep.

Places to Stay – middle

Funduq ar-Rawdha is a gorgeous-looking two-sheet hotel where an air-conditioned double with private bathroom costs YR 175 a night. While definitely not very clean by Western standards, this one is acceptable if the price suits you and if you don't feel like carrying your baggage any further. There is another place of this type half a km further along, on the same side of the street: the *al-Hudayda Hotel* (☎ 226100). It has similar prices and friendly service but is often full.

The biggest cluster of hotels is on the southern side of the People's Garden. No less than four hotels stand here, side by side. You

might consider investing a few riyals in a local taxi ride instead of walking from the taxi station – the buses take you much closer.

The *Red Sea* (☎ 72507) and *Tihama* (☎ 239558) hotels, both very popular with backpackers and sailors, offer reasonable accommodation in the lower two-sheet category. Prices for a double start at around YR 200 (private bathroom and air-conditioning each add YR 20 to YR 40 to the price). Ask to see the rooms before making a decision, though. I strongly suggest that you don't pay for a private bathroom here – bathrooms in the corridors are no less filthy but at least you have a choice. If you do want one, make sure that the water runs as advertised before closing the deal. The cockroaches are not dangerous.

If you feel uncomfortably warm when looking for a room, it might be wise to get one with air-conditioning because the temperature won't drop when night falls. On the other hand, insisting on hot water doesn't necessarily make sense in the Tihama, since cold tap water is seldom particularly cold. The water has probably been stored in a tank on the roof of the house, with the sun heating it all day, so a shower is warm in the evening and cold in the morning – as it should be.

Places to Stay – top end

If money is of no concern, you'll probably choose either the *Bristol* (☎ 239197, telex 5617) or the *al-Burj* (☎ 75852, telex 5676) and stay in a room with a view of the People's Garden. Both hotels are in the Yemeni deluxe category and you'll get the best al-Hudayda has to offer for YR 200 to YR 250 per person. Presumably what you get for your money is a better level of cleanliness than the previously mentioned places.

The most Western-style hotel in al-Hudayda is undoubtedly the *Ambassador* (☎ 231247), on San'a St, a few hundred metres from the taxi station in the direction of San'a. This hotel is frequented by businesspeople and government officials, and has singles/doubles with bath, air-conditioning and TV for YR 450/550. The Indian bartender prefers Country & Western music in the disco.

Places to Eat

There are some restaurants along San'a St and more in the market area between the Red Sea and the People's Garden. The usual rule applies here: eat what most people eat, in places where most of them eat, and avoid raw vegetables and nonbottled water.

Al-Khayyam Restaurant, on the street running from the People's Garden to Tahrir Square, is popular among the expatriate community of al-Hudayda, though it is not cheap. Tahrir Square has a good no-name fish restaurant. On San'a St you may try the *Royal Golden* or the *Deluxe*.

Fish is a great idea for lunch: fishers bring their catch ashore in the mornings and fish is fresh at noon. I would think twice, however, before eating fish for dinner – the cold storage facility in the fishing port may be the only one in the entire city, and a day in the open in al-Hudayda makes anything stink, especially a dead fish! Lunch is the main meal of the day for the Tihamis. For religious reasons, shellfish is rarely eaten in the restaurants, though you will see plenty of it in the fishing port if you visit early in the morning.

At the market you can buy any fruit, from banana to papaya or watermelon, at prices somewhat lower than in the mountains. The fruit is sometimes fresher, too.

Getting There & Away

There are two practical ways of getting to and from al-Hudayda: bus and taxi. There are also two impractical ways: plane and boat. As few international flights land at the al-Hudayda airport, the issue of flying is a bit theoretical. As for boats, every other visitor to Yemen seems to have contemplated entering or leaving the country by sea. However, there are no regular (nor irregular, as far as I know) passenger routes to al-Hudayda, so the only way to do it would be to board a cargo ship from Port Sudan or some other improbable place. The precious few I know who have actually had the chance to do this

decided against it, since they considered it too dangerous! Judging from their fierce looks, I must conclude that only impractical dreamers or genuine desperadoes actually take this option.

Bus The bus station is on San'a St, some 500 metres from the People's Garden. For schedules, see the Getting Around chapter. The timetable (in Arabic only) is inside the ticket office. The office is open one hour before the buses leave.

The fares to San'a and Ta'izz are YR 80 to YR 90 depending on the type of connection. You can also buy a ticket to an intermediate stop (see table of bus lines in the Getting Around chapter).

Taxi The station for taxis to the east and south is further along San'a St. There are always plenty of taxis waiting for passengers heading in the direction of San'a or Ta'izz. While taxi fares are YR 10 to YR 15 higher than the bus fares, taxis are a viable alternative to buses on these much-trafficked routes. You should not have to wait more than 30 minutes for a taxi to fill up, unless you arrive in the quiet hours of the afternoon or at midnight.

Northern Tihama

You must have more than a passing interest in the Tihama if you want to visit the coastal areas north of al-Hudayda. These are certainly not tourist areas: the few funduqs in the region are definitely of the lowest class, the weather is unbearably hot and humid, and most of the roads (other than the al-Hudayda to Jizan highway) are miserable dirt roads. A trip to al-Luhayya, for example, makes a very long day even if you hire a private car, and you have to find a driver willing to drive from 6 am until late evening. Otherwise you would also have to stay overnight somewhere – and the locals are not used to seeing tourists camping nearby!

Indeed, the General Tourist Corporation

discourages individual visits to northern Tihama and does not issue tour permits to places like al-Luhayya. While Harad certainly belongs to the border area, it should still be possible to visit areas along the main road as far north as Suq al-Khamis, even Suq 'Abs, but if you have no tour permit and are caught by a soldier, you will have to turn back.

Although al-Luhayya is the northern Tihama's main historical attraction, it is not as spectacular as some of the modern settlements you will see along the road on the way there.

Getting There & Away

There is a bus service from al-Hudayda to the northern Tihama up to Harad near the Saudi border. It runs along the asphalted Jizan road to Saudi Arabia. To use the bus (indeed, to get out of the city at all along this road), you need a tour permit to somewhere north of al-Hudayda. You can abandon the bus in az-Zaydiya, al-Qanawis, al-Ma'ras, Suq al-Khamis or Suq 'Abs.

If none of these places is your destination, you could try to get a taxi or hitch a ride from a crossing. However, you would still be better off hiring your own car from al-Hudayda. The bus continues to Harad, though this is unlikely to be your destination, since it is a border station and individual travellers are not permitted into Saudi Arabia.

An interesting alternative exists for those who want no more than a glimpse of the northern Tihama and who are equipped with an adventurous mind and plenty of time: the Hajja taxi.

You can find the Hajja taxi station immediately to the north of the People's Garden. The route from al-Hudayda to Hajja goes 100 km north along the asphalted road past az-Zaydiya and al-Qanawis to Dayr Dukhna (where you may have to change cars and wait for a couple of hours for the next one to fill with passengers). It then turns east onto a dirt road that leads to Hajja, some 70 km away via at-Tur. Expect this latter part of the trip to take at least twice as long as the

first. The so-called road was very bumpy at the time of our visit, 4WD being an absolute necessity, though there are plans to asphalt it in a few years. As matters stand now, the overall cost of the trip is YR 80 to YR 100 per person. The experience is worth it as long as you don't suffer from car sickness.

AS-SALIF الصليف
(as-sali:f)

This old port town, by the strait that separates the Kamaran island from the mainland, is the site of age-old salt quarries, still in operation. Today it stands out as the end point of oil pipes from the Ma'rib/al-Jawf area and is off-limits to tourists. There are no buses and very few shared taxis, but if you have a car, you can approach the town by taking the shoreside road north of al-Hudayda. Turn left some 14 km after al-Hudayda and drive for another 50 km to reach as-Salif. There are several fine beaches along the road, even some pretty desolate ones, which is fine if gawking Yemenis tend to make your swimming uncomfortable.

The Kamaran island has not been developed and is off-limits to tourists.

AZ-ZAYDIYA الزيدية
(az-zaydiya; al-Zaydiyah)

Back on the Jizan Rd, 50 km north of al-Hudayda, the road passes az-Zaydiya, northern Tihama's largest town. This is also the largest brick settlement in the northern Tihama (brick architecture is common in the southern Tihama, with towns such as Zabid and Hays serving as brilliant examples). Az-Zaydiya is said to be a major producer of dhumas (the slightly curved ceremonial daggers of the religious elite).

AL-QANAWIS القناوص
(al-qana:wis)

Al-Qanawis, 20 km further on, is another brick village. From this point on, the typical reed architecture of the Wadi Mawr area becomes dominant, giving the landscape an eerily 'African' feel. Halfway between al-Qanawis and Wadi Mawr is the Dayr Dukhna

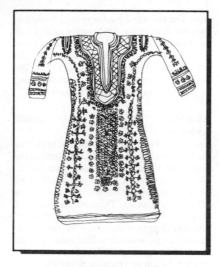

Woman's dress from Tihama

and lively motifs, and household utensils hang handily from the walls.

A few km south of az-Zuhra is the village of ar-Rafi'i (ar- ra:fi'i:). It has a Sunday suq and an old Turkish fort that was later used by the imams as a winter resort.

AL-LUHAYYA اللحيّة
(al-luHayya; Loheyah)
The old port of northern Tihama, al-Luhayya, had its heyday from the 15th to the early 19th centuries. Today it is a small fishing village. Its small rectangular reed houses are built in a completely different style from those in az-Zuhra. The few remaining (and rapidly decaying) Red Sea houses stand alongside the ruins of many others, reminding the visitor of the city's past importance. A major attraction is the central mosque, built by Ottoman Turks in the 19th century, with its three big domes and 14 smaller ones in two neat rows.

SUQ AL-KHAMIS سوق الخميس
(su:q al-khami:s)
About 40 km to the north of al-Qanawis and a couple of km off the main road is a small village that seems completely desolate for most of the week. The name of the village, Suq al-Khamis, literally means 'Thursday Market', and that's what it is – a marketplace with very few permanent dwellers. On Thursday mornings the village abounds with hundreds of traders and their customers from nearby villages. There are several hundred similar suqs in the northern Yemen but this one is the most important in the northern Tihama.

crossroads; the road to the right leads to Hajja.

AZ-ZUHRA الزهرة
(az-zuhra; al-Zuhrah)
Twenty-five km from al-Qanawis, a few km after you cross the Wadi Mawr, you will see a gravel road on your left. The road leads first to az-Zuhra and then on to al-Luhayya, 60 km off the main road.

There is nothing special to see in az-Zuhra, but the region's hundreds of round huts are the finest examples you will find of Tihami reed architecture of African origin. The huts may look primitive from a distance, but if you walk inside the village among the houses you suddenly feel very small. The biggest huts may be up to six metres in diameter and six metres high inside – hardly primitive!

If you are lucky enough to be invited inside a house, you will see that the floors and walls are completely surfaced with mud all the way up to the domed ceiling, leaving no visible sign of the reed structure. The walls are often painted with bright colours

Southern Tihama

The Tihami towns and villages of greatest historical and modern-day interest lie to the south of al-Hudayda.

AS-SUKHNA السخنة
(as-sukhna)
This small, modest bath resort in the foothills

of Jabal Bura' has a few hot springs and used to serve as one of the imams' winter palaces. There are persistent rumours that the present government has plans to develop this place into a tourist attraction.

To reach as-Sukhna you need to drive to the nondescript village of al-Mansuriya, 44 km south-east of al-Hudayda (YR 10 to YR 20 by bus or taxi), then take local transport along the 20-km gravel road north-east to the spa village.

BAYT AL-FAQIH   بيت الفقية
(bayt al-faqi:h; Bait, Beyt)

The system of weekly markets is well established in many countries and has operated for thousands of years. For obscure reasons, this system has developed to its extreme in the northern part of Yemen. In the early 1980s Western specialists and explorers doing fieldwork in the YAR catalogued more than 300 weekly markets, and the number is currently estimated at well over 500.

Contrary to expectation, the custom did not wane after the revolution and the result ing upheaval in the YAR's economy. (The system is not in use in the southern part of the country but I lack information on whether or not it existed there before the Communist revolution.) The street markets you see in those towns or villages which have asphalted roads operate every weekday. These markets are a new element in the economy, having developed mainly in the 1970s, but they have not suffocated the weekly markets. Instead, the systems seem to complement each other and, when the economy is boosted, both types benefit. In fact, both the number of weekly market sites and the number of traders operating in existing markets have been steadily rising since the revolution.

The goods sold at the weekly markets have traditionally been agricultural and handicraft products, and this remains very much true. In fact, the majority of traders at the weekly markets still belong to the subsistence sector of the economy. However, the relatively few traders who offer imported commodities already reap most of the riyals.

The Friday market of Bayt al-Faqih, established in the early 1700s as a trading point for coffee, is by far the most famous of Yemen's weekly markets. There was already a very small village here, founded in the 13th century by one Sheikh Ahmad ibn Musa of the 'Akk tribe from Wadi Zabid. Sheikh Ahmad travelled a great deal and was famed as a very wise man – hence the name of the town: 'House of the Wise Man'.

The town's location in central Tihama made it an ideal trading centre: it was easily accessible from the coffee-growing mountain areas and the ports were not far away. Trade in mocha coffee soon made Bayt al-Faqih famous among coffee-consuming Arabs all over the world. Carsten Niebuhr describes the place:

Traders from Hijaz, Persia, Egypt, Syria, Constantinople, Habash, Tunis, Fez and Morocco come to the market of Bayt al-Faqih to purchase the coffee beans, to send them from there via the ports of al-Makha and al-Hudayda further. Even buyers from India and sometimes from Europe meet here.

There are far fewer restrictions on photography in the Tihami culture and attitude than you'll find in the mountain villages, and the businesspeople of Bayt al-Faqih certainly understand the value of advertisement. Most people here are too busy to take up those horrible poses young Yemenis are so fond of and they are not likely to get angry at your camera exploits.

The cuppers are an exception to this rule. They practise their ancient art in open houses in the middle of the market. You can see several customers lying on beds, their naked backs covered with half a dozen or more small horns. The cupper sucks blood up into these horns through small incisions into the skin. The idea is to free the patient from 'bad blood' (considered to be the source of various ailments). The process is unquestionably somewhat intimate and photo-taking will definitely not be appreciated.

Orientation & Information
If you arrive by taxi, the driver will probably

take you straight to the 'supermarket'. If you come by bus, you will be left at the crossroads and will have to walk a km or so from the main road. The taxi fare to the market area should not be more than a couple of riyals.

Modern facilities are found along the main road, though there aren't too many of them here: a hospital for emergencies, a pharmacy and a petrol station – no post, no money exchange.

Apart from the market, there is little to see in Bayt al-Faqih. The town has rather modest Tihami brick houses; in the vicinity are hamlets of reed houses with mud walls. The Turkish-built fortress named Husn Uthman, in the centre of the town, can hardly be considered a sight.

The Market

The market is the attraction of Bayt al-Faqih. The market area is huge, consisting of both open-air spaces and covered alleys, with different areas for each type of goods. You can easily walk around for more than an hour without passing the same place twice. There must be well over 1000 traders.

Today coffee no longer makes up the bulk of the trade in Bayt al-Faqih. Instead, you can buy whatever products the Tihami agriculture or handicraft industry has to offer. Here's your chance to find some Yemeni pottery, colourful Tihami clothes and baskets. How about a camel, cow, donkey, lamb or chicken? All are going cheap. Fruit, vegetables or cereal? Anything you can imagine.

Places to Stay

I would not recommend that you stay overnight in Bayt al-Faqih. There is little to see on Friday evening, so why loiter around here after the market? On the other hand, if you are coming from Ta'izz, you might want to

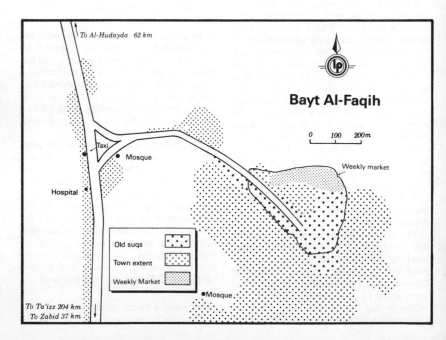

Bayt Al-Faqih

To Al-Hudayda 62 km

Taxi

Mosque

Hospital

0   100   200m

Weekly market

Old suqs

Town extent

Weekly Market

Mosque

To Ta'izz 204 km
To Zabid 37 km

arrive in Bayt al-Faqih Thursday evening to get an early start for your adventures in the marketplace. Be warned that you will not be the only one wanting accommodation then, so the places to stay will be crowded.

There really is nothing more than bottom-end accommodation in Bayt al-Faqih. There is no streetside hotel offering private rooms by the highway, just basic dormitories near the suq. YR 20 will get you a no-sheet bed, but don't ask for anything more.

Places to Eat

Lunch in Bayt al-Faqih is not such a bad idea – you are certainly not the only hungry person around, so food should be fresh and safe. Elsewhere in Tihama, eating would be a greater risk than in the highlands. Choose anything that boils, eat snacks from the market stalls and take full meals indoors – there is an alley full of restaurants. Try the soups; you are unlikely to be disappointed. If it is not a market day, you might want to resort to biscuits.

Getting There & Away

The easiest way to get to Bayt al-Faqih is from al-Hudayda; buses (YR 15) depart from al-Hudayda at 7 am and taxis (YR 25) leave at any time. The 55-km trip along a good asphalted road takes only an hour. En route you will see typical Tihama scenes but no particular sights – even the bigger town of al-Mansuriya lies a little way off the road. Some people count the Tihami petrol stations as sights. They are certainly quite imaginatively decorated, with their colourful neon lights making a very impressive display at night.

Coming from the direction of Ta'izz is less practical because it means that you have to stay overnight in some small Tihami town (offering only very modest accommodation) in order to get a glimpse of the market. The trading activities peak between 7 and 10 am, and even if you start from Ta'izz at 6 or 7 am (the first bus leaves at 7 am), it takes three or four hours to reach Bayt al-Faqih. By Friday afternoon the town is almost as quiet as it is during the rest of the week.

It is easy to leave Bayt al-Faqih at noon on Friday. There is no need to wait for a bus – just go to the taxi station and climb into a taxi that's headed in the right direction. It will start in a couple of minutes. Be sure to negotiate the price first; YR 15 should take you to Zabid, YR 25 to al-Hudayda and YR 60 to Ta'izz.

ZABID زبيد

(zabi:d; Zebid, Zebed)
About 37 km south of Bayt al-Faqih lies Zabid, a town with a remarkable past. It is one of the oldest towns in Yemen.

History

Little is known of life in the Tihama before the arrival of Islam, though it is certain that Wadi Zabid has been under cultivation from time immemorial. The Asha'ir tribe, who lived in the Tihama south of Wadi Rima' (the next major wadi north of Wadi Zabid), and the 'Akk tribe, who occupied the central Tihama north of Wadi Rima', adopted Islam during the Prophet's lifetime. The leader of the Asha'ir tribe, Sheikh Abu Musa bin Ash'ari, even visited the Prophet Muhammad in Madina; after his return, the sheikh built one of Yemen's very first mosques, near a well in Wadi Zabid.

Adopting Islam did not mean being loyal to the central rulers, and three major uprisings of the Tihami tribes were recorded in the earliest centuries of Islam. The first was put down in the days of Abu Bakr, the first of the Umayyad caliphs. In 819 AD the third revolt occurred. It was against the Abbasid caliphs and resulted in the appointment of Muhammad ibn 'Abdullah ibn Ziyad as governor of the region. It is to this man that the founding of Zabid town in 820 is credited. Eventually he made his rule independent of the caliphs who had given him power and, before long, he ruled 'the whole of Yemen' (whatever is meant by that – obviously, at least the Tihama).

Muhammad ibn Ziyad not only founded a town – he also founded a dynasty that lasted 200 years (820-1012) and an Islamic university that still partly functions.

The Arabic words for mosque (*ja:mi'*) and university (*ja:mi'a*) both derive from the same root verb (*jama'a* – to gather, collect, bring together), and the concepts are indeed intertwined. Within every mosque is a Koran school, its main function being to teach boys and girls to read and write. The final exam involves a recitation of the Koran in its entirety – by heart! The students learn this easily, as it is the only task they practise, even if the secrets of the alphabet are not fully grasped. Before the revolution, this was the only kind of education in Yemen. The illiteracy rate is still high, some 70% to 80%, even after more than a decade of modern schooling.

The university of Zabid was not just a Koran school but an ever-growing compound of all the schools and mosques of the town, leading to higher and higher education. Muhammad ibn Ziyad did not found the university alone; he brought a prominent Mufti, at-Taghlabi, from Baghdad for this task. Zabid soon became a famed centre of learning, attracting scholars from abroad. Some stayed for a short while, others for the whole of their lives. Those who left spread Zabid's fame – and Sunni teaching – across the Muslim world.

Naturally it was mostly questions relating to the creed and interpretations of Islamic law that were studied and taught in the university of Zabid. However, other disciplines included grammar, poetry, history and mathematics. The word 'algebra' has been attributed to a Zabidi scholar named Ahmad abu Musa al-Jaladi, who created a mathematical system he called al-Jabr.

The Ziyadid dynasty eventually ended and was replaced by lesser ones like the Najahids (1012-1153) and Mahdi'ids (1153-1173). Although Zabid was no longer the capital of 'the whole of Yemen', the university prospered. Even when the Ayyubids ruled Yemen from Egypt (1173-1229), the university continued to expand, reaching its peak during the Rasulid era (1229-1454). It is said that during this period, some 5000 students occupied the more than 200 schools and mosques of Zabid; the town was the absolute centre of learning for the southern part of the Islamic empire.

During the Tahirid rule (1454-1526) and the following decades of disorder, and especially during the first Ottoman occupation (1545-1636), the activities of the Zabid university began to diminish. The following centuries brought the Tihama several interregnums, when foreign conquerors landed in Yemen. Only the Zaydis of the mountains were finally able to successfully resist the outside forces, so the centre of Sunni teaching gradually lost its importance. Although there are still many mosques and Koran schools in Zabid today, they certainly don't form a university any more.

Orientation

The Zabid junction on the al-Hudayda to Ta'izz road will attract your attention because of its many trees. Wadi Zabid obviously has enough water to grow some pleasant shade trees – much needed, since the climate of Zabid is the hottest of the hot. Indeed, when the Tihamese around Zabid heard we were heading for Zabid, they warned against it and recommended a visit to al-Khawkha instead.

The town itself lies on the western side of the road, leaving only a few newly built commercial buildings and shacks by the roadside (though this area will no doubt develop into a modern housing centre in the far-too-near future). Walking along the alley that leads directly to the suq area of Zabid, you will notice a large square to your left, just before the town itself, with some imposing buildings behind it. This is the new government 'centre' of Zabid – the old centre is the suq.

Once you dive into the town, you'll find it easy to get lost. The alleys are winding and the blocks are closely built, with no visual axes or hills. Don't panic. Getting lost here is not a serious matter because the town is not that big; you will soon reach open fields, so it is not difficult to find your way back.

The city itself, inside its remaining walls, is quite a sight. Walking in the covered,

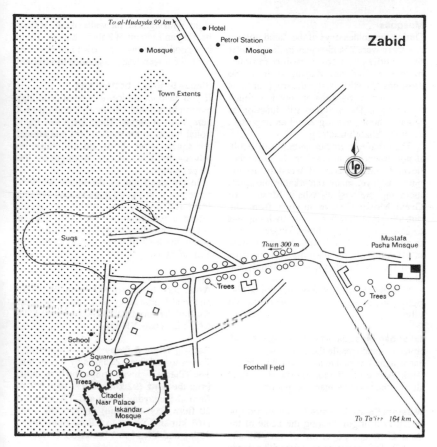

winding suq alleys, where small shops alternate with eating houses and tearooms, your sense of direction and dimension is soon distorted, making you very receptive to Zabid's atmosphere.

Houses

Once you're out of the suqs, the city appears reserved, with only a few children chasing you. This impression is created by the Zabid architects, who developed a unique style while trying to hide the wealth of the house-owners from passers-by: the bigger the house and the more splendid its interior, the more modest the street façade. The outer walls of the one or two-storey brick houses show little decoration or paint.

If you get a glimpse of the inner courtyards of the houses, the dazzling white, richly ornamented walls reveal the aesthetic preferences of the Zabid elite. Better still, if you get invited into a Zabid home (not very probable), you'll be struck by the great contrast between the inner grandeur and the outer simplicity of the construction and decoration.

Mosques

During the golden days of the Zabid university there were 236 mosques in Zabid. Over the centuries two out of every three mosques have vanished but Zabid, with its 86 mosques, is still extraordinary (San'a is famous for its 64 minarets but is a much larger city). The mosques still function as Koran schools, making Zabid an important centre of Shafa'i teaching.

The usual rule applies here: it is difficult, if not downright impossible, for a nonbeliever to enter places of worship. To the untrained eye, many remarkable mosques, including the vast al-Asha'ir Mosque, or Great Mosque, seem modest from the outside, since they don't raise their cupolas to great heights. Instead the mosques extend themselves over a wide area, but this feature is difficult to grasp when looking at a mosque from the nearby alleys; you're simply too close.

Perhaps the easiest mosques for a layperson to appreciate lie just outside the old city:

Iskandar Mosque with its 60-metre-high minaret stands inside the citadel walls, near the square. It is said to have been built by the Turk Alexander Ramoz (hence the name) during the first Ottoman occupation.

Mustafa Pasha Mosque is another mosque of Turkish origin, bearing the name of the first Ottoman governor of the Tihama (1540). This imposing mosque with a dozen cupolas stands on the eastern side of the Ta'izz to al-Hudayda highway, half a km out of town. It was one of the city mosques in earlier times but much of the city has since vanished, leaving only the mosque standing solemnly.

Nasr Palace

The palace by the citadel draws the attention of travellers because of its central location on the site of a much older Turkish building. The palace itself was built in the late 1800s and today serves as a government building, though it is obviously perceived as a tourist sight, with signs on the walls of the 1st floor bearing an account of Zabid's history. There is a good view over the town and environs from the tower. Entry is granted to visitors.

Places to Stay – bottom end

If you have no choice, it is possible to stay overnight in Zabid. However, it is always hot here, even at nights. There are a few traditional hotels in the market area and around the square – no sheets, no tap water, no privacy, but you can stay overnight for YR 20 per person.

In the small inn by the square we were presented with a guest book to sign. Judging from the mostly unprintable comments recorded by German travellers, the place was not up to middle-European standards. Still, this is the kind of hotel you will find near Yemeni markets (if you find anything at all).

Places to Stay – middle

A one-sheet hotel was built in the late 1980s on the al-Hudayda to Ta'izz Rd, a bit to the north of the petrol station. A quadruple room with a fan costs YR 120.

Getting There & Away

Travel to and from Zabid is by bus or taxi. The Tihama highway brings you here, either from the north (92 km and YR 30 to YR 40 from al-Hudayda, 37 km and YR 15 to YR 20 from Bayt al-Faqih) or from the south (161 km and YR 50 to YR 60 from Ta'izz, 35 km and YR 15 to YR 20 from Hays).

HAYS حيس
(Hays)
As you continue south from Zabid, you will pass a couple of towns with more examples of south Tihami brick architecture. Fourteen km from Zabid you reach Suq al-Jarrahi, a town with a Monday market, and 21 km further on is the town of Hays.

While neither of the towns possesses a glorious past, Hays is well worth visiting if you have a couple of extra hours. Sunday, market day, brings even more people into this very densely built, busy little town. Keep an eye open for those yellow and green glazed clay pots common in the northern part of Yemen; plenty of them are manufactured here, utilising techniques introduced by the Mamelukes in the 14th century.

Although the houses of Hays are smaller, on average, than those in Zabid, they are plastered very white with gypsum, causing the whole city to shine brightly in the sun. As in Zabid, the houses have rich decoration only on walls facing the inner courtyard.

AL-KHAWKHA الخوخة

(al-khawkha; al-Khokha, Khokhah, Cocha)
Al-Khawkha is the biggest fishing village on the southern coast of the Red Sea. The Yemenis, especially the Tihamese, are very fond of the place and many will highly recommend a visit to al-Khawkha if you talk with them about your travel plans. Guided tours that include the Tihama usually visit al-Khawkha, too.

Palm groves decorate the shores, the climate is more pleasant than that of inland Tihama (not so hot, though still windy), the waters lend themselves to a nice swim (but don't risk swimming past the reefs because there are sharks) and grilled fish is fresh and cheap. Moreover, camping is no problem here: the locals are used to it, and after a walk of a few km along the shores, you should be able to find a suitable place – if your tent is strong enough to withstand the wind.

On the other hand, this may not be what you came to see in Yemen. Al-Khawkha certainly is a sight to the Yemenis because it is very different from anything else in their country. Government tourist officials have seen how Europeans flock to places like the Seychelles or Maldives, so al-Khawkha seemed a way to make some bucks. However, they haven't invested a buck in the place themselves. If I were after this kind of holiday, I would choose the Seychelles instead.

Places to Stay
Although al-Khawkha is touted as a major holiday resort, the accommodation offered is primitive, to say the least. There are three main alternatives: sleep in the open, camp in your own tent or stay in a filthy no-sheet YR 10 funduq in the market area.

The General Tourist Corporation recommends a so-called *tourist village* (YR 100 per person per night, including meals) five km north of al-Khawkha. However, the walls of the huts are skeletal and the ground is bare, so staying here is almost the equivalent of sleeping in the open.

Some travellers report having found a new hotel about an hour's walk from the village, not far from the beach. This place, the *Abu Shar Hotel*, offers no-sheet dormitory beds for YR 20. While a few people have enjoyed their stay there, most visitors report that they would rather have slept in the open. However, even a hemp-strung Tihama bed is better than lying on the ground because it allows air to circulate freely around your body and keeps some distance between you and the scorpions.

Getting There & Away
The easiest way to reach al-Khawkha is to take a taxi from Hays. A seat should not cost you more than YR 15 but a whole taxi may be as much as YR 100. The trip is only 29 km and the road, while not asphalted, is rather good – though some may try to tell you otherwise.

Another road runs along the shore from al-Makha. This route is twice as long and carries virtually no regular traffic, so you would almost certainly have to hire a very expensive private car.

Ta'izz

The province of Ta'izz occupies the southernmost part of the former YAR, extending to the southern Tihama. Its port is al-Makha. A great part of the province is mountainous, with most towns and villages at an altitude of 1000 to 2000 metres. The mountains catch the first rains brought by the monsoon winds, so the climate is pleasant and the province is quite fertile, with great agricultural potential.

The region's inhabitants have long enjoyed a cosmopolitan status among the Yemenis because of the proximity of two main ports, al-Makha and Aden. For generations people from the Hujjariya district, to the south of Ta'izz city, have sailed to remote destinations, returning years, even decades, later. After the oil boom, they were among the first to join the mass migration of labour. Today the high mobility of the Hujjariya people also benefits domestic activities: plenty of shopkeepers and craftspeople in various northern towns and villages turn out to be of southern origin.

For the traveller, the province includes several historical sites, from the al-Makha port to the al-Janad mosque. You can also take scenic drives in the Hujjariya or Jabal Sabir, although they offer nothing especially breathtaking – certainly there are more spectacular mountains and villages with older buildings in the upper Yemen. However, if you have the time, you will find spending a couple of days in the province of Ta'izz interesting.

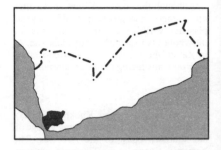

AL-MAKHA المخا

(al-makha:; al-Mukha, Mocha, Mokka)
This old coffee port in the southernmost part of Tihama continues to attract visitors because of its fame from times long gone. Al-Makha today is a small village with few (if any) attractions. As one disappointed visitor put it, al-Makha is 'for name-addicted romantics only'. A couple of hours should be enough to walk through all the streets and still leave you plenty of time to admire the waves of the Red Sea. But hopefully not the sunset, beautiful as it is, because there are no facilities for an overnight stay.

Al-Makha was the YAR's second most important international port. Even so, its importance was negligible and the village's main claim to fame was as the Republic's main smuggling port, especially for booze from Djibouti. Plans to develop the port were scrapped after the unification in 1990, when Aden became the most important port of the new Republic of Yemen. The major power plant, built nearby in the mid-1980s, will probably never be needed for the port of al-Makha.

History

There was already a major port somewhere around here in Himyarite times, before Islam. Little is known of al-Makha's early development, however; the first written documents date from the early 1400s. By the time Europeans appeared in these waters, al-Makha was already a prospering city.

In 1616 a Dutch visitor to al-Makha, Pieter van der Broecke, noted a caravan of 1000 camels carrying goods imported from as far away as Hungary and Venice. Exports through al-Makha included fruit, cloth, spices, dyes, pottery and, most importantly, coffee, grown in the Yemeni mountains and the latest craze in Europe.

Two years later the English and Dutch built al-Makha's first coffee factories. They were soon followed by other Europeans, even Americans. By the 1630s coffee houses were being opened in Venice, Amsterdam and elsewhere, and the demand for coffee rose to such heights that Yemen was no longer able, on its own, to meet it. Prices soared, bringing prosperity to the coffee merchants of al-Makha, who built gorgeous villas in the city.

During those years Yemen had a virtual world monopoly on the beans, to the extent that the trade name 'Mocha coffee' has survived to the present day. Eventually, however, the plant was smuggled out of the country, and new plantations were growing in Ceylon (now Sri Lanka) and Java by the early 1700s. The monopoly was broken and the decline of al-Makha had begun. The final blow came in 1839, when the British captured Aden and started to develop it as the main port of southern Arabia, robbing al-Makha of the remaining trade.

Coffee is still grown in the mountains of Yemen, although farmers derive greater profits from qat. The restoration of the coffee trade is a much-argued issue among those foreigners working in development-aid projects and wanting to see coffee plants once again filling Yemeni mountain slopes instead of qat.

Things to See

The ash-Shadhli mosque, with its beautiful Zabid-influenced architecture, is about 500 years old. Ruins of the coffee merchants' villas also bear interesting ornaments in the Tihami style. Most villas have already shrunk to sand-covered rubble – there are many such heaps around.

Studiu Finus (Studio Venus), in the centre of the village, probably exists to offer entertainment to sailors visiting al-Makha; it was closed during our visit.

Places to Stay

There are a couple of teahouses in the centre of al-Makha but the village has no overnight accommodation.

Getting There & Away

Buses don't serve al-Makha. The easiest way to reach the village is by taxi from Ta'izz, a 105-km ride on a good asphalted road. A seat in a taxi should not cost you more than YR 40 to YR 50. However, traffic to al-Makha is not heavy, so you might have to wait an hour or more for the car to fill up – and just as long in al-Makha to get back! I suggest that you leave for al-Makha early in the morning to be sure of getting back without any problems.

If you are travelling southwards along the Tihama highway, you might consider getting out at Mafraq al-Makha (the al-Makha junction), 70 km from Hays, to wait for a ride to al-Makha. The village is actually a couple of km north of the crossroads, so watch for the right place to get out of the car.

TA'IZZ تعز

(ta'izz; Taiz, Tais)

Although it is another former capital of Yemen, Ta'izz is a relatively young city by Yemeni standards and has a mostly modern, almost European appearance. Most of the architecture in Ta'izz is postrevolutionary – concrete apartment buildings with painted walls. However, the town does have very old quarters and many beautiful old mosques dating from the Rasulid era, so a walk in the old town is quite worthwhile.

Ta'izz is dramatically located at an altitude of 1400 metres, in the northern foothills of Jabal Sabir, the province's highest mountain. The city has a definite charm – quite unlike al-Hudayda, for example.

History

Historians are not certain when and by whom Ta'izz was founded. Although Mt Sabir was already inhabited in pre-Islamic times, the first written record of the town named Ta'izz dates from 1175 AD. By then Ta'izz must have existed for 100 years or so, since the Ayyubid ruler Turan Shah, after conquering the Mahdi'ids in Zabid, decided to live in Ta'izz. Zabid remained the Ayyubid capital, but for a man of Egyptian origin, the climate of Ta'izz was much more pleasant, especially during the summer.

After the Ayyubids the southern parts of Yemen fell into the hands of the Rasulids (1229-1454), who ruled the southern mountains and Tihama from Ta'izz. Occasionally their kingdom spread as far north as Mecca and as far east as Oman, so Ta'izz was unquestionably Yemen's capital during the Rasulid era. The city prospered greatly under the Rasulids; fortifications were built, mosques were constructed, water was brought to the city by means of an aqueduct from Mt Sabir and the city became a remarkable trade centre.

The period of Rasulid rule was followed by the 'dark centuries', during which Ta'izz fell to various foreign conquerors and local rulers. The Ottoman Turks often invaded the highlands via Ta'izz and, in the years of defeat, were sometimes able to hold the city even when the northern mountains, with their Zaydi population, were lost.

In the 20th century Ta'izz was again made the capital of Yemen, after a power struggle in 1948. The 'Free Yemenis', a group opposing imamic rule, was organised in Aden. The Free Yemenis consisted mainly of Shafa'i merchants of the south but also included a Zaydi leader, Muhammad Mahmud az-Zubayri. In early 1948 the group succeeded in assassinating Imam Yahya and proclaimed an imam of their own choosing, Abdullah al-Wazir, in San'a. However, with Saudi support, Yahya's son Ahmad soon defeated the rebels and became the imam of Yemen.

Imam Ahmad made Ta'izz his residence and the new capital of Yemen, never returning to San'a. Much of the current prosperity of Ta'izz thus derives from the period between 1948 and the 1962 revolution. Even during the civil war (fought mainly in the north) Ta'izz served as a 'second capital' of Yemen, and most of the foreign diplomatic missions moved to San'a only in the early 1970s.

Orientation & Information

Ta'izz is not the easiest city to find your way around. Because it is built in a hilly area, the streets of this vast city wind up and down, left and right. Without a map, you can easily get lost. Keep in mind that the huge and highly visible Mt Sabir stands to the south.

Two long streets wind their way through the city in an east-west direction. Gamal Abdul Nasser St serves as the main thoroughfare and buses leave you at either end of the street, depending on the direction you came from. The smaller 26th September St passes by the walls of the old city, further to the south. At one point, near the Haud al-Ashraf part of town, the streets run very close to each other. There are plenty of hotels and restaurants in this region.

Tourist Office There is an office of the General Tourist Corporation (spelt Coropration) on Gamal Abdul Nasser St, some 200 metres from its junction with San'a St, where the San'a bus leaves you. The staff here are very helpful; they have few customers and show genuine interest in solving any problems you might have.

Money Banks are the best place to change money in Ta'izz. Yemeni riyals can reportedly be bought from the moneychangers in the old suqs, in the immediate vicinity of Bab al-Kabir, but this has become more difficult since private money exchange was made illegal in 1987. Some of the moneychangers here also run a shop selling silver jewellery – that's called synergy!

Post The post office is in Haud al-Ashraf, opposite the main bus office.

Telephone If you have to phone home or wire for more money, the Cable & Wireless office, on 26th September St, is open from 7.30 am to 8.30 pm – exceptional hours in Yemen, where people only work in the morning!

Maps A map of Ta'izz was published by the General Tourist Corporation in 1982. It details the city in 1:10,000 scale and the centre in 1:5000 scale. On the other side is a map of the province in 1:250,000 scale.

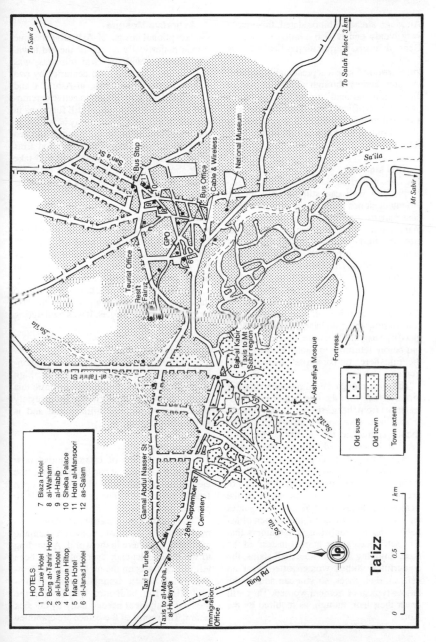

HOTELS

1 DeLuxe Hotel
2 Borg at-Tahrir Hotel
3 al-Ikhwa Hotel
4 Pensoun Hiltop
5 Marib Hotel
6 al-Janad Hotel
7 Blaza Hotel
8 al-Waham
9 al-Habib
10 Sheba Palace
11 Hotel al-Mansoori
12 as-Salam

To San'a
To Salah Palace 3 km
San'a St
Bus Stop
Bus Office
Cable & Wireless
National Museum
Sa'ila
Mt Sabir
GPO
Tourist Office
Rest
Fairuz
Sa'ila
Bab al-Kabir
Taxis to Mt Sabir region
Al-Ashrafiya Mosque
Fortress
al-Tahrir St
Gamal Abdul Nasser St
26th September St
Cemetery
Sa'ila
Sa'ila
Taxi to Turba
Taxis to al-Macha, al-Hudayda
Immigration Office
Ring Rd

Old sucs
Old town
Town extent

Ta'izz

0   0.5   1 km

Although already a bit outdated, this map is very handy and is also available from the General Tourist Corporation office in San'a.

Immigration Since it is presumably possible to enter Yemen through al-Makha port or Ta'izz 'international' airport, the city has an immigration office. This is useful if you need a visa extension. The office is inconveniently located out of the town centre, on the Ring Rd.

Central Market

The old town of Ta'izz was walled and parts of the city wall can still be seen on the mountain slopes south of the city. The liveliest part of the old town is definitely the market area by the northern wall of the old city. The market is not big – just a couple of parallel alleys joining the wall's two main gates, Bab Musa (the Gate of Sheikh Musa) and Bab al-Kabir (the Great Gate) – but it is interesting. Most of the items sold in the San'a suqs can be bought here, some at slightly lower prices. If you are seriously considering the purchase of some pricey piece of Yemeni silverware, check the Ta'izz suq before returning to San'a. Bargaining is the rule here, unlike most other suqs of Yemen.

The wide range of food products on offer includes fish from the Red Sea and subtropical fruits from the nearby wadis and Tihama. If you have developed a taste for qat, you should appreciate the quality of the stuff here. It is advertised that the best qat in Yemen grows on the slopes of Mt Sabir.

By the way, keep an eye on the gender of the merchants in this market; they are not exclusively male, as in most areas of the Yemeni highlands. Most Yemeni tour guides are eager to tell you about the women of Mt Sabir, who are such tough bargainers that they sell goods at the market instead of the men. Enjoying such a 'liberated' status, the colourfully clothed women often wear no veils on their faces, so you can admire the tattoos typical of Yemeni women. They still cover their hair, though, as required by the Koran.

Al-Ashrafiya Mosque

Of exceptional design, al-Ashrafiya mosque stands majestically on top of the old town. The mosque, with its twin minarets, was built in the 13th and 14th centuries by two followers of Turan Shah, al-Ashraf I and al-Ashraf II. It is no longer in active ceremonial use but a Koran school still functions in the side-building. Children may be willing to guide you around in the afternoon. If allowed in, women should cover their hair and arms before entering and all visitors should take their shoes off. From the minaret there are wonderful views over the old town and its many mosques.

Other Mosques

West of al-Ashrafiya is another remarkable mosque, al-Mu'tabiya, built in the 16th century. Although this mosque was built by the Turks, its style, with many cupolas but no minaret, is borrowed from Egypt.

Also visible is al-Mudhaffar mosque, to the south of al-Ashrafiya, with one minaret and more than 20 cupolas. It was built during the 13th century.

The Fortress of Cairo

The fortress, or Qal'at al-Qahira (Unconquerable Fortress), stands on a cliff, high above the city. You will have to admire this much-advertised 'sight' from a distance only because it is still in military use and is impossible to enter.

National Museum

The former palace of Imam Ahmad now serves as a museum. It can be found near the eastern end of 26th September St and is open from 8 am to noon. The entry fee is YR 10 per person.

'The monument of antirevolution', this must be one of the most impressive thematic museums anywhere in the world. According to the official legend, everything has been left just as it was on the night of 26 September 1962, when Imam Ahmad died – including the bedroom filled with the medical equipment needed daily by the sick imam. The rooms of the palace are crammed

Top: Zaydi graveyard in Sa'da
Left: Selling watermelons in Bayt al-Faqih market
Right: Street scene in Say'un

Top: Typical old settlement on the slopes of Mt Sabir
Left: The Mosque of Arwa in Jibla
Right: The solemn beauty of al-Janad Mosque

with an astonishing abundance of earthly wealth – wardrobes, perfumes, guns, radios, presents from contemporary rulers – obviously preserved on an 'as is' basis to demonstrate the social injustice of imamic rule.

Visitors born before the early 1950s will experience an eerie sense of *déjà vu* here, since many common Western household utensils from the 1940s and 1950s are on show as exotic parts of a rare collection.

Salah Palace
Another former palace of the imam since converted into a national museum, Salah Palace stands on the eastern outskirts of Ta'izz. A taxi will take you there from anywhere in the city for about YR 15. Minibuses shuttle continuously along Salah Rd; the fare is YR 2.

This museum is planned more traditionally than the National Museum; there are glass showcases with old silverware like jambiyas and dhumas, a collection of coins, manuscripts of the Koran, clothes, original government documents and photographs of Imam Ahmad. Note the bulging eyes; Ahmad was famed as a cruel ruler and it was generally believed that as a young man, he had practised throttling himself to cultivate this fierce appearance.

On the walls, aerial photographs from around the early 1960s show the former YAR's major towns: San'a, al-Mahwit, Hajja, Sa'da, Dhamar, Yarim, Ibb, al-Hudayda, Zabid, Ta'izz, even al-Makha. These very interesting photos give the layouts of all the old Islamic cities for which you can't buy a map. Too bad snapping photos in the museums is mamnu'.

The only zoo in Yemen is part of the Salah Palace. The few small cages feature (offspring of?) the lions of the imam, as well as a couple of other species, like jackals. You can't blame the Yemenis for not having a bigger zoo – theirs is one of the poorest countries in the world as far as wildlife goes.

Both the museum and the zoo charge separate entry fees of YR 10 and are only open before noon.

Places to Stay
As the third largest city in Yemen and with well over 300,000 inhabitants, Ta'izz has plenty of hotels to choose from.

Places to Stay – bottom end
Between the San'a bus stop and the central bus office, there are plenty of cheap, one-sheet hotels with double to quadruple rooms. *Al-Waham*, for example, offers beds in quadruple rooms for YR 30 each; the common bathrooms are filthy, with cold shower only. Around the corner the *al-Habib* offers double rooms with private bathrooms for YR 80 ; it's much cleaner but has cold showers only.

At the corner of San'a St and Gamal Abdul Nasser St is the *as-Salam Hotel*, tempting tourists getting off the San'a bus. The hotel has obviously improved its sanitary standards since the first edition of this book, since many travellers have reported it to be clean. A single goes for YR 60, a double for YR 100.

At the very bottom end, no-sheet dormitories are easy to find in the vicinity of the bus stops from both the San'a and al-Hudayda directions. Just ask anybody: *mumkin tiqu:l-li wayn funduq rakhi:s?*

Places to Stay – middle
If you get into a taxi and ask for a hotel, you will probably be driven to the *DeLuxe Hotel* (☎ 226251), on Gamal Abdul Nasser St, north of Bab al-Kabir. This huge hotel with plenty of rooms is conveniently situated near the old town. While there's nothing deluxe here, this is an acceptable two-sheet hotel with private bathrooms. Prices are in the YR 80 to YR 100 per person range. Check the boiler before accepting a room.

Nearby is *Borg at-Tahrir Hotel* (☎ 221482), on at-Tahrir St, some 100 metres north of the Gamal Abdul Nasser St intersection. This two-sheet hotel has clean common bathrooms and charges YR 150/250 for singles/doubles.

Other similarly priced hotels in the upper middle range include the *Blaza Hotel* (Plaza? ☎ 220224) and the *al-Janad Hotel* (☎

210529) close to the bus office, towards the centre of the city. These comfortable hotels are smaller, however, and tend to be fully booked in advance. Prices for a double are around YR 200.

Heading towards San'a St from the bus office there are a couple of satisfactory two-sheet hotels: *Sheba Palace* and *Hotel al-Mansoori*.

Places to Stay – top end
There is a concentration of more expensive hotels on the al-Dabwa mountain, a hill north of the Haud al-Ashraf, on the opposite side of Gamal Abdul Nasser St: the top-class *Marib Hotel* (☎ 210350) offers you Western-style accommodation for up to YR 600 per person. The *al-Ikhwa Hotel* (or *al Ekhoh*, as the Ta'izz map spells it, ☎ 210364) is cheaper, at YR 350 a double, but definitely not as clean. Both hotels have singles and doubles available.

The *Pensoun Hiltop* (or *Hel Top Hotel*, according to the Ta'izz map) is on the same hill. This is a slowly decaying place, originally in the same category as the other two, but neglected ever since it was built. However, it's much better value for money: YR 185 for a double with private bath.

An additional benefit here is a nice view over the city. Even if you stay elsewhere, it pays to visit this hill with a camera.

In 1990 an old building on the way to Mt Sabir was being renovated into a new deluxe-class hotel.

Places to Eat
Ta'izz has plenty of eateries evenly distributed around the modern city. There are several on Gamal Abdul Nasser St, ranging from *Superman* to simple shacks selling grilled chicken on the street. Uphill from the DeLuxe Hotel, a place named *Restaurant* serves pretty good French-style food at prices only slightly higher than those of the Yemeni eateries.

A Ta'izzian phenomenon are the so-called 'park restaurants' – there are a few within easy reach of the DeLuxe Hotel.

The exceptionally tidy *Restaurant Fairuz*, in the Haud al-Ashraf area, serves Lebanese food. It lies on the nameless street that continues down the hill from the Ma'rib and al-Ikhwa hotels, across Gamal Abdul Nasser St.

Getting There & Away
It's easy to get to Ta'izz from San'a or al-Hudayda. The Ta'izz airport is north of the city, 20 km along the San'a road.

Bus For bus connections, see the table of bus lines in the Getting Around chapter. Several buses leave daily for al-Hudayda and San'a. Tickets can be bought in the bus or from the bus office before you enter the bus.

Taxi Taxis are also easy to find, with fares 10% to 15% above those of the buses. If you come from San'a, I recommend that you sit on the right-hand side of the vehicle. This makes it easier to watch the spectacular scenery of the mountain stretches, especially the Sumarra Pass.

There are separate taxi stations for taxis heading in different directions. Taxis to al-Hudayda (and to al-Makha and at-Turba) wait at the corner of 26th September and Gamal Abdul Nasser streets, while taxis going in the San'a and Aden direction wait at the junction of the San'a and Aden roads.

When trying to get a city taxi to the station, be careful not to accept offers to drive you all the way to your destination (YR 1500 to San'a, for example); YR 10 should be enough to reach the station.

Getting Around
Unlike San'a, Ta'izz has no city buses. Instead, black-striped minibuses shuttle along Gamal Abdul Nasser St, 26th September St and other longish streets. The fare is YR 2 to YR 4 per person, according to the length of the ride. If you don't fix the price beforehand, you may well pay YR 6.

AROUND TA'IZZ
You can make a couple of short excursions in the area around Ta'izz.

Jabal Sabir   جبل صبر

The high mountain to the south of Ta'izz has been inhabited from times beyond living memory and, even today, it is under heavy cultivation, with terraces of qat and other crops stretching to the very top of the 3006-metre peak. Depending on the weather, the views to the Ta'izz area can be extraordinary or completely obscured by clouds. In the rainy seasons, however, the weather changes rapidly.

The 1600 metre change in altitude means a significant drop (between 8°C and 16°C) in temperature, so be sure you have enough clothing when starting for the windy mountaintop.

The road up the mountain is not asphalted; in fact it is very bumpy. The 4WD taxis start their 1½ hour climb from Bab al-Kabir, and a seat may cost you YR 30. This is not robbery, given the circumstances, although the trip is only six km. Ask for a village called al-Ar'us – it is nearest to the summit. Army camps are often held somewhere near the top of the mountain, making it impossible for a tourist to ascend to the highest peaks.

Sitting in a taxi is not exactly enjoyable here, so you might consider walking back. This also gives you a better chance to admire the green terraced slopes covered in roses and other bushes. However, remember that if it rains here, it will rain in the afternoon.

Hujjariya   حجرية

(Hujjariya; Huggariyah)

A trip to the Hujjariya countryside can best be made by visiting at-Turba, the southernmost town in the area of the former YAR to which you can travel.

Taxis to at-Turba leave from the western taxi station in Ta'izz (see the Ta'izz map). A seat for the 1½ hour trip should not cost more than YR 40. Beside the road you can see perhaps the biggest tree in Yemen, a baobab (Adansonia digitata) with a trunk circumference of 20½ metres. There are some other places of interest, too.

Suq adh-Dhabab   سوق الضباب

After the at-Turba junction the asphalted road soon descends into a very green wadi (one of the upper branches of the Wadi Bani Khawlan) between Jabal Sabir and Jabal Habashi. The Suq adh-Dhabab village has a lively Sunday market here. As you pass through this valley, with its palms and philodendrons, you will find it easy to guess the origins of the subtropical fruits in the Ta'izz market. Many families from around Ta'izz like to come here to wash clothes or just to have a nice time.

Yifrus   يفرس

(yifrus; Yufrus, Yafrus)

A few km further on, the road again descends to cross the Wadi Bani Khawlan. Twenty-two km from the at-Turba crossroads, a small dirt road crosses to the right. This road leads to a village named Yifrus, famed for its 500-year-old mosque. The white mosque is a real beauty, visible long before you reach the village, even from the at-Turba road.

According to the scriptures, this mosque was built by the last Tahirid ruler ('Amir bin 'Abd al-Wahab) to honour a learned man and scholar, Ahmad ibn Alwan. Ahmad lived in Yifrus during the Rasulid era and wrote many books on Sufism and Sunni law.

The mosque is still in full operation, and the original three-km aqueduct brings water to it. You will probably not be allowed in (we were allowed into the courtyard, by the ablution pool), but the mosque is a sight anyway, with its beautifully balanced cupola and minaret.

At-Turba   التربة

(at-turba; al-Turbah)

Beyond the Yifrus junction, the at-Turba road rises through Naqil Hasus (the Hasus Pass), at 1400 metres, to the very stony Hujjariya plateau. The name Hujjariya literally means 'stony' and you will easily grant this name to the region during the next 50 km to at-Turba. The tree species around at-Turba are perhaps more reminiscent of African savanna than any other area in Yemen.

The at-Turba village is not very big. Its modest stone houses, few more than three storeys high, have few decorations, the most notable curiosity being the clearly protruding waste shafts on many of them.

More spectacular than the village is its location on a steep cliff. The huge Wadi al-Maqatira, which flows towards the Indian Ocean, has eaten its way some 800 metres into the base rock, and many houses have been built on the very edge of the cliff. Here more than anywhere, the Yemeni fondness for dramatic locations has dictated the site. In clear weather you can see deep into the Lahej governorate in southern Yemen.

Al-Janad الجند

(al-janad; Ganad)

Al-Janad, near the Ta'izz airport, is a poor village with only a few clusters of modest, one-storeyed houses. It attracts a steady flow of travellers, both Muslim and non-Muslim because it is the site of Yemen's oldest mosque – or a mosque at least as old as the Grand Mosque of San'a. Both were originally built before the Prophet's death in 632 AD and, since then, have been renovated and enlarged many times.

The mosque has a 70-metre-high minaret. Inside, a tranquil atmosphere prevails, encouraged by a certain asceticism of construction. An open rectangular square is surrounded by halls with white stone arches and pillars. There is almost no decoration – just the solemn feel of a holy place.

Many tourist groups are shown this mosque, so the imam of al-Janad has grown used to visitors. If it is not prayer time, you will probably be allowed to enter, as long as you are properly clothed. Take your shoes off first, and give the imam some baksheesh as you leave.

Getting There & Away It is fairly easy to reach al-Janad from Ta'izz. From the San'a taxi station, get a seat in a short-haul taxi up to Mafraq al-Janad. (In this region, to the south of the Sumarra Pass, 'j' is pronounced like the 'g' in 'girl'.) A typical price is YR 10 to YR 15 (six km). No taxis go to al-Janad, but for a few YR (or even for free), virtually any passer-by will take you on the five-km ride.

Coming back, you can return to Ta'izz or go on in the direction of Ibb. The taxis will probably take you from Mafraq al-Janad to al-Qa'ida for YR 10 to YR 15 (12 km). From there you can continue to Ibb (YR 20 for the 36-km trip is typical).

Ibb

The province of Ibb, to the north-east of Ta'izz, stands at the top of the lower Yemen. Most of its area is at altitudes above 1500 metres and some of it is more than twice that high. The highest peaks are Jabal Ta'kar (3230 metres), south of the town of Jibla, and a 3350-metre mountain no map seems to know the name of, north-east of the town of Ibb.

Ibb is known as 'the fertile province' because it gathers most of the rains brought to Yemen by southern winds, five to 10 times more than Ma'rib. Ibb receives rainfall of 1500 mm between late May and early September, when it rains almost every afternoon. There are also occasional showers during the winter months. On a typical summer afternoon, moving around in the open is very impractical because torrents of water flood the streets and roads – something you'd hardly anticipate in Arabia!

Nicknames like 'the Green Land of Arabia' do not exaggerate – the slopes are terraced from the bottoms of the valleys to the tops of the mountains, where it's not too steep. The terraces are very old and some have been here for 1000 years. With water available throughout the year, the fields are harvested three or four times annually. Every imaginable crop, from dates and grain to coffee and qat, can be cultivated somewhere in this province which serves as the granary of Yemen.

IBB اب

('ibb; Ebb)

The capital of the province, Ibb, was built on a hilltop (altitude 1850 metres) near a valley that cuts through the mountain ridge from north-west to south-east. Recently the growing town has spread all the way down to the valley, transforming arable land into streets and buildings – a common occurrence in growing Yemeni cities and towns, which originally served as settlements for farmers cultivating the surrounding land. The busy

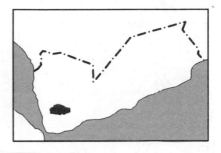

town had 35,000 inhabitants in 1981 but probably has many times that number now.

The architecture of Ibb features the stone tower houses common in the Yemeni mountains. Traditionally, buildings have been made from local grey or pink-toned stone but postrevolutionary construction favours the more easily cut orange lava rock which is transported 80 km from the north.

Orientation & Information

The tarmac road between San'a and Ta'izz no longer passes through the modern centre of Ibb. When the Ibb to al-'Udayn asphalt road was built in the late 1980s, the highway was diverted to pass a couple of km west of Ibb. If you arrive by bus, you will get off at the junction of these roads; look for a black-striped taxi to take you to the town centre for a few riyals.

Basic services (restaurants, hotels and petrol stations) can be found in the centre, within 10 minutes walk of the al-'Udayn road's junction with the old highway. The new centre, just below the old town, is rapidly expanding along the al-'Udayn road. Eventually the road may continue to Suq al-Jarrahi, near Zabid, where a dirt road already leads from al-'Udayn, but I know of no plan as yet.

Market day in Ibb is Saturday, when you

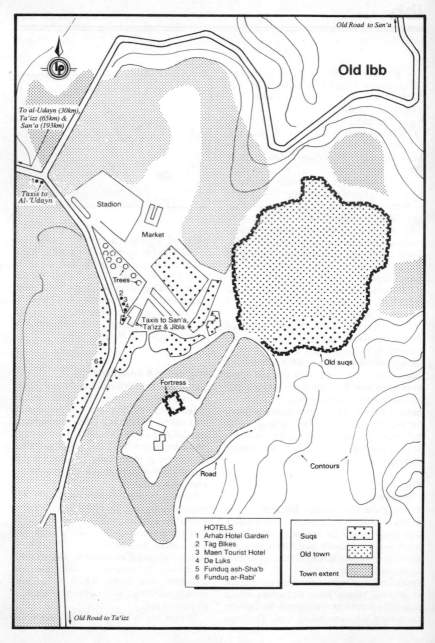

Old Road to San'a

Old Ibb

To al-Udayn (30km),
Ta'izz (65km) &
San'a (193km)

1
Taxis to
Al-'Udayn

Stadion

Market

Trees

2
3
4
Taxis to San'a,
Ta'izz & Jibla

5

6

Old suqs

Fortress

Contours

Road

Old Road to Ta'izz

HOTELS
1 Arhab Hotel Garden
2 Tag Blkes
3 Maen Tourist Hotel
4 De Luks
5 Funduq ash-Sha'b
6 Funduq ar-Rabi'

Suqs

Old town

Town extent

can observe the province's great variety of agricultural products.

Things to See

Ibb is often neglected by tourists, even though many travellers stop here en route to nearby Jibla. However, the old town inside the almost intact city wall is certainly worth a walk. Take the uphill street from the central market area or from the taxi station.

The stone-paved streets that crisscross the hilltop are often so narrow that you can't pass around a donkey. The four or five-storeyed stone houses are unpainted, with occasional lime plastering in the footings and window openings. Decoration is sparse but effective: friezes and tiny, round, alabaster-paned windows grouped in twos, threes or fives in arched openings. Old Ibb is a very well-preserved example of the traditional rock architecture of the Yemeni highlands.

The old fortress on top of the neighbouring hilltop is for government use and cannot be entered nor approached too closely.

Places to Stay

As a rapidly developing provincial capital, Ibb has a selection of hotels, most of them along the old San'a to Ta'izz road. There are no top-end hotels.

Places to Stay – bottom end

There are plenty of one-sheet and two-sheet hotels within 100 metres of the street junction which is used as a station by taxis to Jibla and San'a. These places offer beds in double or triple rooms for around YR 20 to YR 40. Here are some examples.

De Luks, nearest to the taxi station, is entered from the upper street. This is certainly not a deluxe-class hotel, lacking more than a little in the area of cleanliness. One-sheet doubles go for YR 80, with common bathrooms in the corridors. The staff advertised hot water but were not able to demonstrate its existence.

The two-sheet *Maen Tourist Hotel* and one-sheet *Taj Blkes* (Ma'in and Taj Bilqis), the next hotels along the San'a road, are

essentially the same as De Luks, though they do offer private bathrooms (cold water only).

Continuing in the Ta'izz direction, *Funduq ash-Sha'b* (winding stairs to the 2nd floor from the street), is what its name promises: a people's hotel. A bed in the dormitory costs YR 10, while a bed in a quadruple room is YR 20. There is no shower but a cold-water tap and bucket are provided. The neighbouring *Funduq ar-Rabi'*, another choice in this category, has nothing smaller than triple rooms.

Places to Stay – middle

At the time of our visit there was only one hotel offering a warm shower: the *Arhab Hotel Garden*, which also spells its name *Alrehab*. This two-sheet hotel was built in the late 1980s and was very clean at the time of our visit in 1990. A double costs YR 120. The 'garden' is probably the modern teahouse between the hotel and the junction of the old San'a to Ta'izz Rd with the new al-'Udayn Rd.

Places to Eat

Try any crowded restaurant on the main road; I found no difference between them. *Mat'am biswas (Restaurant Hot Pepper)*, a km or so in the Ta'izz direction on the old San'a to Ta'izz Rd, lives up to its name, offering very tasty food. Spend YR 2 to get there in a black-striped minibus.

Getting There & Away

You will arrive in Ibb along the north-south highway. The bus fare from San'a (193 km) is YR 60 to YR 65, from Ta'izz (65 km) YR 40. Buses leave you at the new San'a to Ta'izz road's junction with the al-'Udayn road; take a black-striped taxi or minibus into the centre *(markaz)* of Ibb. Green-striped taxis also run frequently along this stretch and will often take you to the very centrum. For a seat in a shared taxi, add YR 20 from San'a and YR 10 from Ta'izz.

About 10 km before you reach Ibb, the views from the road are spectacular, with some of the most dramatic mountains in all of Yemen. Approaching Ibb from the north, the road ascends to an altitude of 2800 metres at the Sumarra Pass, about 45 km before Ibb; 20 km to the south of Ibb there is the Sayyani Pass at an altitude of 2400 metres. For photographs, it is best to sit on the western side (right-hand side from San'a).

For transport from Ibb to either Ta'izz or San'a, go to the new San'a to Ta'izz Rd and hail a bus there.

The green-striped taxis are a more convenient alternative if you are leaving from the very centre of Ibb.

Getting Around
Walk. Black-striped taxis also shuttle along the main roads.

JIBLA جبلة
(jibla; Jiblah, Giblah)
A small town with a big history, Jibla is only eight km from Ibb and three km from the Ta'izz road.

History
Jibla is another former capital of Yemen, or at least of the highlands. From 1064 to 1138 the region was ruled by the Sulayhids, a dynasty founded by 'Ali as-Sulayhi. He was a devout Muslim whose doctrine was called Fatimism, an Ismaili branch of the Shi'a sect of Islam. In 1064, after 15 years of preaching, he had attracted enough followers to proclaim his way the right one. Eventually, he founded an independent state, his immediate rivals being the Najahids of Zabid and the Zaydi imams of Sa'da. After starting his revolution on Mt Masar, in the Haraz region near present-day Manakha, he ruled the country from San'a.

In 1067 King 'Ali was killed while on pilgrimage to Mecca and his son Mukarram became the new king. However, when Mukarram became seriously ill soon afterwards, his wife, Arwa bint Ahmad, took over the role of head of state. When Mukarram died a few years later, she became queen, ruling until her death, in 1138, at the age of 92. Although she died without issue and the Sulayhi state soon dissolved, her influence was profound.

One of the very first tasks Queen Arwa performed was to move the capital of the Sulayhi state to Jibla. During her reign the town flourished and the foundations of the Big Mosque of Jibla, enlarged many times since, were laid. The ancient terraces on the slopes of the neighbouring mountains were greatly developed in Queen Arwa's days. She was a learned and wise woman, spending the state budget for the common benefit of her people. After 850 years the region of Jibla still bears signs of prosperity and welfare.

Things to See
Jibla is attractively located on a basalt hill between two wadis that join immediately under the town. After crossing the bridge you come to a road leading into the town. Take the first street to the left, just after the town funduq and before a small mosque. You will come to the suqs and, eventually, to the Mosque of Queen Arwa.

The mosque is a big one with two minarets. It was built by Queen Arwa, who is buried by the northern wall of the prayer hall, next to the mihrab, which is decorated in Persian style. Her gravestone bears inscriptions in Qufic and old Naskhi calligraphic styles.

The mosque and the attached Koran school are still fully functioning, but since the place is frequented by tour groups, you may be allowed to enter the mosque if you are lucky and don't arrive at prayer time. The visit is certainly worthwhile – this is one of the most remarkable and beautiful mosques in Yemen. Even if you're not allowed to enter, you can see the mosque from the slopes of the hill.

As you enter the town you can choose to continue straight through, past the beautiful small mosque, Qubbat Bayt az-Zum, which many visitors mistake for the Mosque of Queen Arwa. The houses of Jibla are stone towers built in the same style as those in Ibb, though many of those in Jibla are more richly ornamented. The road leads to the upper slopes of the hill. From here you can admire the aqueduct built in the days of Queen

Arwa. It still brings water from the mountains past the graveyard to the town. On top of the hill you will also find the ruins of the palace of Queen Arwa.

Places to Stay

It is possible to stay overnight in Jibla. There is a small one-sheet hotel as you enter the town. It has doubles for YR 60 and common cold-water bathrooms only. Because it's rather clean, this one is definitely worth considering as an alternative to the similarly priced hotels in Ibb – there is certainly less street noise.

There is also the *Jibla Baptist Hospital*, staffed by American, Dutch and Filipino volunteers. This one is not for casual overnighting, but if you find yourself disabled by illness or injury, this is the place to go in the region.

Getting There & Away

From Ibb, you can get a seat in a shared taxi for YR 10; the taxis depart from the main taxi station. Coming from Ta'izz, you could get off at Mafraq Jibla and walk the unpaved road (three km).

AL-'UDAYN

(al-'udayn; Odein)

Thirty km west of Ibb, this very friendly small town by the nearly tropical outskirts of Wadi Zabid is well worth visiting, even though it offers no special sights and is not a good place for an overnight stay. If you enjoy travelling the less visited roads of Yemen, though, the journey to and from al'Udayn certainly makes the trip worthwhile.

Getting There & Away

The easiest way to reach al-'Udayn is via the tarmac road built from Ibb in the late 1980s. The road quickly descends more than 1000 metres, meaning a rapid change of atmosphere. There are old stone watchtowers all along the hilltops. A seat in a shared taxi only costs you YR 20; taxis leave from the junction of the old San'a to Ta'izz road and al-'Udayn road.

Alternatively, you can travel to al-'Udayn

from Ta'izz via the picturesque mountain town of Mudhaykhira – warmly recommended if you have enough time. The taxis leave from in front of the central suqs and charge YR 100 per seat for the 60-km trip to al-'Udayn. Since the new Ibb to al-'Udayn road was built, fewer taxis serve this route. The mountain roads are very hard to drive when compared to the asphalted ones, and you may have to use separate taxis to and from Mudhaykhira. Allow one day for the trip.

The third route to al-'Udayn takes you from the Tihami towns of Hays or Suq al-Jarrahi (near Zabid) via al-Mabraz (59 km from al-'Udayn and 36 km from the Tihama highway). This alternative route is not served by regular taxis at all, though you might succeed in travelling the distance in smaller stretches, walking and getting occasional rides from village to village.

DHAFAR ضفار

(zafar; Dhofar, Zafar, Zofar)

The capital of the once mighty Himyarites is today a forgotten small village on the northern border of the Ibb province. If you ask a Yemeni where Dhafar is, the most likely answer is Oman, meaning the western province of that country. Few Yemeni maps show Dhafar, yet it is an officially recognised site of antiquity, with one of the less than 10 museums in Yemen.

History

The Himyarite state was born in the 2nd century BC, when after a civil war in the state of Qataban, two provinces – Himyar and Radman – became independent. They occupied the region at the very south-western end of the Arabian Peninsula, controlling the Bab al-Mandab strait. This strait was soon to become very strategic when new discoveries in the field of navigation made it possible for the Romans to send ships to India and back through the Red Sea.

Around 20 BC the Himyarites began to build a new capital, Dhafar, on the high plateau (3000 metres above sea level) near present-day Yarim. The flourishing state kept extending its power and, in 50 AD, there was a profound change in the Southern Arabian balance of power: the Sabaean state collapsed. It had been weakened by continuing wars with its neighbours and internal power struggles, and faced diminishing income because the new sea routes stole traffic from the old caravan routes. The age-old Sabaean dynasty was replaced by rulers from the highlands.

Although the Sabaeans were able to successfully revolt against the Himyarites in 190 AD, the Himyarite hegemony was restored barely 100 years later. In the end, the Himyarite king Shammar Yuharish ruled an area that encompassed both of the present-day Yemens. He called himself 'King of Saba, Dhi Raydan, Hadhramawt and Yamna'.

The Himyarites later moved their capital to Ma'rib; after all, Saba had been the spiritual centre of the region for centuries, lending its gods – the Moon, Sun and Venus – to its rivals. The holiest temples were also in Ma'rib. Dhafar took a step backwards in importance. The next centuries before the arrival of Islam saw the destruction of the Himyarite kingdom in continuing wars between Ethiopian Aksumites and Persians on Yemeni soil.

Things to See

Dhafar is a small village. Some nice guys make money by acting as guides (very rare in Yemen) but you hardly need a guide. Still, you may find it difficult to refuse one!

Dhafar is an impressive example of the spontaneous preservation of antique items – every other modest stone house seems to have a Himyarite sculpture (or a piece of one) used as a building block, often above the main entrance. You can see bulls' heads, reliefs of other beasts, plants and human motifs. The small government-built museum in the centre of the village seems to open its doors whenever there are customers. Entry costs YR 4.

A walk past the village is also worthwhile; the rock is full of caves, used as houses or as donkey stables. The disparity between these

rough dwellings and the fine sculptures demonstrates the enormous timespan over which the hill has been used.

Getting There & Away

Visiting Dhafar is a problem if you are travelling on your own. It should be easy, since the village lies only 30 minutes ride from the San'a to Ta'izz road (4WD needed). The small village of Kitab is served by the short-haul taxis that operate between Ibb, Yarim and Dhamar, some five km south of Yarim. The fare from Ibb is the same to either Kitab or Yarim: YR 30.

It is here that the problems begin. Dhafar is a very small village and very little traffic heads from Kitab to Dhafar in the mornings or early afternoons. This makes it impossible to get a seat in a shared taxi. The drivers know your predicament and charge absurd sums like YR 400 for the return trip to Dhafar. They simply don't offer a one-way ticket for the seven-km trip. If you are in a group of six, YR 200 would be fair, with one hour in Dhafar, but you are unlikely to get a bargain like this.

We chose to hitchhike instead. After passing the first village in the midst of the fields, a conical mountain serves as a good landmark; behind it, the mountains embracing Dhafar begin. Finding the village by the cave-dotted slope was the easy part of the job, riding on the platform of a Toyota van. We walked back down the mountain road between impressive volcanic formations, then along the desolate mud road running through the fields. Heavy rain fell from the clouds that came from the south, through the Sumarra Pass. I don't recommend doing this during the rainy season.

An alternative route is from Yarim. Take the road east to Qa'taba and get off at a village named Chaw. Then walk or drive south some 10 km to Dhafar. It might be interesting to combine these routes, using one to reach Dhafar and a different one to leave. The region is sparsely populated, however, so if you get lost, you may walk for hours before meeting anybody to ask for directions.

YARIM

يريم

(yari:m; Yerim)

Yarim, in the fertile Yarim basin, is the northernmost town in the province of Ibb. At 2550 metres above sea level, it is the highest-standing town in Yemen. Although Yarim is a very old settlement, most of the structures were built after the civil war. When the famous Danish expedition's botanical expert, Finnish-born Peter Forsskal, died here in 1763, Yarim was just a tiny village.

The Yarim and Dhamar basins are in the most volcanically active area of northern Yemen. There are many hot springs, with bathhouses built around them. Look out for very low buildings with small cupolas on the roofs; the hammams are built partly below street level to better preserve heat, while the openings on top of the cupolas let sunlight in.

Modern-day Yarim is another roadside market, with plenty of eateries and a few modest no-sheet hotels (prices about YR 40 per person) along the main road.

HAMMAM DAMT

حمام دمت

(Hamma:m damt)

This bath resort is near an extinct volcano 47 km to the east of Yarim. The asphalt road continues on to the town of Qa'taba, near the former YAR-PDRY border;it isn't open to tourists for the time being.

Things to See

Your first impression of Hammam Damt will probably be the volcano on the eastern side of the road, to the south of the village. The village itself is modest, with small modern buildings scattered here and there.

It takes only a few minutes to climb the volcano; steel stairs on the volcano's village side help you up the steepest part. There is a police station at the bottom of the stairs – you must ask for permission here (they might ask to see your tour permit). At the time of our visit, there was no entrance fee.

The volcano is by far the freakiest 'sight' Yemeni nature has to offer. A very even pathway leads almost all the way around the crater, on top of the volcano, with only 20 metres impossible to walk. Deep in the crater, a small lake with green water shimmers in the sun – magical!

Hot springs abound on the northern side of the volcano, many with bathhouses built around them. The big bathhouse by the creek is accessible to both men and women but at different times of the day. On the other side of the creek are a couple more tiny craters.

The place is obviously frequented by Yemenis, since there are more restaurants and hotels than you would normally find in such a tiny village. The government probably has great plans to develop the site into a major tourist attraction, but when we visited, little had been done except the new road to Qa'taba, built in the mid-1980s.

Places to Stay

Damt Tourist Hotel on the main road is quite a clean one-sheet hotel offering doubles for YR 120. No hot water is available – you are expected to use the bathhouses! More basic accommodation, intended for Yemenis coming for a healing bath, is available in the village proper.

Getting There & Away

Hammam Damt is served by buses and taxis. From San'a take the Qa'taba bus, which departs from Bab al-Yaman at 7 am. The fare is YR 75 for buses and YR 100 for taxis. Alternatively you can get to Hammam Damt from Yarim by bus or pay about YR 40 for a seat in a taxi.

Beyond Yarim the road soon descends into a steep gorge, which subsequently opens into a densely populated and extensively cultivated wadi. Here are the headwaters of Wadi Bana, a huge wadi that flows through the Abyan governorate in the southern part of the country, reaching the Indian Ocean near the town of Zinjibar. About 34 km from Yarim there is a village named ar-Radhma. Hammam Damt is 13 km further on.

QA'TABA

قعطبة

(qa'taba; Qatabah)

Some 35 km beyond Hammam Damt, you will reach Qa'taba, an old border town by the now defunct YAR-PDRY boundary. In 1990 this was the terminus of the bus line from San'a. However, a road does continue on to Qa'taba's South Yemeni sister town, adh-Dhalla', which stands on a mountain slope on the other side of the former border (see Lahej). This route between Yarim and Aden is, in fact, shorter than the usual one via Ta'izz.

Dhamar

The province of Dhamar lies in the central highlands; the important agricultural basins of Ma'bar and Dhamar are at an altitude of almost 2500 metres. Irrigation has been practised in this region from ancient times and wide areas are under intense cultivation. The surface is relatively flat, so the large terraces are well suited to the use of modern machinery, making the region ideal for grain production.

To the west the province descends all the way down to the Tihama east of Bayt al-Faqih and Zabid. Although it has few places worth visiting, the province serves as a thoroughfare for most tourists and does have a few sites of interest.

DHAMAR

ذمار

(dhama:r)

The town of Dhamar, in the centre of the Dhamar basin, is of ancient origin. It was founded by the legendary Himyarite king Dhamar 'Ali, renowned for restoring the great dam of Ma'rib. Dhamar is the only town in the northern Yemen which is not surrounded by a wall or natural defensive formations; it is just a settlement on the plain. Centrally situated with good connections to the nearby provinces, the town has prospered as a market and meeting place for tribes living nearby.

Architecturally the houses of Dhamar are a mixture of the stone tower house and the mud house of the eastern plains, combined with the brick construction method common in bigger towns. The stone walls often have inlaid arches and fanlights of brick. To give a smoother appearance, brick walls may be plastered, inside and out, with mud. The decorations are not as rich and fancy as those in San'a.

Qa' al-Yahud is the former Jewish quarter of Dhamar. This closely walled section of mud houses demonstrates the isolation in which the Yemeni Jews lived.

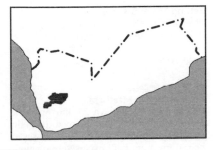

Orientation

The San'a to Ta'izz road passes through narrow 'modern Dhamar'; the old town is to the east. Although, seen in isolation, Dhamar would be a remarkable place, you would probably not rate it as a 'sight' after a week in Yemen – there's nothing too special about it.

Places to Stay

Dhamar has no nice hotels but you will find some one-sheet hotels on the San'a to Ta'izz road. These places have quadruple rooms (YR 25 a bed) and common bathrooms (cold showers only).

There is a big, modern hotel, known by the names *adh-Dhubay* and *'Ayman*, in the new residential area. This two-sheet hotel has only triples but does offer large-sized beds – quite uncharacteristic of Yemeni hotels. The common bathrooms at the end of the corridor have hot water (if you remember to switch the boilers on). At YR 225 a room, this one is far too expensive for the budget traveller, but if you are a family or three young couples willing to share a room, it might be a bargain. You can find the hotel by taking the al-Baydha road (the junction with the main road is clearly marked), then the first street to the right. The hotel is on the right-hand side, a few hundred metres from the street corner.

If you really have to stay overnight in this

173

region, I highly recommend that you take the one-hour ride to Rada' (see al-Baydha), where there is much more choice.

Getting There & Away
Dhamar is on the San'a to Ta'izz highway, 99 km from San'a and 139 km from Ta'izz, so it is an easy place to reach by bus or taxi – and even easier to go straight past.

MA'BAR معبر
(ma'bar; Mabar, Maabar)
Ma'bar is a small town 31 km north of Dhamar, on the San'a-Ta'izz road. Its main peculiarity is that the two-storeyed houses in the old town are built exclusively of mud. While this kind of architecture is common on the eastern plateaus, it is rare in this area of stone or mixed construction.

The road to al-Hudayda, completed in the mid-1980s, branches to the west in Ma'bar.

DHAWRAN ضوران
(zawra:n; Dawran)
Dhawran, a small town some 15 km west of Ma'bar, once served as a royal town. The partly ruined old mosque here is built to the same plan as the mosque at ar-Rawdha, near San'a.

HAMMAM 'ALI حمام علي
(Hamma:m 'ali; Hammam Ali)
This famous bath resort 35 km north-west of Dhamar owes its existence to the countless hot sulphurous springs on the southern slopes of Jabal Dhawran. The numerous bathhouses here are eagerly visited by Yemenis from near and far. They believe that the hot water is good for their health – it probably is. The high season is January to February, the coldest part of the winter, when a hot bath is a most welcome contrast to the raw mountain climate.

Apart from the bathhouses, which are scattered along the lower slopes of the valley, there is little to see in the small village of Hammam 'Ali. The tiny stone huts higher up on the slopes serve as temporary shelters for the customers. During the high season all the

huts are occupied; at other times most of them stay empty.

The typical bathhouse here is a longish one-storey building divided into a row of small bathing chambers. The water runs through the building from one chamber to the next and small openings in the ceilings let in the sunlight.

If you decide to take a relaxing bath, it should not cost you more than a few riyals. There are separate bathhouses for men and women.

Market day in Hammam 'Ali is Monday.

Places to Stay
There are plenty of modest, traditional Yemeni hotels in the village. This is one place where you don't have to worry about the hotel washing facilities – just go to a bathhouse for a hot bath!

Getting There & Away
There are two ways to get to Hammam 'Ali: the old, interesting way and the new, easy way.

The interesting way starts from Dhamar, where 4WD taxis wait to transport bathers to Hammam 'Ali for YR 30 to YR 40 per person. The route takes you first along the highway; eight km north of Dhamar you branch west onto a dirt road and head towards a conical mountain far on the horizon. After a 30-minute ride, past a hilltop village that was badly damaged in the 1982 earthquake, the road descends to a steep wadi. From here it is a one-hour drive to Hammam 'Ali.

The easy route uses the new Ma'bar to Bajil road, which passes near Hammam 'Ali before reaching Madinat ash-Sharq further in the same wadi. If you continue beyond Hammam 'Ali you will end up on this road.

BAYNUN بينون
(baynu:n)
For history freaks only, the ruins of still another Himyarite capital, Baynun, lie east of Dhamar. The town was completely destroyed in about 525 AD by Aksumites, or Ethiopians. Today only the ruins remain,

interesting mainly to archaeologists. Impressive structures that are more easily appreciated by a layperson are the nearby irrigation channels and tunnels. These are about 1500 years old but are well preserved, even though they do not carry water anymore. It is possible to walk through one tunnel that is 150 metres long.

Getting There & Away

Take the al-Baydha road east from Dhamar for some 30 km, then turn left onto the dirt road towards Isbil mountain. The road eventually turns north-west, and after an hour's ride you should find the ruins between the Isbil and Dhi Rakam mountains. A 4WD vehicle and a local guide are strongly recommended.

Al-Baydha

The relatively sparsely populated province of al-Baydha is in the south-eastern part of the former YAR, east of Dhamar and Ibb and to the south of Ma'rib. The provincial capital, al-Baydha, lies at the very south-eastern tip of the province, next to the town of Mukayras, in the Abyan governorate of the southern part of the country.

Before unification of the two Yemens the province's southern and eastern borders with the PDRY were undemarcated and tourism in the province was understandably restricted. Such obstacles should no longer exist, though the infrastructure to support tourism will take some time to develop. An asphalted road leads through the province and links its two major towns, al-Baydha and Rada', with Dhamar.

In the towns, stone and mud architectures coexist, often within a single house – stone in the lower storeys and mud in the upper ones. Along the road there are a couple of larger villages between the towns but most of the settlements in the south-eastern mountains are small hilltop clusters of one and two-storey houses, built in stone and surfaced with mud. Here and there you will see towers built of schist stone, with their characteristic sharply raised corners.

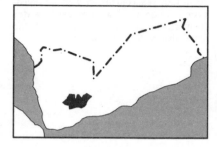

RADA' رداع

(rada:'; Radaa, Rida)

Although Rada' does not have the status of provincial capital, it is the more important of the province's two towns. The latest available population figure, 30,000 inhabitants, is from 1986 and is now clearly obsolete, the town having experienced explosive growth. The large town lies on a plain and there is a fortified rocky hill at one side of the old town. Parts of the town wall, together with the western gate, still stand. Although the town is mainly built of mud, the wall is made of stone.

Orientation

Buses and taxis leave you by the Dhamar to al-Baydha road, with old Rada' to your left. The first stop will probably be in the midst of the new town, which materialised out of nowhere in the latter half of the 1980s. You'd do better to ask for the Brother's Hotel (Funduq al-Ikhwa). You will then be dropped off at a junction only a couple of hundred metres from the old town. The road leads you straight to the centre, where you'll find all the travellers' facilities, from hotels and pharmacies to police and restaurants.

Things to See

You'll find it rewarding to walk around the very large old centre, built of brick and mud. The houses present a striking contrast to the stone architecture of the midlands – compare Rada' with Ibb, for example. Although the ground floor may be of stone, the next floors are usually built of brick and finished with a beautiful, smooth mud surfacing that needs to be renewed every year. If you are lucky, you may see this elaborate manual process. The local mud has an odd greyish tone, unique in Yemen.

Keep an eye open for the windows and fanlights. The double or triple-arched fanlights with huge alabaster panes and mud-and-brick framing are unique to Rada' and cannot be seen anywhere else in Yemen. A walk in the old suq next to the al-Amiriya mosque is also rewarding.

The new town is a pleasing example of the Yemeni respect for local conditions and tradition in architecture. Compare the mud-covered houses along the Dhamar to al-Baydha road with the new houses in San'a or Ta'izz, for example.

Al-Amiriya Mosque This exceptional mosque with grooved cupolas at the corners stands in the centre of the old town. It was built, in a style unique in Yemen, by 'Amir bin 'Abd al-Wahab, the same Tahirid sultan who built the Yifrus mosque in the Hujjariya. Almost 500 years old, the mosque is no longer in active ceremonial use and was even in severe danger of collapse in the late 1980s. Fortunately a restoration project has finally commenced but it will probably be well into the 1990s before work is complete.

Places to Stay

The *Brothers* hotel, visible from the Dhamar to al-Baydha road, was built in 1986 in modern style and is obviously targeted at foreigners. With triples for YR 100, it is an economical one-sheet hotel. There is a bathroom (with warm shower) for every two rooms, and a dormitory on the ground floor caters for those travelling on a tight budget.

If you prefer an old Yemeni-style house, just look some 300 metres further – to the left is a tower house with the clear sign 'HOTEL' on the roof. This is the *'Arsh Bilqis* hotel, with doubles, triples and quadruples for YR 30 a bed. Common bathrooms in the corridors have showers; boilers will be switched on upon demand. This place has a very amiable atmosphere but is not quite clean.

Places to Eat

There are several restaurants along the main road, between the Brothers hotel and the central market. When we visited, three of them were serving huge whole fish, grilled over a roaring fire – why so far inland, I can't figure.

Getting There & Away

Rada' is served by regular bus connections from San'a (see the table of bus lines in the Getting Around chapter). From Dhamar, the easiest way to get to Rada' is by shared taxi. The 55-km ride on the very good road across the plain costs YR 25 per person and takes less than one hour.

AL-BAYDHA البيضاء

(al-Bayza:; al-Bayda, al-Beida)

Many tourists think that al-Baydha must be very exotic because of its remote location and they are disappointed if the General Tourist Corporation won't grant them a tour permit. I can offer some consolation: there's nothing so special about it. The town is just a small, albeit fast-developing provincial capital with plenty of stone buildings in postrevolutionary style, often painted in strikingly inappropriate colours.

Older houses are built either of stone or of mud. Combinations also occur, with lower floors built of stone and perhaps the uppermost floor made of mud. Windows are small and waste shafts are replaced by protruding drainage pipes.

The road to al-Baydha does not offer many surprises, either. Apart from a couple of bigger villages by the road and some hilltop hamlets here and there, you will mainly see desolate stony stretches with the occasional shrub. A few very small wadis cross the road in this watershed between the drainages of Wadi Bana, which flow towards the Indian Ocean, and those of Wadi Adhana, which flow to Ma'rib. In the vicinity of al-Baydha, some very beautiful mud villages draw your attention.

Getting There & Away

You can get to al-Baydha easily from San'a on the twice-daily bus. From Rada' it's best to take a taxi – YR 35 will buy you a seat for the 125-km ride. Traffic is not heavy on the tarmac road that passes through this sparsely populated province.

It remains to be seen which kind of road

connections will be developed between al-Baydha and al-Mukayras; before the unification not even a donkey could cross the YAR-PDRY border most of the time.

Ma'rib

Ma'rib is the easternmost province of the former YAR. Only its western border is clearly defined; no boundary stones mark the sands of ar-Ruba' al-Khali desert, nor have the borders been drawn on a map. This is the land of Bedouin tribes. Only a few villages line the wadis that descend from the eastern mountains to spill their scanty waters in the sands.

Sparse vegetation and an equally sparse population make the province look like a developing area, a burden to the country. And yet it was here that the mightiest kingdom of ancient Arabia flourished. This is also the site of the 1980s oil finds that promise to save the Yemeni economy.

There are not many places you can visit in Ma'rib province. Tour permits to the village of Ma'rib are granted only through tour operators, and you have to hire a car with a driver. The rest of the province is off limits, probably because local tribes hold more power than the central government. Before the tarmac road from San'a to Ma'rib was built in 1980, visitors usually had to fly to Ma'rib. Today the airport is for military and industrial use only.

MA'RIB

مأرب

(ma:'rib; Mareb, Maarib, Maareb)

Ma'rib is the most famous archaeological site in Yemen. Once the capital of the kingdom of Saba, the city was reduced to a small village in the 6th century AD after the final collapse of the kingdom. For hundreds of years the village remained basically the same; the earliest European expeditions to reach it depicted 19th-century Ma'rib very much as it appeared in the mid-1980s.

Ma'rib is often a destination for foreign tourists. It is easily reached from San'a and can be visited hurriedly in a single day, possibly combined with a visit to Baraqish. Tour operators usually recommend that you spend two days. Yemenis expect every traveller to see Ma'rib, though many have not been there

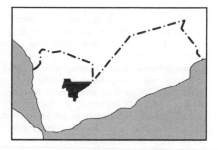

themselves; sightseeing is a concept to which they seldom relate personally.

It is possible to hurry through the sights of Ma'rib and Baraqish in a single day, starting early (6 or 7 am) from San'a and being back by sunset. However, a lazier pace is certainly worthwhile – and also gives your driver some time to recuperate before the drive back.

History

Ma'rib was probably inhabited much earlier than the oldest written accounts testify. Human survival in the eastern escarpment, where annual rainfall is scanty (below 300 mm), is based on the existence of wadis that collect their waters from large areas. One of the greatest of these wadis, Wadi Adhana (or Wadi Dhana), by which Ma'rib lies, has a catchment area of 10,000 sq km, reaching all the way from the Dhamar basin in the southwest.

In the 8th century BC a great dam was built in Ma'rib, at that time called Maryab. The wadi flowed through a gorge between two mountains, Jabal Balaq al-Qibli and Jabal Balaq al-Awsat. Between these mountains was built a 680-metre wall of sand, mud and gravel, strengthened by rocks of lava and limestone. Over the centuries the wall was gradually enlarged and strengthened until, finally, its height reached 16 metres in the middle of the wadi. This remarkable feat of ancient engineering was so dominant a feature that it gave the entire wadi a new name: Wadi as-Sudd, or the Wadi of the Dam.

Sluice gates were constructed at the northern and southern ends of the dam to divert water to the fields that were cultivated on both banks of the wadi, known as the North and South Oases. In fact, the dam was not for collecting water in a huge reservoir but, rather, was designed to steer water to the terraces and fields higher up on the wadi banks. Even so, silting was a major problem (the water carried heavy sediment loads that caused the fields of the oases to rise more than one cm a year), so the dam eventually had to be raised and constant care was needed to guarantee proper irrigation of all fields.

The system was nonetheless effective; for more than 1000 years it provided irrigation to 96 sq km of fields, sustaining a population of 30,000 to 50,000 people. Excess water was no doubt used by smaller settlements down the wadi. Cereals such as teff, millet, barley and oat were grown, as well as broom-corn, grape, cumin, flax, garden sorrel and sesame.

There were even palm plantations in the capital of Saba, providing travellers along the incense route with welcome shade on the long desert road. By virtue of this strategic location on the incense road, Saba's fame spread across the civilised world, from Rome to India. The chance to collect taxes from the caravans that passed by with their precious loads gave Saba a prosperity that would not have been possible for a purely agricultural settlement.

Over the centuries the kingdom of Saba waged several wars against neighbouring rival states. In about 500 BC Ma'rib was fortified with a wall. Then around 400 BC the northern tribes freed themselves from Sabaean rule, founding the state of Ma'in. To the east, the Hadhramawt also gained independence. Although Saba was meanwhile able to destroy the kingdom of Awsan, Qa'taban (to the south) simultaneously

gained strength. Wars against Qa'taban, Ma'in and Hadhramawt continued through the 5th century BC.

During the following centuries peaceful periods alternated with wars. New enemies appeared; in 25-24 BC even the Romans, led by Aegius Gallius, carried out a military expedition in southern Arabia. They reached the walls of Ma'rib but were unable to conquer the city. By around 50 AD the rise of the Himyarites and the subsequent wars against them greatly weakened the kingdom of Saba. In the 2nd century AD the traditional dynasty of Saba was brought to an end and was replaced by rulers from the highlands. Later on, when the Himyarite state was at its largest and during the Ethiopian occupation in the 5th and 6th centuries, Ma'rib was ruled from distant capitals in the mountains.

Maintaining a structure as sophisticated as the Great Dam of Ma'rib called for a strong central authority. The decline of the kingdom of Saba and the subsequent failure to maintain the dam led to several disasters in which the dam was greatly damaged, even partly washed away by floods after exceptionally heavy rains. The earliest such occasion was recorded in 319 AD. In 542 the dam broke completely but the Ethiopian ruler of Yemen, Abraha, ordered 20,000 workers to do repairs and they succeeded in restoring the dam.

The final catastrophe occurred in 570, when the dam was irrevocably washed away. Most of the inhabitants of Ma'rib fled to various parts of the Arabian Peninsula. Many Arabians today carry the surname 'Yamani', indicating that they are descended from ancient Sabaeans.

After the dam's collapse only a few families stayed in Ma'rib and nearby villages. The incense trade had long since vanished, and the region became 'far from everywhere'. Little is known about the apparently scanty developments of the next 1400 years.

During the civil war of the 1960s Egyptian forces made Ma'rib a base for their operations. The village was heavily bombed in the intense battles and its future looked grimmer than ever. However, in the 1970s, pump irrigation revived agriculture in the region – even in the absence of the dam, ground water had been able to accumulate. By the mid-1980s, the population of the region had grown to about 13,000, far too many for the area to support. The level of ground water sank, drying up the wells.

Ma'rib's future nevertheless seems prosperous for two main reasons. First, in the early 1980s Hunt Oil Corporation found oil east of Ma'rib. Yemen's first oil well went into production in 1986 and a pipeline was built from Ma'rib to as-Salif, north of al-Hudayda; the YAR was already an oil-exporting country before the unification of the Yemens, though the exports were modest in scale.

Second, the government of the YAR, conscious of tradition, had an ambitious plan to revive agriculture in the region by means of a new Ma'rib dam, to be built a few km upstream from the site of the ancient dam. Although the economic sanity of the plan was much disputed, the project went ahead and Ma'rib is now a much greener place than it was in the mid 1980s.

The Ma'rib of today is a bustling town, with heavy trucks raising dust in the windy air a common sight. One wonders what will remain of the ancient relics which probably lie buried in the sands.

Orientation & Information
If you have hired a car and a driver you will not have to worry about orientation. However, should the current restrictions be lifted and you arrive by bus or shared taxi, you will be left at what is called 'New Ma'rib', a collection of shops, petrol stations, government offices and other houses just past the Ma'rib airport. Here you can have something to eat and buy bottles of fresh water for the visit to old Ma'rib. Buy plenty of that water; in case you have not noticed it yet, the air is extremely hot in Ma'rib and you will sweat a lot more here than in San'a. If you plan to do a lot of walking, take some salt tablets with you to restore your salt balance.

The road continues to the old village of Ma'rib, a couple of km away on the bank of Wadi as-Sudd. Just before the village a new road branches to the right, leading to the sites of the old and new dams a little way upstream. The archaeological sites are widely scattered around the wadi, so you will need a car to see everything. This involves a 30-km round trip along the asphalted roads built through the sands in the late 1980s.

If you are travelling on your own, you should be able to get lifts with the Toyotas passing by. Another possibility is to hire a car locally; YR 100 should be more than enough.

Things to See
The usual schedule for tourists includes the old village of Ma'rib, three archaeological sites and the new dam, though the banks of the wadi probably conceal many other sites worth excavating. If you take a walk around here you will see many small heaps of sand – closer inspection shows them to be the ruins of ancient houses.

In addition you will probably see several sand-carrying whirlwinds. I have seen more of them here than anywhere else in Yemen.

Old Ma'rib The village stands on a tiny hill and can be seen from the new Ma'rib. Old Ma'rib is an impressive place, with its small-windowed mud skyscrapers, their stone basements often sporting stones from ancient monuments. You will see Sabaean inscriptions, ornaments and figurative motifs, such as ibex heads, on these stones.

Many of the houses lie in ruins following the bombings of the civil war, while many more have been damaged by a lack of the care and maintenance that is needed by mud buildings. Very few people live in old Ma'rib anymore and you might think the place deserted were it not for the goats and children greeting you. By the mid-1990s old Ma'rib will probably be totally abandoned.

'Arsh Bilqis On the other side of the wadi, just a couple of km south-southwest of old Ma'rib, you will find the remnants of remarkable Sabaean temples, now half-buried in a sand dune and surrounded by a

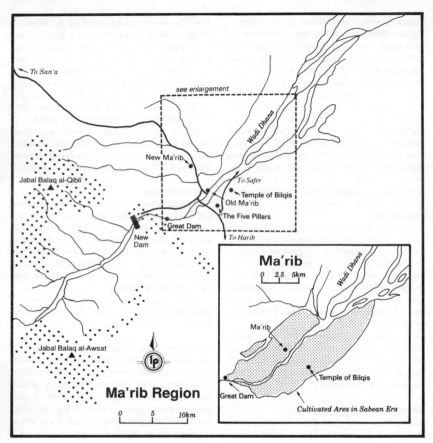

Ma'rib Region

0   5   10km

Ma'rib

0   2.5   5km

Cultivated Area in Sabean Era

wire fence. Before the building of the new dam it was possible to walk the distance during the dry season. Nowadays water flows all year round, making walking impractical.

A longer but easier route takes you along asphalt roads. As you head along the road from new Ma'rib to the dam, turn left to Jaw al-Ubar, over the wadi. Turn left again at the Safir-Harib junction, eight km from new Ma'rib, and you will soon see a sign pointing left to the 'Balqis Palace'.

A few hundred metres to the west stand the five pillars of the Temple of the Moon.

The sixth pillar is broken in the middle, as if to remind you of the five undisputed pillars and the one disputed pillar of the faith of Islam (see the Religion section). Local people call this 'Arsh Bilqis, or the Throne of Bilqis. Bilqis is the Yemeni name for the legendary queen of Saba, who visited King Solomon in the 10th century BC.

Archaeologists disagree with this view, holding instead that the pillars once belonged to a temple consecrated to the moon god Almaqah (Ilumquh). Further research on the question is needed, and excavations were under way when we visited in 1990.

Mahram Bilqis An even more imposing site can be reached by continuing further in the direction of Safir and turning right at the sign reading 'Sun Temple'.

Yemenis call this temple Mahram Bilqis, which translates as 'Temple of Bilqis'. Again, this attribution is probably wrong, since archaeological studies indicate that the temple was actually built around 400 BC and was originally known as the Temple of Awwam. The word *maHram* means 'Temple of Refuge', indicating that it was not an ordinary temple but one which enjoyed so-called *Haram* (taboo, forbidden) status. Persecuted people could take refuge inside, and even the worst criminal could obtain temporary shelter.

American archaeologists performed excavations here between the years 1950 and 1952, exposing most of the temple from the sands. Their work was, however, interrupted by local tribespeople whose suspicions of the oddly behaving strangers finally turned to open hostility. Today the desert has reclaimed much of the temple, leaving only pillars rising from the sands. The temple's oval form is not easily perceived; it is surrounded by a wall nine metres high and four metres thick. After visiting this place, you wonder what other surprises Yemen's dunes might hide.

The Great Dam Back on the road that leads to the dams, you come to the ancient Great Dam of Ma'rib, some eight km upwards by the wadi. Little of it remains; there is no trace of the dam in the bottom of the wadi, just the ruins of the sluice gates on each bank. Looking across from one sluice to the other gives you an idea of the immense scale of the ancient construction.

The northern sluice was originally the bigger of the two, although less remains of it today. If you wander around it you can clearly see the canal system that distributed water to fields at different heights. Nearby are the so-called 'Stones of King', with

Himyarite inscriptions from the 4th century AD describing dam repairs.

The southern sluice is in better condition, although the sluice was apparently the smaller one in ancient times. The site is well worth a close study. Some of the carefully cut stones carry Sabaean inscriptions.

The New Dam Continuing just a couple of km along the green wadi from the old dam, you will come to the vast new dam, which connects the two mountains like a giant ruler. Walking on top of the huge structure, 40 metres high and 760 metres long, gives you ample time to contemplate this incredible combination of respect for ancient history and confidence in modern technology.

In the first place, the whole thing is a gift from Sheikh Zayid an-Nahayan, the ruler of Abu Dhabi, whose ancestors lived in Wadi Nahayan, near Ma'rib, and migrated to the shores of the Persian Gulf after the great disaster of 570 AD. In the 1980s Sheikh Zayid donated US$75 million to the government of the YAR to develop the Ma'rib region.

The dam was built by 400 Turkish workers to plans drawn up by a Swiss company. It is capable of storing 400 million cubic metres of water in the artificial lake. After years of work, the dam itself was finished in 1986, although construction of an elaborate system of irrigation channels and some 20 smaller dams in the region is still going on.

Whether the money could have been used more reasonably is not a question you should raise with the Yemenis. Today's problem is where to find families who are willing to move to Ma'rib and start taking advantage of the agricultural opportunity created by the dam.

Places to Stay - bottom end

Although the tour operators will want to book your accommodation in one of the top-of-the-line hotels, there are cheaper alternatives. The one-sheet *Brothers* hotel, by the gasoline station in the centre of new Ma'rib, offers quadruples (YR 50 per bed) with shared bathrooms. The place also has a dormitory filled with pipe smoke in the grass-roots Yemeni style.

Places to Stay - top end

Perhaps partly as a result of recent oil finds and partly in appreciation of the tourism potential of the archaeological sites, there are a couple of higher standard hotels in the rapidly expanding new Ma'rib. A 1st-class hotel opened on the south-western side in 1986. Head towards old Ma'rib until you reach the *Funduq al-Jannattayn* sign by the roadside. The hotel even has a swimming pool in the garden – a most unexpected sight in the middle of the desert, even if it is seldom filled with water. The name literally means 'Hotel of the Two Paradises', reflecting the Koran's description of ancient Saba. A double costs YR 330, YR 385 with air-conditioning.

Another holiday resort hotel, the even more gorgeous *Bilqish Mareb Hotel* (☎ 2666, telex 4033 BQSHT YE), offers doubles for YR 600 to YR 700. As you arrive from San'a, turn right beyond the bus station – the hotel approach is marked by double gateways.

Places to Eat

For simple eating, there are quite a few Yemeni-style restaurants near the bus station. These are all about the same.

Getting There & Away

Usually you won't have to think about how to get to Ma'rib – your transport will have been arranged by the travel agency for YR 1500 per group. If it should again become possible to visit Ma'rib on your own, you will need at least 10 copies of your tour permit to get there back.

Getting to Ma'rib from San'a is easy. Buses leave from Bab ash-Sha'ub at 8 am and 2 pm; the 158-km trip takes 2¾ hours and costs YR 70. Yellow-striped taxis offer an alternative to the buses; they charge YR 80 a seat and are a useful option if the bus timetable doesn't suit you. However, traffic to Ma'rib is not very heavy, the buses run

half-empty and I would not recommend that you rely on getting a taxi at 9 or 10 am.

The road first heads north-east, leaving ar-Rawdha and its grape gardens to the west. Then it gradually ascends from the San'a basin to a pass, Naqil bin Ghaylan (altitude 2300 metres), 35 km from San'a. Soon thereafter the road crosses the upper parts of Wadi al-Jawf, then winds through the eastern mountains, turning east. About 70 km from San'a you reach another pass, Naqil al-Farda. The final descent to the eastern deserts now begins, very steeply at first and offering spectacular views to the north. Shortly after Naqil al-Farda a tarmac road branches to the north, leading to Baraqish (see al-Jawf).

The rest of the road is rather straight, descending to an altitude of 1100 metres and passing through dry lands where rocky hamada-type semidesert alternates with deserts of sand dunes and protruding black lava rocks. Small wadis cross the road here and there. Vegetation consists of small shrubs and grasses, with acacia and tamarisk trees growing where there is enough moisture in the ground. Local tribes practise goat-herding here; you can witness their influence from the many checkpoints en route.

SIRWAH   صرواح

(sirwa:H)

The asphalt road from San'a to Ma'rib takes the northern route around the mountains to the east of San'a. The old road to Ma'rib took a more southerly course, past the ancient town of Sirwah.

Sirwah lies by Wadi Ghada, south-west of Jabal al-Barra and 37 km west of Ma'rib, surrounded by mountains. It was the capital of the Sabaean kingdom before the construction of Ma'rib's irrigation system in the 8th century BC. Exactly when the city was established and when the capital was transferred to Ma'rib is still to be determined by archaeological research, which has been hampered by the suspiciousness of local tribes. However, the reason for the transfer of the capital is clear: the tiny Wadi Ghada was not able to sustain as large a population as the bigger Wadi Adhana.

Modern-day Sirwah, like Ma'rib, is only a shadow of its past self, a mere village near the ruins of the ancient capital. You cannot visit it alone: the Yemeni tourism officials will probably tell you that there is 'nothing left of Sirwah' and deny you a tour permit.

Sirwah does still have ruins but it might be true that you have to be a real buff of archaeology to appreciate them.

If you decide to visit Sirwah, you will need a local guide. It might be a good idea to consult the tourist agencies in San'a; in recent years no tour operators have been willing to organise a car to Sirwah.

Al-Jawf

The last province of the former YAR is al-Jawf, the north-eastern region of semidesert and total desert formerly inhabited only by nomadic bedouins. Tourists are usually neither allowed nor wanted in the province. This was the stronghold of Royalists during the civil war of the 1960s; the local sheikhs still consider themselves to be in charge and are hostile to strangers.

Oil explorers of the 1980s and the subsequent flow of government and foreign oil workers did not help the situation. The bedouins' share of the wealth brought by oil is nil, yet their way of living is being destroyed. They see every 4WD vehicle as a potential threat, bringing disorder and disturbance to their world. Whether it carries oil workers or tourists makes little difference. Some have even dealt with the situation by forcing the car to stop at gunpoint and taking it over.

However, should the province be open to foreign travellers, there are a couple of places of interest.

The province gets its name from Wadi al-Jawf, a giant wadi originating in the mountains north-east of San'a, south-east of Sa'da. The region may not always have been as arid as it is today; in antiquity an important kingdom called Ma'in flourished here, with Saba and Hadhramawt as its foes. Also known as Minaeans, the people of Ma'in were originally subordinate to Ma'rib but, in the course of centuries, gained strength and independence.

Ma'in is the least researched of the ancient kingdoms of southern Arabia. What is known is that it was at its strongest between the years 410 BC (when it started to cause severe trouble for the Sabaean rulers) and 120 BC (when it was conquered by the kingdom of Saba). In its heyday Ma'in controlled a large stretch of the incense route between Ma'rib and Najran.

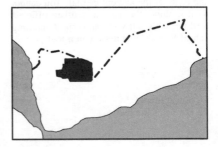

BARAQISH
(bara:qish)

براقش

The original capital of the kingdom of Ma'in and also known as Yathil, Baraqish stands on the eastern bank of Wadi Farda, a tributary of Wadi al-Jawf. Even today the ruins are most impressive, though the centuries have not been kind to the place. It is the only historic site in al-Jawf province that can occasionally be reached by ordinary travellers.

Baraqish served as the capital for just a few decades around the year 400 BC. It was a very tightly built urban settlement. The 14-metre-high city walls are still mostly intact; the dozens of impressive watchtowers were once visible from a distance of many kilometres. The wall certainly had a defensive function but was even more important as a demonstration of wealth.

Little is known about developments in Baraqish after the capital was moved to Ma'in. However, the city remained inhabited for centuries, with new houses built on the ruins of old ones.

Old stones with Minaean inscriptions have been used to repair the city wall here and there. The top layer of the now deserted city almost reaches the top of the surrounding walls, with the remaining few houses built in the Islamic architectural style. In the centre of the area are the ruins of a mosque, with a deep well in the middle.

The city is today surrounded by a wire fence with a gate on the northern side. Make sure you stay on friendly terms with the bedouins guarding the site; they only get paid by the tourists visiting Baraqish.

Getting There & Away

Seeing Baraqish can be conveniently combined with a visit to Ma'rib, since it only adds about an hour to the driving time. In the late 1980s a tarmac road to al-Hazm was built from the San'a-Ma'rib highway, 35 km south of Baraqish. The new road passes through Baraqish and Ma'in. You can only get a tour permit to Baraqish through a tour organiser – the site cannot be visited on an individual basis.

MA'IN   معين
(ma'i:n)

The less intact ruins of the subsequent capital of the kingdom of Ma'in, also known as Qarnawu, are only some 20 km north of Baraqish but have never been included on the list of permissible tourist destinations.

AL-HAZM AL-JAWF   الحزم الجوف
(al-Hazm)

The modern capital of the province of al-Jawf, al-Hazm al-Jawf is today served by domestic Yemen Airways flights. The town, only a few km north-west of the ruins of Ma'in, serves as the base for the oil drillers and explorers in the region and is of no particular interest. To the west, along the wadi, the ruins of two ancient towns, as-Sawda and al-Bayda, are not currently accessible to travellers.

The Southern Governorates

Until 1990, it was next to impossible to visit South Yemen, then the PDRY (People's Democratic Republic of Yemen). This Communist country remained extremely reclusive throughout its existence, being one of the world's most inaccessible countries. Many an intrepid traveller spent weeks visiting some African embassy of the PDRY trying in vain to get an entry visa. Some adventurers even managed to get themselves into an aeroplane without a visa, only to be mercilessly deported from the Aden international airport on the next plane flying back to where they came from.

Apart from those employed in development projects or otherwise visiting the country at the invitation of the PDRY government, only tour groups paying extortionate prices were allowed in. Even then, prearrangements were extremely time consuming, and few Western tour operators took the trouble to include the PDRY on their programmes. The US$3000 to US$4000 price tag for a 16-day tour from Western Europe further served to scare off potential visitors.

But those select few with enough patience, time and money to make their dream come true never confessed it if their visit to the country was a disappointment. The PDRY was a unique experiment in Marxism in a hostile environment, a poor and underdeveloped country striving to shape its future while simultaneously carrying a glorious if distant past with incomparable pride – a strange collision of very different ideas and eras.

Today the PDRY makes up just six more provinces, or governorates, in the multiparty Republic of Yemen, paling in comparison with the northern part of the country because of its more modest mountains and its fewer, smaller and often less spectacular cities. Long distances and your limited time may make you want to skip the south altogether. However, if you are interested in various aspects of Arab lifestyles and in the history of the peninsula as a whole, then the southern governorates are a must. Your perception of Yemen is certain to be incomplete if you only visit the mountains of the north.

Some basics here are very different to the everyday routines in the northern provinces. Both riyals and dinars are valid currencies everywhere in the country, though you will probably have to deal with dinars in the south only. By the end of 1990 no schedule or details were available of the imminent monetary union, so dinars, shillings and fils will no doubt remain in circulation for some years yet.

The legislation of the southern governorates reflects a mixture of British, Socialist and Arabic concepts of law. The 1990 unification has not yet altered the peculiarities of the south, and different legal systems will probably continue to coexist for years. One outstanding example of British heritage is the fact that alcohol is freely available in many hotels, restaurants and shops of the south, and the Seera brewery still operates in Aden. The chewing of qat (which only grows in the mountains by the northern border of the Lahej and Abyan governorates) was formerly allowed only on Thursdays and Fridays but was legalised at the end of 1990. Expect the ban on the public carrying of jambiyas to be lifted soon, too.

Reflecting the liberal ideals of Socialism, some Arabic customs and shari'a rulings concerning women were outlawed. For example, a man is permitted to have only one wife. Furthermore, women are allowed to appear unveiled in public and their participation in urban working life is encouraged. This, however, affects mainly women living in Aden; traditions are still strong in the hinterlands, where many people prefer to live according to local customs rather than by the rulings imposed by short-lived governments.

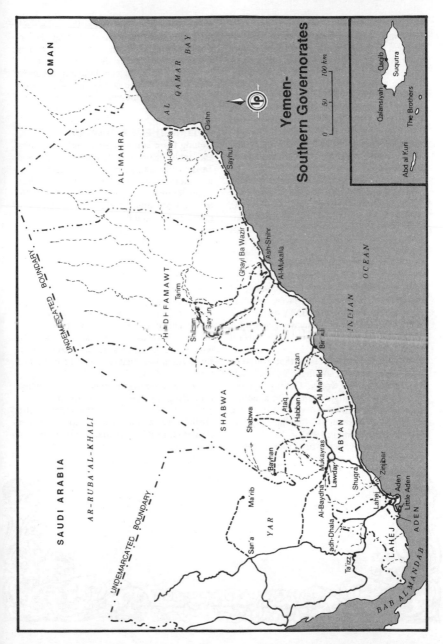

PLACES TO STAY

As things stand now, the most serious problem an independent traveller will face in the southern governorates is lack of accommodation. During the Marxist era, travelling was limited and the country needed very few hotels. Those hotels that did exist were all run by the state-owned Public Corporation of Tourism. Most of the hotels were inherited from the colonial era, but after the revolution, some residences of the former feudal sultans were transformed into hotels and rest houses.

Similar standards were applied to each type of accommodation, regardless of their origin. All hotels sported two sheets on the beds, private bathrooms and air-conditioning (at least fans), and the prices did not differ much. The hotel restaurants all had similar menus (tasteless dishes served with date juice) and alcoholic drinks were available in the bars. Also, most of them were badly neglected during the 23 years of Marxist rule. As a result there were less than 20 hotels operating in the PDRY by the time of Yemeni unification. Many were closed for renovation projects that will take several years.

You will therefore find that southern hotels tend to be full and that booking hotels in advance rarely works. Getting a hotel room in Aden is a nightmare but the situation is even worse in other governorates. In the second biggest town, al-Mukalla, only one hotel was operating in 1990.

Things may get better once market forces start to have an impact. Because there is such a drought of capital in the southern governorates, I expect that some of the hotel chains already established in the former YAR will be the first to build new hotels in the most visited areas of the southern governorates. This will take some years, however.

GETTING THERE & AROUND

Getting there is no longer a problem: buses and taxis drive to Aden from San'a and Ta'izz daily, and getting a tour permit is as easy here as anywhere else. Huge Yemen Land Transport Company buses shuttle between the major towns of the southern governorates, and the system of shared taxis works smoothly in the south, as it does elsewhere in the Arabic world, linking small villages, towns and cities within and between the governorates.

Air travel is a viable alternative. The Aden international airport actually has a greater capacity than the San'a airport, and the huge passenger terminal, built in the 1980s, could easily handle all visitors to Yemen for years to come. However, it remains to be seen which foreign airlines actually continue to fly to Aden now that San'a is the capital of the unified Yemen.

Domestic air flights are most usable when travelling to the eastern governorates. Several weekly flights serve the Hadhramawt and al-Mukalla; for a traveller short on time it is convenient to fly in at least one direction.

Aden

The Aden Governorate has the smallest area of the southern governorates, comprising just Aden, its immediate surroundings and the island of Suqutra.

ADEN
عدن

('adan)

The most important sea port and the new economical capital of Yemen, Aden is built on a site of past volcanic activity. The huge lava mountains by the shore shelter a natural deep port that is capable of handling even the largest of vessels.

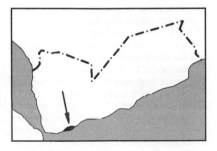

History

Thus it is not surprising that the site has been inhabited for so long, having served as the port of the ancient kingdom of Awsan between the 5th and 7th centuries BC. The site of this kingdom's capital has yet to be discovered.

In 410 BC Awsan was defeated by Saba, starting a long sequence of changes in the sovereignty of Aden. Ancient kings, local sheikhs and sultans of the Islamic era, and distant colonists from Egypt and Europe all ruled over or enjoyed the benefits of this natural port's convenient location on the major sea route between India and Europe. After 1497 AD, when Vasco da Gama discovered the alternative route around Africa, the importance of Aden began to diminish, only to be revived when the Suez Canal was completed in 1869. The British, who had held Aden for 30 years at that time, remained in control until 1967 when the independent South Yemeni state was born.

During its years of independence the PDRY was plagued by political instability, repeatedly manifested in the worst imaginable way: violent unrest either within the country or along its borders. The last such event took place in January 1986, when an 11-day civil war devastated Aden, killed several thousands of people and practically closed the country to foreigners for six months.

When the two Yemens finally united, on 22 May 1990, Aden was declared the 'economic capital of the country', though the new country was to be governed from San'a. Making Aden the trade capital was natural because the city certainly has the best natural port anywhere on the Yemeni coast.

For a tourist entering the southern governorates today, Aden is a necessary stop because it is the hub of all transport routes whether by air and by land. It is probably also here that foreigners must register to get tour permits if the system of the northern provinces has been extended here – the situation was somewhat unclear in 1990.

Orientation

Despite the long history and cosmopolitan flavour of this very old seaport, Aden is not exactly the place to go in search of *l'exotique*. The population consists of Arabs, Bedouins, Somalis and other Africans, Pakistanis and Indians. Even someChinese have found their way here.

Aden actually consists of several towns: the classical port city of Aden on the cape, the industrial Little Aden with its huge oil refinery on the western shores of the Bay of Aden and the new government centre, Madinat ash-Sha'b (also spelt al-Shaab).

This centre, the 'people's city', was sometimes referred to as the actual capital of the PDRY during the years of Communist rule. To the north of the old city are the suburbs of Khormaksar, in the neck of Cape Aden, and Sheikh Othman (named after the founder of Aden), a few km inland. Between them is Aden's international airport. Salt works can be seen on the plains between the towns.

The old city is scattered around the almost 600-metre-high volcano that forms Cape Aden. The oldest and biggest subcentre is the Crater (also spelt Critir or Critire) area, on the eastern part of the cape, surrounded by majestic lava rocks. To the east Crater opens to the sea at Holkat Bay, with the mountainous Sira Island topped by an old Turkish fort on the left.

To the west of Crater is the central Ma'alla, facing the harbour to the north, and around the western tip (the colonial Steamer Point) of the cape is at-Tawahi, where you'll find most of the city's hotels. Here you may also observe some tax-free shops. Although an oddity today, these shops have a remarkable past: during the last years of British rule in the 1960s, more than 200,000 transit passengers and tourists visited Aden each year, and the city's duty-free trade was the fourth largest in the world (after London, Liverpool and New York). In an effort to regain its former status, Aden was declared a free town again in May 1991.

Continuing along the coast you finally arrive at Gold Mohur Bay, a fine beach frequented by residents of Aden. The rest of the southern coast is rocky and undeveloped.

In spite of the city's age, Aden has relatively few old buildings. The strong British influence in architecture was replaced by an even stronger Russian one during the existence of the PDRY. As an official leaflet from the early 1980s proudly puts it, 'Aden is a clean, well-organized city with many modern buildings'. There are dozens of blocks of these modern buildings in the Ma'alla district.

Information

Banks in Aden are open from 7.30 am to 12.30 pm; all hotels also exchange money. For tour permits, the General Tourist Corporation branch office is at the Crescent Hotel. Yemen Airways' (al-Yemda) office for domestic flights is on Main Ma'alla St in easstern Ma'alla; for international flights go to Queen Arwa Rd in central Crater.

The Cisterns of Tawila

The so-called Tanks of Aden are among the very oldest sights in Aden. These huge cisterns are high on the slopes of Jabal Shamsan, with excellent views over Crater to the north-east. The 18 cisterns, probably built by the Himyarites in the 1st century AD, can store a total of 45 million litres of water. The official brochures give 427 BC as the date of construction, but any project of this magnitude must have taken decades, and the 'BC' probably means 'Before Hijra' rather than 'Before Christ'. The present appearance of the Tanks is the result of renovations carried out by the British in the mid-1800s.

The Ethnographical Museum

This museum, in a garden just by the tanks, offers glimpses of how life was once lived in the South Yemeni hinterlands. Textiles, jambiyas and silverwork are amongst the things that can be seen here. Labels are in Arabic only. The tiny museum is open daily from 8 am to 1 pm.

The Military Museum

The Military Museum is on Sayla Rd in central Crater. This two-storey museum was apparently the pride of the rulers of the PDRY. The war history of the PDRY is pompously presented in various rooms of the museum: early resistance during the colonial days is remembered in the Occupation Hall, suspense thickens in the Revolution Hall and the displays culminate in the Victory Hall. Several rooms feature present-day Land, Air and Sea forces and show equipment that is still in use. The story ends in the 19th of January Hall, which documents the tragic events of the 1986 civil war in painful detail. The keepers of the museum are obviously

Top: Thousand-year-old terraces near Ibb
Left: Crater Lake in Hammam Damt
Right: Minaret of the al-Janad Mosque

Top: Casting bricks of sandy clay, straw and water
Left: The five pillars near Ma'rib
Right: Children sitting under Sabaean inscriptions, Ma'rib

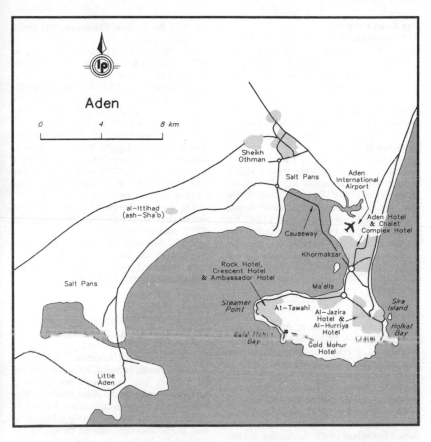

very proud of Yemeni military might, even when it is used against the Yemeni people.

The museum is open from 8.30 am to 1.30 pm and from 3 to 5 pm every day, except Thursdays, when it stays closed. The admission fee is 25 fils and cameras are strictly prohibited.

The National Museum

Located at at-Tawahi, this is one of Yemen's largest museums, second only to the National Museum in San'a. It has numerous treasures from excavations at Awsan kingdom towns, such as Qa'taban, Shabwa and Hadhramawt. The exhibits include impressive half-life-size alabaster statues of people. The museum is open daily from 8 am to noon and 3 to 5 pm, closed on Thursdays.

Al-Aidrus Mosque

The al-Aidrus (al-'idru:s) Mosque, on Aidrus St, is one of the oldest mosques in Aden. First built in the 14th century AD, it was rebuilt after being destroyed in 1859. Today, however, it is one of the few buildings in Aden constructed before 1900.

The Aden Minaret

Although the 8th century mosque to which it belonged is long gone, this blazingly white minaret still stands among the modern houses of the central Crater area, not far from the central post office.

Organised Tours

Should you decide that you need and can afford the services of a tour agency, you will find some in Aden.

Arabia Felix Tourist (AFT for short) was the only tour operator in the former PDRY. Their office is in eastern Ma'alla, on the northern side of Ma'alla's main street. In the days when they had a monopoly, AFT would not even talk to you for less than $1000, but increased competition will no doubt force them to hunt for smaller prey, too.

An early competitor is Yemen Tourist Company (YTC), the AFT's North Yemeni counterpart. YTC is located in at-Tawahi, opposite the Crescent Hotel.

Places to Stay

Finding accommodation in Aden is a real problem because the few hotels are always overbooked. Trying to confirm your reservation beforehand is not reliable, and you might end up phoning other hotels from the reception area of one you thought you had booked! If you do, here is a selection:

Aden Hotel (☎ 32947) in Khormaksar, near the airport, was being extensively renovated in the late 1980s. According to 1990 plans, the Swiss Moevenpick chain should start operating it. This luxury hotel is definitely not cheap but you could conveniently stay here if you visit Aden in transit. Facilities are Western-style, and even before renovation singles/doubles cost YD 38/45.

The *Chalet Complex Hotel* (☎ 341301) at Khormaksar is cheaper than the Aden Hotel, if you like listening to aircraft during the night. Singles/doubles are YD 13/20.

The 200-room *Gold Mohur Hotel* (☎ 324171), the largest hotel in Aden, is very luxurious and clean. Managed by Bulgarians, it is near the at-Tawahi area, at the southern end of Gold Mohur Bay, and has views of the harbour. Rooms are YD 19/22 a single/double.

The *26 September Hotel* (☎ 322266), at at-Tawahi, was known in the colonial era as the Rock Hotel at Steamer Point and is still better known by this name. Foreign journalists used to frequent this place and it's recommended if you like a sense of history. Singles/doubles are YD 8/11.500.

The *Funduq al-Hilal* (☎ 323471), or *Crescent Hotel*, is the biggest hotel in at-Tawahi, comprising two separate buildings. It offers singles for YD 7 or YD 8 and doubles for YD 8 to YD 11. This, too, is an old hotel with some class but is rapidly rotting away.

The *Ambassador* (☎ 324431) is the third and smallest at-Tawahi hotel. Singles go for YD 6, doubles for YD 8.

The *al-Jazira* (☎ 321234) and *al-Hurriya* (☎ 3252217) are the only hotels in the Crater area. They are both modest establishments, with doubles going for YD 8.

Places to Eat

Every hotel in Aden has a restaurant, though the food is not of a high standard. The restaurant on the roof of the *26 September Hotel* is recommended for its views.

In at-Tawahi, between the hotels and the bus station, you can't miss the *Cafeteria Broast Roasting*, in the Aden Gardens. The very popular open-air cafe next to it is highly recommended. Here you can sip coffee or tea and, in the evenings, admire the incredibly colourfully lit fountain nearby. The *Ching Sing Restaurant*, behind the bus station, serves excellent tandoori fish.

In Crater, the best teahouses and small restaurants are in the suq area around the Ma'in Bazaar Rd. Several confectionery shops here sell traditional Arabic sweets, too.

Getting There & Away

Aden is served by regular long-haul buses and taxis heading north and east. Alternatively you could fly there, using domestic flights from San'a or from other southern governorates. Flying directly to Aden (instead of San'a) from other countries is also possible. Finally, Aden is effectively served by numerous cargo ship lines.

Aden's main bus station is in Sheikh Othman, which is connected with Aden by both the blue city buses and the taxis. A private taxi should cost a couple of dinars. Buses leave at 6 am for al-Mukalla (YD 5 per person), at 6.30 am for Ataq (YD 3) and Azal (YD 3), and at 7 am to Ta'izz (YD 4). You have to buy your ticket by 4 pm the previous day and reconfirm your booking at least 30 minutes before the bus leaves. Buses are often fully booked a couple of days in advance.

Next to the bus station there is the taxi station of Sheikh Othman, serving more spontaneous travellers and those who have just missed the bus. Shared taxis operate to the places already mentioned; fares are 20% to 100% higher than bus fares.

More conveniently, some taxis also leave from the city bus station in Crater. It is advisable to be here early in the morning, no later than 7 am, to be sure of getting a seat.

Getting Around

Aden has a very functional public transport system, with large and small blue buses shuttling between the subcentres. I recommend using only the small buses because they go straight from the bus station of one subcentre to that of another. The large buses, on the other hand, seem to drive around every possible corner, making them very slow. Tickets cost 1.50 to three shillings per person.

The ticket control system is an excellent demonstration of the workings of a centrally planned economy, creating jobs for several people. First, you cannot buy tickets from the buses – only from small kiosks at the bus stations. Between the stations, along the bus routes, you can also buy tickets from selected small shacks selling foodstuffs and the like (supermarkets in local parlance). Second, on entering the bus, you have to cancel your ticket by pushing it into a piercing device by the door. Third, before the bus leaves the station, a controller checks all the tickets, tearing them in two. Finally, somewhere between stations, a second controller enters

the bus and collects the tickets. I wonder how long it will stay this way postunification.

Using taxis is also affordable in Aden but, unlike in the North, you have to bargain hard. The yellow taxis should take you between any two points on the cape of Aden for one dinar and to Sheikh Othman for two, but you will often be asked for five. Because of the efficient bus system you will not find shared taxis with regular routes as you will in the towns of the northern provinces; instead you hire a whole car for yourself or your group.

SUQUTRA سقطرة

(suqutra; Socotra)

The Horn of Africa points towards Suqutra, in the Arabian Sea. Yemen's largest island is 350 km off the southern coast of the Arabian Peninsula and almost 1000 km from Aden. It is part of the Governorate of Aden and is of significant strategic interest because it is the only island of any considerable size in this area, through which so many ships pass. It was the entry point to the area for European colonialism in the 16th century, when the Portuguese first occupied it, and was under British rule from 1876 to 1967. During the Cold War era the importance of a reported Soviet naval base here was much disputed.

Suqutra has been inhabited for at least a few thousand years but written accounts are scanty. It is known that the Sabaeans occupied the island in the 6th century BC and that the population was converted to Christianity around 600 AD. Even today, most of the island's 30,000 inhabitants are Christian, though the form of Christianity they practise is greatly influenced by Islam.

The island, with its many rare plant and bird species, was dutifully listed as one of the 'tourist sites' of the former PDRY, probably because its sandy beaches and the many fish in its waters offered considerable potential for a tourist resort. No steps, however, have been taken to develop the island in this direction, and today it is virtually inaccessible. To book a seat on the weekly flight to Suqutra you must have a confirmed reservation at the only guesthouse on the island – and this is impossible to get.

Lahej & Abyan

The westernmost of the southern governorates, Lahej and Abyan (directly to the east of Lahej) occupy the area between the former YAR and the Gulf of Aden. These are the most fertile governorates in the southern part of the country and the only ones with mountains high enough for qat cultivation. Several wadis flow into the region from the mountains of the north; the most important of them, Wadi Bana, forms the border between Lahej and Abyan.

If you arrive in Aden from the north by bus or taxi from Ta'izz, the road to Aden descends from the mountains and along the beautiful Wadi Tuban through the central part of the Lahej Governorate.

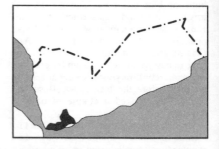

LAHEJ لحج
Lahej
(laHij; Lahij, Lahaj)
Lahej, the capital of the governorate, is some 45 km north of Aden. Before the 1967 revolution the Sultan of Lahej lived here. He was one of the mightiest sultans in the southern part of Yemen and his palace, now a school of agriculture, is worth seeing.

Adh-Dhala' الضالع
(az-za:la:'; Dhala, Talla)
At the northernmost tip of the governorate, very close to the town of Qa'taba in the province of Ibb, adh-Dhala' is 96 km from Aden. If you visit the town try to do it on a Thursday, the market day in adh-Dhala'.

Adh-Dhala' has a museum which features ancient relics as well as monuments to the 1967 revolution.

ABYAN أبين
The Abyan Governorate is to the north-east of Aden, bounded by the al-Baydha province to the north, Lahej and Aden governorates to the west and Shabwa Governorate to the east, with the Gulf of Aden to the south. The

governorate has relatively few sites of interest to the tourist.

If you travel to the east using land transportation, you are bound to visit the capital of the governorate, Zinjibar, as well as fishing villages such as Shuqra, further to the east – the whole South Yemeni coast is very good for fishing. Beyond Shuqra the road turns inland to the north-east, entering the green town of Lawdar. Although it is a few km off the Aden to al-Mukalla tarmac road, Lawdar is nevertheless a stop for the buses and taxis passing by.

Mukayras مكيراس
(mukayra:s; Mukairas, Mukeiras)
From Lawdar you might visit Mukayras, which stands on the slopes of Jabal Thira (also called az-za:hir), 28 km from Lawdar and only 18 km from the town of al-Baydha. This genuine Yemeni mountain town has a very pleasant climate because of its altitude of more than 2000 metres (the highest town in the former PDRY). Its orchards produce peaches that are famous in the region.

During the days before unification of the two Yemens, this town was listed as a major sight of the Marxist PDRY and even boasted a tourist hotel. Today it is just one more mountain town in Yemen.

Shabwa

Shabwa, the fourth of the southern governorates, stretches from the southern coast of the republic, east of Abyan and al-Baydha, to the deserts of ar-Ruba' al-Khali east of Ma'rib, where the border between Yemen and Saudi Arabia lies undrawn and unmarked in the sands.

For a traveller who is genuinely interested in the history of the region, there is plenty to see in Shabwa – if you have enough time and determination. In the northern part of the governorate there are the upper stretches of Wadi Hadhramawt, where major kingdoms once flourished along the incense route – the ruins of the ancient capitals Shabwa and Tinma have been explored by 20th-century archaeologists. The ancient town of Qana, on the southern coast, is at one end of these ancient caravan routes; it is nowadays known by the name Bir 'Ali.

The northern area of the governorate is not a common tourist destination but it is sometimes possible to arrange a visit to one of the ancient capitals if you show that you know what you are after. Don't count on this, though, since even professionals usually have to engage in years of negotiations.

The road from Aden to al-Mukalla, built by the Chinese in the 1970s, is some distance from the coast for most of its course through Shabwa Governorate, running across the foothills of the coastal mountain ridge of Southern Arabia at altitudes of less than 1000 metres. The road passes quite a few villages and small towns built on wadi banks.

A distinctive feature of houses in Shabwa and parts of Hadhramawt are the highly protruding corner peaks on the roofs. These are often chalked white and are of age-old design. The material of these houses is mud brick, even when the buildings stand on rock.

HABBAN   حبان
(Habba:n)
Some 340 km from Aden, just beyond the Ataq junction, is the smallish town of

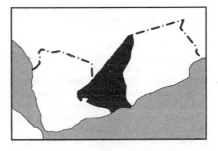

Habban. It is noted for its Jewish inhabitants who, along with their silversmithing traditions, are now mostly gone.

Habban has a most impressive appearance. Traditional mud brick houses of four to five storeys are larger than those in most other Yemeni towns. The town is built low on the banks of Wadi Habban, framed on all sides by majestic table mountains. Over millions of years, the wadi has eaten its course deep into the chalk stone. The setting is a typical South Yemeni one, reminiscent of the landscapes of Wadi Hadhramawt.

'AZAN   عزان
('aza:n; Azzan)
'Azan, the next town to the east of Habban and some 390 km from Aden, is in the region of Wadi Mayfa'a, along with Mayfa'a, the former capital of lower Hadhramawt. Mayfa'a had its heyday in the last three centuries BC and, if you have the time, the ruins are reportedly well worth seeing. They can be found in the vicinity of the present-day village of Naqb al-Hajar, a few km from 'Azan.

BIR 'ALI   بر علي
(bir 'ali; Bir Ali)
This fishing village on the coast of the Gulf of Aden is the last one along the Aden to al-Mukalla highway before the road enters

the Hadhramawt Governorate. It is easily visited en route between Aden and Mukalla – the road passes right by it. There is a rest house in Bir 'Ali and it is possible to stop here for a meal. Although there are no facilities for overnighting, you can camp by the shore.

There is a strong sense of history in this village, which stands on the site of ancient Qana, the principal southern point of the incense route. The ruins of Qana itself are on a hill called Husn al-Ghurab (Crow Fortress), to the west of the present village. The remains of a 1st century temple are amongst the best preserved sights.

The location of Bir 'Ali can be counted as more of a sight than any of the ruins, however. Black volcanic rock extends to the horizon in all directions, contrasted by the white sands of Bir 'Ali – sheer magic. It is easy to understand why the ancient traders chose this natural port site as the end point of the incense route.

SHABWA شبوه

(shabwa; Shabwah, Shabwat)

Shabwa is the ancient capital of the kingdom of Hadhramawt. The early history of the kingdom is poorly recorded, so it is not known when Shabwa was founded, let alone when it became capital.

A kingdom named Hadhramawt was first mentioned in scriptures dating from 750 BC, and Greek historians record their knowledge of the place in the 4th century BC. Shabwa is first described by the Greek Eratosthenes, in the 3rd century BC, under the name 'Sabota'. According to the Roman historian Pliny, writing in the 1st century BC, the flourishing city had 60 temples inside its walls. At its largest, the irrigated and cultivated area is said to have comprised 15,000 hectares.

During the 220s AD Shabwa was defeated by the Sabaeans. The final blow was the emergence of a Central Arabian nomadic tribe, the Kinda, 30,000 of whom arrived in the Shabwa region. The original population eventually fled east to the town of Say'un.

Towards modern times only a few families have inhabited the site, living on salt-mining.

Even today the central government has no firm control over the local nomads in northern parts of the Shabwa Governorate. This is cited as one of the main reasons for the authorities' extreme reluctance to let tourists visit Shabwa. French archaeologists conducted excavations here between 1975 and 1985, exposing much of the western part of the ancient city. The other parts lie beneath the present-day villages of Matha and al-Hajar.

Shabwa is in the westernmost part of Wadi Hadhramawt, some 500 km from Aden. Although it once derived its wealth from its strategic location on the incense route, Shabwa today is not well connected to anywhere, and nothing but tracks and paths lead to the ruins. The route crosses 100 km of desert from Ataq in the south.

BAYHAN بيحان

(bayHa:n; Beihan, Bihan)

Before the unification of the two Yemens, Bayhan, the westernmost part of the Shabwa Governorate, was a cartographic anomaly: in a region where no borders between the YAR and the PDRY had been drawn, Bayhan belonged to the PDRY as indisputably as al-Baydha, to the south of it, belonged to the YAR. The nearby oil finds of the late 1980s would finally have forced the countries to define the border, had they not decided in 1990 to kick away the empty oil barrels that marked the temporary dividing line.

Bayhan is the site of ancient Tinma, the capital of the state of Qa'taban (not to be confused with the present-day town of Qa'taba). Tinma was built on the incense road, halfway between Shabwa and Ma'rib. With only 60 to 80 km between Tinma and Ma'rib, the three towns were surprisingly close to each other for the capitals of three rival kingdoms. It is thought that Tinma was originally founded by the Sabaeans in around 400 BC and that it later grew in power by exploiting periods of weakness in the kingdom of Saba. Some accounts give even earlier foundation dates, and official brochures claim that the ruins are 4000 years old! The kingdom of Qa'taban existed for 500 years until it was defeated by Hadhramawt in the year 100 AD.

For 12 months in 1950 and 1951, large-scale excavations were conducted in Bayhan by the American archaeologist Wendell Phillips. Consequently Tinma is the best known ancient capital in Southern Arabia – in Ma'rib, only nine months work was possible. Russian archaeologists have been continuing the explorations in the 1980s. The Bayhan Museum is said to house finds from the excavation sites in and around Tinma.

In the days of state monopoly on tourism, Bayhan (unlike Shabwa) was on the list of the PDRY's tourist sites. In 1987 a project to build an asphalt road to Bayhan was started, making the site more accessible, though the road obviously does not yet extend all the way to Bayhan – in 1990, we found it impossible to get a car which would take us beyond the village of Ataq.

Should you succeed in making your way to Bayhan, there are several sites of historical interest in and around the town. The official list includes:

Tinma تمنع

Tinma is also spelt 'Tamnou' but its modern name is Hajjar Kuhlan. The site, some 30 km east from the present town of Bayhan, consists of 21 hectares of ruins, including 10-metre pillars and other stone remnants of temples, houses and bastions, with a wealth of Qa'tabanian inscriptions.

Jabal Aqil جبل عقل

This mountain is to the north of Tinma. The cemetery of Tinma was found here, 1½ km from the town itself.

Jabal an-Nasr جبل النصر

There is a large water cistern on this mountain, to the west of Tinma.

Hajr Hanu az-Zuri حجر حنو الزوري

This ancient town is in nearby Wadi Ayn.

Hajr bin Hamid جحر بن حميد

Hajr bin Hamid, another historical town, is halfway between Bayhan and Tinma.

Hadhramawt

The biggest province in Yemen, the Hadhramawt Governorate extends from the coast of the Arabian Sea to the southern deserts of ar-Ruba' al-Khali. Apart from the port of al-Mukalla and the historic towns of Wadi Hadhramawt, there is little to see. You could visit a couple of coastal towns but few visitors regret skipping them.

The climate of the Hadhramawt governorate, like that of most of the southern governorates, is very hot. Summer is definitely not a time to visit, with daily temperatures approaching 50°C and nights hovering above 30°C; coastal areas are very humid as well. Winter is most suitable for a visit: the dry climate of Wadi Hadhramawt in the inland is very pleasant then.

Getting There & Away

There is only one tarmac road, which covers the 620 km from Aden to the coastal town of al-Mukalla. This stretch takes nine hours by taxi or 12 hours by bus, with just one obligatory meal stop (at the Restaurant of the Sons of Hadhramawt). If you wish to make sightseeing stops you will have to allocate more days. Continuing another 300 km over the mountains, you finally reach the Hadhramawt valley and the towns of Shibam, Say'un and Tarim. Buses and taxis make this five-hour trip. The tarmac road, built in 1982, runs straight across the table mountains.

It is also possible to fly the 550 km from Aden to Say'un, one of the remarkable historical towns of Wadi Hadhramawt. A flight connection from San'a to al-Mukalla is also planned but had not yet been implemented in 1990.

AL-MUKALLA   المكلا
(al-mukalla; Mukallah, Makallah)
The capital of the governorate, al-Mukalla is a prosperous seaport and an important centre for fishing, one of the main export industries of the southern part of the country. With

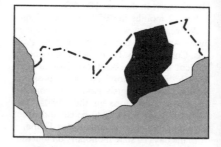

100,000 inhabitants, al-Mukalla is the second largest city in the southern governorates.

Al-Mukalla is a very old town, having served as the port of Hadhramawt for hundreds of years. It was founded as a fishing village in 1035 AD but only acquired town status in 1625. In the 18th and 19th centuries al-Mukalla's importance grew as the economy of the Wadi Hadhramawt area strengthened, and this growth has continued since the 1967 revolution as new suburbs have been built.

Things to See

The most impressive sight in al-Mukalla used to be the coastline of the old town. The chain of white houses, built next to the waterfront, seemed to rise straight out of the water. Unfortunately the scene was effectively demolished in the late 1980s by the construction of a gigantic mole. This now embraces all of al-Mukalla, from the new western suburbs to the harbour east of the town.

Still, the town is impressive, squeezed between the sea and huge volcanic mountains. The old part of the town is certainly worth seeing – take a walk and look for the finely engraved wooden window blinds and balconies. Much of the al-Mukalla Cape is occupied by the town cemetery, which is surrounded by a high wall so that you can hardly see it. A walk around the cape is rewarding, though. The style of the white buildings, with their turquoise decorations, is a fascinating mix of Yemeni, Arabic and Indian elements, as you might expect from an old port town on the south coast of the peninsula.

Mosques Al-Mukalla has some beautiful mosques. Most notable of these is ar-Rawdha Mosque, in the centre of the old town, next to the al-Mukalla Hotel.

On Main al-Mukalla St is the Mosque of 'Umar. At night both these mosques are illuminated in a most bizarre way. An evening stroll along the main street is pleasantly accompanied by the scent of dhoop and incense burned by the merchants.

Al-Mukalla Museum By the bay of al-Mukalla stands the former palace of the sultans, the last of whom, Sultan Ghalib, emigrated to Jedda in 1967. In the days of the PDRY the building served as a 'folklore and antiquities' museum and exhibited some finds from the old town of Shabwa. The museum was closed in 1990 because the building was under renovation, and it is uncertain whether it will be opened again.

Husn al-Ghuwayzi Topping an imposing cliff just out of the town on the Riyan road, this tiny fortress is a perfect example of the bizarre imagination of the Yemeni architect. It was built in 1884 and is irresistible to any visitor with a camera, even if you can't visit the military museum it houses.

Places to Stay
There are a couple of hotels in al-Mukalla: the more expensive *Funduq ash-Sha'b* and the more modest *Funduq al-Mukalla*. In 1990 the ash-Sha'b Hotel was closed for renovation. The al-Mukalla Hotel, attractively situated by the coast with good views over the bay of al-Mukalla and the old town, has doubles for YD 7.300. It, too, could do with some renovations.

Places to Eat
Avoid the al-Mukalla Hotel restaurant – the food is safe and nutritious but definitely not tasty. Instead, try the numerous small restaurants both in the old town and the new suburbs; they serve excellent fish as well as the ubiquitous chicken. Tuna, pilchard and lobster are common here but the real winner in al-Mukalla is dried shark.

Next to the Mosque of 'Umar is a traditional teahouse with a fine atmosphere.

Getting There & Away
Buses and taxis arriving from the direction of Aden enter the town through the modern western suburb of al-Mukalla, named Hai al-Omal (Hay al-'uma:l). The al-Mukalla bus station is here. Buses for Aden and for Say'un (in Wadi Hadhramawt) leave daily at 6.30 and 7 am. As in Aden, you have to buy your ticket by 4 pm the day before and arrive at the station 30 minutes before the bus leaves. A ticket to Say'un costs YD 3.

Taxis continue down the wadi that separates Hai al-Omal from the old town of al-Mukalla, then turn left towards the taxi station in the northern suburb of Hai Ukiubi. Here you can get a shared taxi to Aden or Wadi Hadhramawt any time in the morning, though there are hardly any in the afternoon. The trip to Say'un costs YD 7 and takes six hours.

Flying to or from al-Mukalla means using the desert airport of Riyan, some 20 km north-east of al-Mukalla. No buses seem to serve the airport; try to find somebody to share your taxi, since the fare for the 30-minute ride is YD 6. The Yemen Airways (al-Yemda) office is on Main al-Mukalla St, near the Mosque of 'Umar.

Getting Around
The old town of al-Mukalla is squeezed between the mountains and the bay of al-Mukalla, an area easily covered on foot. The suburbs and the nearby towns and villages are served by an extensive bus network. There are schematic line maps at the main bus stops with captions in Arabic only. The station at the eastern end of the Main al-

Mukalla St is conveniently close to the al-Mukalla Hotel.

AROUND AL-MUKALLA

Around al-Mukalla are some old towns and villages that you can visit by bus or taxi.

Ghayl Ba Wazir   غيل باوزير

Some 30 km to the north-east of al-Mukalla in Ghayl Ba Wazir, the former sultan's summer palace has been converted into a tiny rest house. It has five rooms and one swimming pool, and is warmly recommended by those who have spent a night there.

Ash-Shihr   الشحر
(ash-shiHr)

This small fishing port, 54 km east of al-Mukalla, is a very old settlement. Already known in the days of antiquity, ash-Shihr is also mentioned in the writings of Marco Polo. Still in existence are parts of the town wall and a couple of its gates, originally built in the 13th century. You might also appreciate bathing at the nearby hot springs or watching local beekeepers practise their profession.

The old dirt road to Wadi Hadhramawt starts from ash-Shihr and winds its way along Wadi 'Adim to al-Ghurfa, east of Say'un. It has been all but abandoned since 1982, when the western tarmac road from Riyan was finished, cutting some 10 hours from a 16-hour drive. Until Toyotas replaced camels as the beasts of burden, the trip used to take seven to nine days.

Burum   بروم
(buru:m)

Some 20 km west of al-Mukalla, this small old village is easily spotted from the main road. Pillars of smoke rise from the ovens where gypsum is burned.

Wadi Hadhramawt

Wadi Hadhramawt (wa:di: Hazramawt), the biggest wadi in the Arabian Peninsula, is one of the major attractions of southern Yemen. This famous valley runs for 160 km, west to east, amidst most arid, stony desert plateaus (called *ju:l*) about 160 km from the coast. At the western end is the sandy desert of Ramlat as-Sab'atayn. Downstream the wadi joins with the dry and inhospitable Wadi Masila, which connects the system to the sea.

Wadi Hadhramawt with its numerous tributaries, however, is very fertile, making it possible for a population of 200,000 to live on agriculture and goat-herding. Formed by erosion of the sandstone bedrock over millions of years, the main wadi is today some 300 metres deep and two km wide on average, with the wadi bottom at an altitude of 700 metres. Ground water is available throughout the year; the rainy seasons bring abundant floods to replenish it, creating this most unexpectedly green land between the desolate tablelands.

History

The abundance of archaeological sites in the Wadi Hadhramawt area shows us that the region has been settled throughout human history and that it prospered greatly in ancient times. Indeed, some historians argue that the place was mentioned in the Book of Genesis, with its name spelt 'Hazarmaveth'. According to local tradition the earliest inhabitants of the wadi were descendants of Joktan, a grandson of Noah, through the prophet Hud.

Wadi Hadhramawt is located on the ancient incense route. The oldest archaeological finds here date from the 9th century BC, and Hadhramawt was known to Greek historians of the 3rd century BC. Shabwa, at the far western end of the wadi, was halfway between Qana and Ma'rib, and Wadi Hadhramawt was ruled from this city for centuries before the 3rd century AD. Elaborate irrigation systems were developed and maintained throughout the centuries of the frankincense trade. Even frankincense itself was grown in Wadi Hadhramawt, as well as on the southern coast (the bush still grows wild in some of the side wadis).

The history of Hadhramawt between the demise of Shabwa and the entry of Islam is obscure. Certainly the Persian Sassanids, who were invited by Yemeni kings to fight against Ethiopians in the 6th century AD, also presided in Hadhramawt. Evidence of this can be seen in the Persian style of the ruins in Husn al-'Urr, in the eastern part of the wadi.

Records of early Islam's influence here are fragmentary and very few original documents remain. Although Hadhrami soldiers were among the Muslim troops who conquered Egypt, there was also resistance to Islam in the wadi. Only the holy town of Tarim is said to have followed the Islamic faith continuously through the centuries.

In 746 AD a man called 'Abd Allah ibn Yahya, from Basra, Iraq, introduced the Ibadi school of thinking to Hadhramawt. The Ibadi sect survived in the wadi for at least 450 years, although Yemeni caliphs set to conquer Hadhramawt on several occasions. Most importantly, in 951 Sayyid Ahmad ibn 'Isa al-Muhajir, a descendant of the Prophet Muhammad, came here with 80 families and settled in Hajrayn, in the eastern part of Wadi Hadhramawt, establishing Shafa'ism in the region. The tomb of al-Muhajir is still an important place of pilgrimage, and the town of Tarim has remained the centre of Shafa'i teaching in Hadhramawt.

In the 10th century a Ziyadid ruler of Yemen, Husayn ibn Salama, allowed the building of many mosques and wells along the caravan route between Hadhramawt and Mecca, including the Friday mosque in al-Huraydha, in the western part of the wadi. The first centuries of the 2nd millennium saw the conquest of Hadhramawt by rival Yemeni dynasties. Following the demise of the Ayyubids in the 13th century, the wadi was ruled by the Rasulids who presided over an era of great stability and prosperity for the region.

The year 1488 was an important one for Wadi Hadhramawt. The Kathiris of Hamdanis, a San'a tribe, conquered Hadhramawt and eventually settled permanently in the wadi. The Kathiri Sultanate was founded in the eastern part of the wadi, first with Tarim and subsequently with Say'un as its capital.

In the 16th century the western part of the wadi fell under the rule of the Qu'aitis, a Yafi'i tribe originally brought to the region by the Kathiris as paid soldiers. The Qu'aiti Sultanate made the town of al-Qatn their capital. The constant warring between the rival tribes had, by now, greatly reduced the wadi's agricultural output, resulting in famines.

While the subsequent centuries brought increasingly long periods of peace, a severe setback occurred in 1809, when the Sa'udi Wahhabis looted the wadi and destroyed all the tombs and prestigious buildings (including mosques) they could find. Innumerable manuscripts were burned or dumped into wells during this ghastly episode.

A century-long period of hostilities started in 1830, when the Qu'aitis and the Kathiris again fell into dispute. The confrontation was over who would rule the town of Shibam, located between al-Qatn and Say'un, the capitals of the sultanates. Twenty-seven years of war left the impoverished city, previously under the joint rule of the two sultans, in the hands of the Qu'aitis.

Wadi Hadhramawt remained thus divided, with the border between the Qu'aiti and Kathiri sultanates drawn to the east of Shibam, for almost a century. The colonial power of Great Britain was slow to extend its rule this far in the hinterlands. Hadhramawt and al-Mahra formed the so-called Eastern Aden Protectorate, and the British ruled through protection treaties with the local sultans. In 1888 one such treaty was signed with the Qu'aiti Sultan in al-Mukalla, but the Kathiris did not follow suit until 1918. It was only in 1934 that the British finally extended their control to Wadi Hadhramawt, mediating between the warring tribes and signing hundreds of treaties with them, as well as half a dozen or so with the most important sultans.

Thus the isolation between the sultanates of al-Qatn and Say'un was lifted by the 1940s. The 1967 revolution brought a final

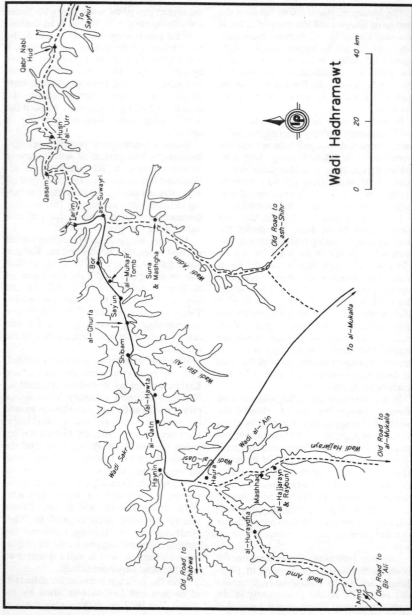

Wadi Hadhramawt

resolution to the dispute: with the sultans fleeing to Saudi Arabia, the central government of the new republic was able to completely replace the age-old ruling institutions.

Architecture

Tower houses are an invention of Hadhramis, original in style and unchanged by the centuries. The buildings are made exclusively of mud bricks. This applies not only to old tower houses but to all constructions, even today: mosques, tombs, wells, walls, everything.

If you spend a few days in Wadi Hadhramawt during the dry season you can hardly avoid witnessing the making of those mud bricks. Wet mud is mixed with some straw to give strength. The mixture is spread out on the bare earth and shaped into bricks using wooden frames that mould two thin rectangular bricks at once. The size of the bricks varies from 25 to 50 cm on the longer side, to be used at various heights of the wall, since this is thicker for the ground floor and thinner for the top floor.

After the walls have been built from bricks, they are plastered smooth. Two main types of plaster are used: brown earth (for most walls) and light lime plaster (for top floors). For decorative purposes an even whiter plaster was achieved using egg shells as a component. The parapets on the roof terraces of many houses are often whitewashed and shine magnificently at sunset.

Orientation & Information

The unofficial capital of Wadi Hadhramawt is Say'un, in the middle of the wadi, with an airport and other central traffic facilities. If you arrive by car, you travel through much of the wadi before entering Say'un.

The tarmac road from al-Mukalla descends to the wadi through one of its western tributaries, Wadi al-Qasr, by the town of Haura (Hawra). A little beyond Haura is a junction − dirt roads to the left lead to other side wadis where important historic sites can be found: al-Hurayda in Wadi 'Amd and al-Hajjarayn and Raybun in Wadi Hajjarayn.

From Haura the main road continues to the wadi proper, passing the towns of Haynin, al-Qatn, al-Hawta and Shibam before reaching Say'un. From there the road continues to Tarim. Beyond Tarim there are still sites of historical interest along the road to Wadi Masila − Husn al-'Urr and Qabr Nabi Hud, among others.

Places to Stay

Finding a hotel room is either easy or impossible in Wadi Hadhramawt. There are only three hotels in the entire area: one each in al-Qatn, Say'un and Tarim. Together, they have a total of about 40 rooms, more than half of them in Say'un. If you arrive without a reservation the usual procedure is to try the *as-Salam Hotel* in Say'un first because the staff speak English, so they may be able to phone other hotels for you if there is nothing available in Say'un.

Getting Around

Blue buses shuttle along the tarmac road that links the towns of Wadi Hadhramawt all morning and during the early afternoon. Tickets, which are bought on board, cost four shillings per person from Say'un to Shibam and six shillings from Say'un to Tarim. Service taxis do the same job for half a dinar per person. They have more flexible schedules and also operate later in the day. You can also hire a private taxi at any time for a negotiable fare of a few dinars.

AL-QATN القطن
(al-qatn)

Although not celebrated for any ancient monuments, al-Qatn is a fine example of a traditional town in the Wadi Hadhramawt style. Should you arrive in a private car from the direction of al-Mukalla, this place is well worth a stop. If you manage to get accommodation here it could be a good idea to start early the next day for Shibam and Say'un instead of heading straight to Say'un.

Places to Stay

The *Red Line Hotel* in al-Qatn is actually a tiny rest house, with only a few rooms for an overnight stay. Not for those appreciating cleanliness and quality, it offers doubles for less than YD 8.

SHIBAM
شبام

(shiba:m)

Shibam is to the south what old San'a is to the north: the most celebrated Arabic Islamic city built in traditional style. Shibam is a tight collection of some 500 skyscrapers, five to seven-storeys high, crammed into an area of perhaps only half a sq km. Aptly dubbed 'the Manhattan of the desert', the town rises straight from a slight elevation in the central part of the valley; it is not on the wadi bank, like Say'un for example. Shibam is a sight you will never forget – entering the town for the first time is guaranteed to make you forget the trouble you may have had getting here. You may have seen pictures of Shibam but the reality is likely to exceed your expectations.

Shibam is a very old city. It was already the capital of the Hadhramawt area in the 3rd century AD, after the fall of Shabwa, and served as the capital several times until the 16th century. Today it has a population of around 7000.

Shibam, with its extremely compact layout, is a remarkable example of ancient town planning. It has an earth wall and the houses are built with mud bricks and wooden superstructures on stone foundations. The highest house has eight storeys, with a height of almost 30 metres above street level and 39 metres from the wadi bottom. Most of the houses have four to seven storeys, depending on the height of the elevation on which they stand, so that the roofs of the buildings are all at the same level. Because the town is built so low, at the bottom of the wadi, it is vulnerable to floods and was, indeed, partly destroyed by floods in 1532-33 AD.

In the 1980s Shibam, like San'a, was the target of a US$40 million UNESCO programme to safeguard the cultural heritage of the human race. There was plenty of work to do. Many of the houses had been badly damaged by heavy floods in 1975 and 1982 (and again in 1989). Building costs have been steadily rising, so the owners cannot afford the necessary repairs after such damage. Outside help is still badly needed. Projects include restoring the dams that protect the city, building drainage and sewerage systems, restoring individual houses, and so on. There are plans to spend another US$40 million on other sites in Wadi Hadhramawt.

Things to See

You should try to see Shibam from within and from without. You can explore the town's narrow streets or admire it from a distance, from the sandy wadi bottom to the south or from the palm groves in other directions. If you fly to the Hadhramawt from Aden try to see Shibam from above as well.

Seen from the wadi bottom in front of the town, Shibam's appearance is somewhat nondescript because of the white-chalked newer houses built in the mid-1900s between the road and the town wall. The traditional tourist practice of photographing the town at sunset from the cliffs above the new suburb of Sihayl, on the southern side of the wadi, puts things nicely in perspective.

A walk among the goats in the streets of the town is recommended. Most of the present houses date from the 16th century AD, many having been rebuilt about 100 years ago. Look for the finely engraved wooden doors; the locks of them are also made from wood.

The citadel by the main square is quite old, dating from the 13th century AD. It is not to be confused with the neighbouring Sultan's Palace, which was not built until the 1920s.

Mosques The biggest of the six mosques of the walled city is the Friday Mosque, built in 133 AH (904 AD) by Caliph Harun ar-Rashid on the site of a still earlier mosque. Since then it has been rebuilt several times, most recently in the 1960s.

The mosque you see first as you enter the city through the main gate is that of al-

Khawkha, also more than 1000 years old. It was last rebuilt in the 1940s.

In the western palm grove stands the splendid white Mosque of Shaykh Ma'ruf, more than 400 years old.

SAY'UN سيئون

(say'un; Saiwun, Seiyun, Siun, Sayaun)
This town of 30,000 people is the largest in the Hadhramawt valley and was the capital of the northern Hadhramawt Protectorate during the final years of British rule. It is the entry point for tourists visiting the area by plane or by car. Say'un is 320 km north of al-Mukalla, in the middle of Wadi Hadhramawt, and is called 'the town of a million palm trees' – you certainly don't want to check the count but it seems easy to believe!

Say'un, an age-old market place, is situated on a major caravan route. Its economy was greatly boosted in 1490 AD, when some 10,000 members of a North Yemeni tribe, the Kathiris of Hamdanis, immigrated to the town and made it their capital, ruling it until the 1967 revolution. The imposing buildings of the town are excellent examples of the clay brick architecture of Wadi Hadhramawt. Some of the most beautiful mosques and minarets in all of Yemen can be found in Say'un.

The choice of personal vehicles demonstrates the influence of the Soviet-style centrally planned economy, introduced by the 1967 revolution. Motorbikes, as ubiquitous as date palms, were invariably Suzukis in 1990 because, for 23 years, no other brand was available.

Orientation & Information
Say'un is an easy town to find your way around. Most of the activity is within a couple of hundred metres of the taxi and bus stations by the old gorgeous Sultan's Palace, visible from anywhere. The main road passes through Say'un from west to east, making some turns in the centre, leaving most of the town on the southern side of the road.

The Say'un airport is to the north, only 10 minutes from the town (one dinar by private taxi); the road parts from the western main road. The Yemen Airways (al-Yemda) office is within walking distance of the town centre; go east along the main road until you come to the first junction. Turn right along the boulevard, go past the main post office and you will find the airline office in the 3rd block, on the opposite side of the street.

The Sultan's Palace
The Sultan's Palace in Say'un is perhaps the most pompous of all South Yemeni palaces, a multistoreyed white-plastered colossus with light-blue window decorations. You can't miss it – it stands on an elevation next to the town's central suqs.

The palace is now mostly empty, having been converted into a museum after the 1967 revolution. The museum, open daily from 7.30 am to noon, occupies several halls and rooms on various floors but leaves plenty of space unused. The permanent archaeological show includes several maps and aerial photos that illustrate the sites of the finds. Raybun appears to have been a very productive site, and there are Semitic and Himyarite writings and artefacts from the Raybun excavations on display. This is a very interesting show if you read either Arabic or Russian, the only languages of the exhibit labels.

On the top floor you will find various departments dedicated to folkloristic themes, such as handicraft, marriage and birth, coffee and tea customs, and Arab medicine. Of special interest are the coins and banknotes from the days of the sultanates; a passport from Say'un, Kathiri State, Aden Protectorate vividly illustrates the nearness of the period of British occupation, which has left almost no signs outside the building. The department of the Liberation War as well as the Say'un Library were closed at the time of our visit.

Other Sights
The turquoise Tomb of Habshi is the next most eye-catching structure in the centre of Say'un. It dates from the 1910s. The nearby Mosque of al-Haddad is much older, dating from the 16th century AD.

On the southern side of the palace you will find the old suq of Say'un. The shopping malls of the new suqs, to the east of the palace, by the bus and taxi stations, clearly owe their design to the old suq.

On the far southern edge of the old suq, next to the residential area and the graveyard, you can find what is probably the best cassette shop in Wadi Hadhramawt. Here you can buy the works of singers born in various Hadhrami towns, some of them now famous all over the Arabian Peninsula.

Places to Stay

The only place to stay overnight in Say'un is the modern *as-Salam Hotel* (☎ 2341, 2401), a couple of km from the town centre in the direction of Tarim. A double with air-con goes for YD 13, including breakfast. The hotel complex also boasts a swimming pool and a souvenir shop.

Places to Eat

In the very centre of Say'un, next to the new suq and the taxi station, a pleasant cafe serves both tea and cold drinks. Sitting there, you can watch the traffic of Say'un and can also see the town's only noteworthy restaurants: the *ash-Shaab* restaurant, on the 1st floor of the building opposite, and the two better no-name places by the park.

TARIM   تريم
(tari:m; Terim, Trim)
Tarim is the last of the three important towns in Wadi Hadhramawt. This town of 15,000 inhabitants is some 35 km to the east of Say'un. It is overshadowed by vast rock cliffs on one side and surrounded by palm groves on the other.

Tarim has long been an important centre for the Shafa'i school of the Sunni Islamic teaching. From the 17th to the 19th centuries the several hundred mosques of Tarim (the official count today is 365!) were as important in spreading the Shafa'i teachings in and from Hadhramawt as those of Zabid were in the Tihama.

Architecture

A striking feature of Tarim's architecture is its distinctively South-East Asian flavour, introduced in the 19th century by Hadhrami emigrants to the region, particularly those from Java. By the 1930s the Hadhrami community of Indonesia and Singapore had grown to 300,000. Many worked as traders, owning significant properties there, before deciding to return to their home country after spending their working years abroad.

The huge palaces they built are now in various stages of decay. Even so, a leisurely stroll through the streets of the town is guaranteed to consume a significant chunk of your stock of film. The finest palace in this 'Javanese Baroque' style is that of Sayyid 'Umar bin Shaykh al-Qaf, near the al-Muhdar Mosque.

Things to See

Tarim is a beautiful town marked by the high minarets of its many mosques. The most famous, the al-Muhdar Mosque, is the symbol of the town, its 50-metre-high square minaret appearing in every pictorial description of Wadi Hadhramawt.

If you enjoy perfection in Arabic calligraphy, the Al-Afqah Library is the place to visit. The library was founded in 1972 to preserve the spiritual heritage of the region's Islamic teachers, and books were gathered from all over Wadi Hadhramawt. Among its 14,000 volumes are some 3000 antique manuscripts, and several brilliant works of art are on show. Unfortunately the books were locked behind glass doors a few years ago, so you need a special permission to get your hands on them. The library is closed on Fridays.

You can find the library on the 2nd floor of the mosque next to the bus stop at which you will be left when you arrive from Say'un. To enter the library go around the mosque and climb the stairs outside the wall, by the suq of Tarim.

Although it is not appropriate for a non-Muslim to actually enter, the graveyards of Tarim, to the south of the town centre, are worth a glimpse or two through the gates.

The uniformly designed sandstone monuments with their deft calligraphy represent a style unique in Yemen.

Places to Stay

If you can arrange it the *Rest House Qasr al-Qubba*, in Tarim, is an interesting alternative to the as-Salam Hotel of Say'un for your stay in the Hadhramawt area. Although not especially clean, this tiny hotel is attractively built in a very green grove of palms and other trees. The rest house was the first one in Wadi Hadhramawt, built in 1955 by a man returning from Indonesia, where he had been introduced to the concept of tourism.

Qasr al-Qubba is a couple of km from the centre of Tarim. From the street where the Say'un bus leaves you, head west by the park, over an open square by which taxis wait for customers, and go between the graveyards. After a km or so there is a Y-fork – take the road to the left and, after another km, you will find the hotel on your left-hand side.

Getting There & Away

To get to Tarim from Say'un, take the eastbound bus from the Sayun centre past the as-Salam Hotel. The fare is six shillings. A seat in a shared taxi later in the afternoon, when buses no longer drive there, should not cost you more than 10 shillings.

AROUND WADI HADHRAMAWT

Outside the central towns there are plenty of things to see in Wadi Hadhramawt. Historical villages and archaeological sites abound along the tributaries of the main wadi, and innumerable tombs and mosques have been erected in honour of holy men. The abundance of small mosques in the area is explained by the fact that wealthy emigrants each built one upon their return to the homeland. A similar explanation applies to the numerous covered wells (called *siqa:ya*) that dot the landscape.

Some remarkable sites are listed from west to east:

Al-Huraydha الحريذة

Al-Huraydha, by Wadi 'Amd, is some 80 km south-west of Shibam. This village has a peculiar reputation: the best mediators in tribal disputes come from al-Huraydha, and the quarrelling parties take their judgements as final. The first vice president of the unified Yemen, Haidar abu Bakr al-Attas, traces his origins to this village.

The ruins of the town of Madubum, dating from the 5th century BC, lie some three km north-west of al-Huraydha. The site was excavated in the late 1930s by a British archaeological team, who found a large temple dedicated to the moon god. Several tomb caves from the same period were also discovered. Today the drifting sands have reclaimed much of the structures.

Al-Hajjarayn الحجرين

Also called Hagrayn, this is a remarkable stone village atop a rocky slope of Wadi Hajjarayn. Although the name literally means 'two stones' you can actually see millions of stones at a glance in this village. This is one of those ancient villages (it is more than 1000 years old) that Yemenis like foreigners to see, so it is rather easy to arrange a visit here.

Raybun ريبون

Raybun is one of the most important archaeological sites in Wadi Hadhramawt. Close to al-Hajjarayn, this ancient town was demonstrably settled by the 10th century BC. Not much of it remains today but finds from Raybun abound in the Say'un museum.

Mashhad مشهد

Next to Raybun, Mashhad is a village with some fine tombs. The Tomb of Hasan ibn Hasan dates to 1591, while the complex of the five Tombs of 'Ali ibn Hasan (and his family) was reputedly rebuilt in the 1830s. The domed buildings are most imposing.

Al-Ghurfa الغرفه

A town six km to the west of Say'un, al-Ghurfa is the site of the important 16th-century Mosque of Ba'bath. Inside the mosque are well-preserved original ornaments and other remarkable decorations in the Tahirid style. A huge, impressive tomb stands out nearby.

The Tomb of Ahmad ibn 'Isa al-Muhajir
The tomb is about five km east of Say'un, on the southern bank of the wadi bottom. Clearly visible from the main road, this tomb of the 10th-century spiritual leader is, even today, an important place of pilgrimage. It has been well maintained and its beauty is readily apparent to even the untrained eye. In the nearby village of Bor, on the other side of the road, a mosque built by the saint's son 'Abd Allah Ahmad ibn 'Isa is under restoration.

Suna & Mashgha   سونة و مشغة
These two pre-Islamic settlements on opposite banks of Wadi 'Adim are some 20 km to the south of Tarim. They are still waiting for further research.

Husn al-'Urr   حصن العر
This fort is about 35 km east of Tarim, on a hill in the middle of the main wadi. Probably dating from pre-Islamic times, it has reportedly been used for over 1000 years. There is enough left of the fortification and the cistern next to it for even a layperson to appreciate.

Qabr Nabi Allah Hud   قبر نبي لله هود
This tomb, another 35 km to the east of Husn al-'Urr, is one of the most important places of pilgrimage in Wadi Hadhramawt. The town has been built next to the tomb of the pre-Islamic prophet Hud, which has a prayer hall next to it. The amazing thing is that this finely kept town is actually inhabited for only three days a year, during the pilgrimage.

Al-Mahra

The sixth governorate of the southern Yemen, al-Mahra is a distant region inhabited mainly by Bedouins. It has no remarkable towns or major roads, just its small capital, al-Ghayda, and a couple of fishing ports. Al-Mahra is Yemen's most underdeveloped area. During the period of British colonial rule the region was formally under the power of the Sultan of Suqutra, although there was little to rule. Before and after the 1967 revolution the region was the scene of some military action when the Leftist movement tried (in vain) to expand its influence to the Dhofar area of western Oman.

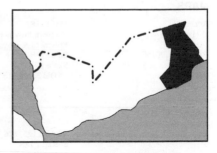

With almost no agriculture, limited livestock herding and some fishing, the conditions of life are hard here. For decades the major source of income for the families of al-Mahra was remittances from relatives who had emigrated to Kuwait. The Gulf crisis of 1990/91 therefore hit this governorate particularly hard, forcing those emigrants to return home in thousands, leaving their property behind.

You are unlikely to visit al-Mahra. You might be able to arrange a trip to al-Mahra if you are an anthropologist or a linguist who specialises in South Arabian people and dialects. The original inhabitants of al-Mahra belong to the oldest tribes of South Arabia; you may still meet people speaking one of the three local dialects. *Mahric, Shahric* and *Suqutric*. All are Semitic dialects but they are so different from Arabic that they are considered to constitute a linguistic group of their own.

Index

MAPS

TEXT

Map references are in **bold** type

Guides to the Middle East

Egypt & the Sudan - a travel survival kit

This guide takes you into and beyond the spectacular pyramids, temples, tombs, monasteries and mosques, and the bustling main streets of these fascinating countries to discover their incredible beauty, unusual sights and friendly people.

Israel - a travel survival kit

Detailed practical travel information is combined with authoritative historical references in this comprehensive guide. Complete coverage of both the modern state of Israel and the ancient biblical country.

Jordan & Syria - a travel survival kit

Two countries away from the usual travel routes, but with a wealth of natural and historical attractions for the adventurous traveller...12th century Crusader castles, ruined cities, the ancient Nabatean capital of Petra and haunting desert landscapes.

Turkey - a travel survival kit

This acclaimed guide takes you from Istanbul bazaars to Mediterranean beaches, from historic battlegrounds to the stamping grounds of St Paul, Alexander the Great, the Emperor Constantine, King Croesus and Omar Khayyam.

West Asia on a shoestring

Want to cruise to Asia for 15 cents? Drink a great cup of tea while you view Mt Everest? Find the Garden of Eden? This guide has the complete story on the Asian overland trail from Bangladesh to Turkey, including Bhutan, India, Iran, the Maldives, Nepal, Pakistan, Sri Lanka and the Middle East.

Also available:

Egyptian Arabic Phrasebook & Turkish Phrasebook.

Where Can You Find Out.........

HOW to get a Laotian visa in Bangkok?

WHERE to go birdwatching in PNG?

WHAT to expect from the police if you're robbed in Peru?

WHEN you can go to see cow races in Australia?

In the Lonely Planet Newsletter!

Every issue includes:

- *a letter from Lonely Planet founders Tony and Maureen Wheeler*

- *a letter from an author 'on the road'*

- *the most entertaining or informative reader's letter we've received*

- *the latest news on new and forthcoming releases from Lonely Planet*

- *and all the latest travel news from all over the world*

Lonely Planet Guidebooks

Lonely Planet guidebooks cover every accessible part of Asia as well as Australia, the Pacific, South America, Africa, the Middle East and parts of North America and Europe. There are four series: *travel survival kits*, covering a single country for a range of budgets; *shoestring guides* with compact information for low-budget travel in a major region; *walking guides*; and *phrasebooks*.

Australia & the Pacific
Australia
Bushwalking in Australia
Islands of Australia's Great Barrier Reef
Fiji
Micronesia
New Caledonia
New Zealand
Tramping in New Zealand
Papua New Guinea
Papua New Guinea phrasebook
Rarotonga & the Cook Islands
Samoa
Solomon Islands
Sydney
Tahiti & French Polynesia
Tonga
Vanuatu

South-East Asia
Bali & Lombok
Burma
Burmese phrasebook
Indonesia
Indonesia phrasebook
Malaysia, Singapore & Brunei
Philippines
Pilipino phrasebook
Singapore
South-East Asia on a shoestring
Thailand
Thai phrasebook
Vietnam, Laos & Cambodia

North-East Asia
China
Chinese phrasebook
Hong Kong, Macau & Canton
Japan
Japanese phrasebook
Korea
Korean phrasebook
North-East Asia on a shoestring
Taiwan
Tibet
Tibet phrasebook

West Asia
Trekking in Turkey
Turkey
Turkish phrasebook
West Asia on a shoestring

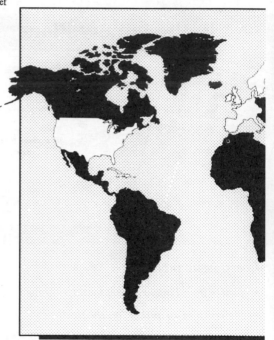

Indian Ocean
Madagascar & Comoros
Maldives & Islands of the East Indian Ocean
Mauritius, Réunion & Seychelles

Mail Order

Lonely Planet guidebooks are distributed worldwide and are sold by good bookshops everywhere. They are also available by mail order from Lonely Planet, so if you have difficulty finding a title please write to us. US and Canadian residents should write to Embarcadero West, 112 Linden St, Oakland CA 94607, USA and residents of other countries to PO Box 617, Hawthorn, Victoria 3122, Australia.

Europe
Eastern Europe on a shoestring
Iceland, Greenland & the Faroe Islands
Trekking in Spain

Indian Subcontinent
Bangladesh
India
Hindi/Urdu phrasebook
Trekking in the Indian Himalaya
Karakoram Highway
Kashmir, Ladakh & Zanskar
Nepal
Trekking in the Nepal Himalaya
Nepal phrasebook
Pakistan
Sri Lanka
Sri Lanka phrasebook

Africa
Africa on a shoestring
Central Africa
East Africa
Kenya
Swahili phrasebook
Morocco, Algeria & Tunisia
Moroccan Arabic phrasebook
West Africa

North America
Alaska
Canada
Hawaii

Mexico
Baja California
Mexico

South America
Argentina
Bolivia
Brazil
Brazilian phrasebook
Chile & Easter Island
Colombia
Ecuador & the Galápagos Islands
Latin American Spanish phrasebook
Peru
Quechua phrasebook
South America on a shoestring

Central America
Costa Rica
La Ruta Maya

Middle East
Egypt & the Sudan
Egyptian Arabic phrasebook
Israel
Jordan & Syria
Yemen

The Lonely Planet Story

Lonely Planet published its first book in 1973 in response to the numerous 'How did you do it?' questions Maureen and Tony Wheeler were asked after driving, bussing, hitching, sailing and railing their way from England to Australia.

Written at a kitchen table and hand collated, trimmed and stapled, *Across Asia on the Cheap* became an instant local bestseller, inspiring thoughts of another book.

Eighteen months in South-East Asia resulted in their second guide, *South-East Asia on a shoestring*, which they put together in a backstreet Chinese hotel in Singapore in 1975. The 'yellow bible' as it quickly became known to backpackers around the world, soon became *the* guide to the region. It has sold well over ½ million copies and is now in its 6th edition, still retaining its familiar yellow cover.

Today there are over 80 Lonely Planet titles – books that have that same adventurous approach to travel as those early guides; books that 'assume you know how to get your luggage off the carousel' as one reviewer put it.

Although Lonely Planet initially specialised in guides to Asia, they now cover most regions of the world, including the Pacific, South America, Africa, the Middle East and Eastern Europe. The list of *walking guides* and *phrasebooks* (for 'unusual' languages such as Quechua, Swahili, Nepalese and Egyptian Arabic) is also growing rapidly.

The emphasis continues to be on travel for independent travellers. Tony and Maureen still travel for several months of each year and play an active part in the writing, updating and quality control of Lonely Planet's guides.

They have been joined by over 50 authors, 40 staff – mainly editors, cartographers, & designers – at our office in Melbourne, Australia, and another 10 at our US office in Oakland, California. Travellers themselves also make a valuable contribution to the guides through the feedback we receive in thousands of letters each year.

The people at Lonely Planet strongly believe that travellers can make a positive contribution to the countries they visit, both through their appreciation of the countries' culture, wildlife and natural features, and through the money they spend. In addition, the company makes a direct contribution to the countries and regions it covers. Since 1986 a percentage of the income from each book has been donated to ventures such as famine relief in Africa; aid projects in India; agricultural projects in Central America; Greenpeace's efforts to halt French nuclear testing in the Pacific and Amnesty International. In 1991 $68,000 was donated to these causes.

Lonely Planet's basic travel philosophy is summed up in Tony Wheeler's comment, 'Don't worry about whether your trip will work out. Just go!'